DEDICATION

I dedicate this book to two people without whom none of this would have been possible.

First of all, Al Johnson, my father, my instructor and my mentor. Thank you for your guidance support and passion for flying that has made my career in aviation possible. You are the best pilot I know.

Secondly, my wife Nancy. How do I start to describe her contribution to my career and my life? Let me start with this. When we met in college (at Oshkosh in 1969) and things started to get serious, I told her I was a pilot now and intended to be a pilot all my life and if she had a problem with that say something now and save us both a lot of grief. It has been 50 years and she has not complained about my flying yet, so it is looking good so far.

When I was crop dusting she helped drive the water truck, flagged a field and did the books. When we had to move from town to town for the next job she was ready to go. When I started to apply to the airlines in the days before computers she typed the applications and the updates to the applications. She supported me through my first year with the airline when money was tight. She supported me through the 4 years of furlough and yet more moves for new jobs. She supported me when I retired early and moved to Alaska to be a bush pilot. Over the years of compiling these stories she was my editor and typist. We had many spirited debates over the style and at times sentence construction I used in this book so if there are any errors they are mine not hers. When I use "I" and "me" it is really WE. She is truly my **partner** and the love of my life.

Dan Johnson

TABLE OF CONTENTS
4.2

3

PART TWO

PART THREE

PART FOUR

MD80 Captain

PART FIVE

Alaska

PART SIX

PART SEVEN

Odds And Ends

BushCat ANC to 10C

DUSTER

By A. Dan Johnson

INTRODUCTION

I have written this book in an effort to both entertain and inform the reader about the life and thoughts of a Crop Duster. The stories I have written all actually happened to me during my career as a Crop Duster from 1969 to 1979. They are true and as accurate as the passage of time permits. I have not embellished them and in fact in most cases I have understated the incidents. The actual and factual incidents need no embellishment to be interesting and exciting. I have attempted to put you into the cockpit as well as my mind as I recount some of the most interesting moments of my crop-dusting career. I hope you enjoy the ride.

In subsequent parts, I have recounted some of the more memorable incidents from a flying career of over 50 years including commuter airline, major airline, corporate and Bush flying in Alaska.

LAW

Aviation, like all other things, has laws. The FAA (Federal Aviation Administration) is the principal governmental law enforcement agency for aviation. Violating a law established by the FAA can lead to penalties from $1,000 to $10,000 and/or suspension or revocation of your pilot certificate. The FAA is a powerful organization and not to be taken lightly. However, the really important laws are those established by GOD, and interpreted by Newton and Bernoulli. The penalty for violating these laws includes a sudden, violent, death.

PART ONE

THE BEGINNING

My father, Al Johnson, started in the crop-dusting business in the 1950s with Aerial Blight Control (ABC) out of West Bend, Wisconsin. As far back as I can remember he was a crop Duster. When I was still just a kid, he left ABC and went into a partnership on his own crop-dusting company. It was called American States, Inc. My father eventually bought the company from his partner and operated it himself from the early 1960s until 1973. American States, Inc. (ASI) was based in Racine, Wisconsin but most of the work was done in Parkdale, Arkansas and later in Antigo, Wisconsin. Every spring my father would move his airplanes from Racine to Parkdale for the spraying season. During most of the time that ASI worked in Arkansas the fleet of airplanes consisted of three yellow 220 h.p. Stearmans.

The name crop duster came from the origin of aerial application, as the spreading of a poisonous "dust" over crops to kill insects. Now almost all chemicals are liquids that are sprayed on, but the name "duster" stuck. I had been around crop dusters all my life and I always knew I would be a crop duster. I loved flying and always went with my dad when he went to the airport on weekends to instruct. He taught me to fly in a J-3 Cub. I was ready to solo when I was 12 years old, but the law said I had to be 16, so I had to wait. I was always at the airport. I helped rebuild several airplanes with my dad. If it had anything to do with airplanes it was hard to keep me away from it.

My dad had told me that when I was big enough to touch the rudder peddles and look out of the cockpit of the Stearman at the same time he would let me taxi it. That time came in 1963. It was also 1963 when I went with my father to help set up for the spraying season in Parkdale. It was just my father, two other pilots, and me. I was in charge of mixing the chemicals, loading the airplanes and doing whatever else that had to be done. I was 13 years old.

In 1965, a glider club moved to Sylvania Airport, Sturtevant, Wisconsin. That is where my father based his airplanes and did flight instruction. I was excited about the new club, because you only had to be 14 to solo in a glider and I was 15! It was September, I was back in Racine for school, and my father had just returned from Arkansas. It was Saturday, Dad had some flight instruction to do so I went with him to the airport. I'd hoped I could get some instruction in the gliders. On September 12, 1965 I had my first glider ride. It was 15 minutes of instruction in aero towing turns and traffic pattern procedures in a TG-3, an old military trainer. My next flight was a week later. I stayed up for 30 minutes and practiced stalls turns and traffic pattern procedures. October 10, 1965 was my third instructional ride in the TG-3. My instructor said I was ready to solo! I wasn't going to solo in the TG-3, though. I was to solo in the Schweizer 1-19 single seat, open cockpit glider pulled by a Volkswagen Beetle.

To get a feel for the 1-19, I sat in it facing into the wind and balanced the wings. I must have been doing that for about a half hour before Fred Flood, Günter Voltz and my father came out and told me it was time to hook up the Volkswagen. (I wrote about that day some years ago. That story was published in Private Pilot magazine, and I will include it later in this book.)

I was pulled the length of the runway three times at a height of about 10 feet to get used to the 1-19 and auto towing. After three trips down the runway they hooked on an 1100-foot rope, which would enable me to get to 800 feet. I made a few turns and came in for a landing. I had done it! I was a pilot!

March 14, 1966, a day after my 16th birthday, I soloed in my father's J-3 Cub, N 98200. The medical examiner I went to wouldn't give me a medical until I was 16 years old, and, for some reason, I think because the 13th was a Sunday, I wasn't able to solo in powered airplanes until a day after my birthday. It didn't matter, I had finally soloed!

I took my driver's test a few days later and failed. I had been driving in Arkansas since I was 13 and I think the examiner mistook that experience for a lack of caution he expected in a new driver. He felt I was too relaxed and didn't take driving seriously enough. I was forced to take the bus to the airport after school, so I could go flying.

I worked for my father every summer from 1963 until 1974. In 1967 he moved the business to Antigo, Wisconsin. The competition was pretty stiff in Arkansas and it was hard to make any money. Antigo was closer to home and held the promise of turning a profit. I continued to work mixing chemicals, flagging fields, and doing whatever else needed to be done. It was hard, dirty work, with hours that started at 3:30 a.m. and ended around 10:00 p.m., seven days a week. I didn't mind it though; I was around airplanes and pilots. What more could I want?

When the wind blew, or it rained, all of us would stay around the hanger and wait for a change in the weather. I always listened to the stories the duster pilots told of their close calls and fun moments. There were lessons to be learned from all of them and I was an eager student.

I got my commercial pilot's license when I was 20 years old. I was surprised my father didn't offer me a job crop dusting with him. As the beginning of the dusting season approached, I told my father I wanted to crop dust, and if I couldn't do it with him, I would have to do it somewhere else. He looked at me and a big smile appeared on his face and said O.K. I'm sure my desire to be a crop duster didn't surprise him and I'm equally sure my mother wasn't really pleased with the idea, although she never said anything against it to me. With my ultimatum, my father had all he needed to get my mothers okay. Looking back, I think my mother told my father not to encourage me or offer to teach me to crop dust. My ultimatum made the difference. I knew a lot about crop dusting form all the work I had done on the ground, watching how the other pilots did things, listening to them discuss how to handle a particular situation and what to do if this or that happened.

My father took me up for a couple of hours in the J-3 and taught me some of the finer points of spraying. We flew out to some nearby fields and circled them from 100 to 200 feet, looking for obstructions. He said that every house and most buildings have electricity. Know where the wire is that services the house and barn. Check for guy wires supporting the poles, especially on corners. Check the field itself for obstructions; things hidden, like old machinery or pumps sticking out of the field. Check the surrounding area for hills, towers, power lines or large cross country, (H pole), power lines, and places to land in an emergency. Circle the field once or twice but if you circle more that twice the farmers will think you're lost or confused, and they may lose confidence in you.

He showed me how to read the wind from watching waves on ponds, smoke, leaves on trees, and wind patterns on grain fields. He showed me how to use the wind to help me put the spray where I wanted it to go. He showed me how to use the airplane's wing tip vortices to fight against the wind to force the spray up wind into hard to get places by crabbing the airplane. He showed me how to get around a single tree that was off one wing tip by kicking full rudder **towards** the tree then releasing it. He taught me that timing is critical. He said to be wary of a single tree in a field. If there is a whole row of trees at the end of a field, there was no problem you will remember it. However, if there is only one lone tree, it is easy to forget about it. If you are distracted or the sun is blocking your vision you could forget it is there and hit it. It is one of the most common accidents in crop dusting.

There is a lot to learn and some things need to be taught by experience. The two most dangerous seasons in a crop duster's life are his first and third. The first because he doesn't know anything and the third because he thinks he knows everything. Dad taught me what he could. The rest was up to Time.

ISN'T THAT DANGEROUS?

When I tell people, I work with now that I was a crop-duster for ten years the response I get is always the same, "you crop dusted for ten years and you are still alive! I have to explain that crop-dusting isn't like it used to be. The airplanes are designed for crop-dusting now. They are not modified for it.

The modern Ag-plane is designed with the engine in front followed by the fuel tank, if it is in the fuselage, then the chemical hopper followed by the cockpit in a raised position to give the pilot good visibility all around the plane. The pilot sits in a roll cage to protect him in the event of a crash. The fuel tanks have bladders in them, similar to military planes, to protect the pilot against fire and explosion. The pilot also wears a crash helmet; I prefer to think of it as a safety helmet, along with a seatbelt and shoulder harness. The airplane has wire cutters along the landing gear and vertically across the windshield. They also have a wire deflector from the top of the cockpit to the top of the tail. The aircraft has all of these safety features to protect the pilot, but the one most important safety feature is flying the aircraft, the pilot.

The pilot must know his airplane and its limitations as well as his own. If the pilot knows those limitations and stays within them then it is not very dangerous at all. Sure, the accident rate is a little higher than for general aviation, but the fatality rate is lower.

CROP DUSTER

Crop-duster; that word is used to describe both an airplane and a man. I have given that a lot of thought, crop-duster. It is right that that same word describes both the plane and the man. They need each other to be a crop-duster. The plane needs the man to make it come to life, to give it direction and purpose. The man needs the plane to translate his thoughts and purpose into actions.

It is fitting that the man and the plane share the same name, for in a very real sense they are the same. When they are at work together the airplanes wings become the man's arms, its tips his fingers, its wheels his feet. The man gives the plane a brain and the plane gives the man its freedom and the ability to accomplish his purpose.

The airplane reacts to the signals from the man's brain. The man does not think a thought and then have to wait for the arms and legs to move the controls for the plane to respond. The man thinks, and the plane responds. There is time for nothing else.

Diving into a field to start a spray run the pilot knows within inches how close his wheels are to the telephone wires on the edge of the field, just as he knows where his own feet are when he walks down the street. He can sense the brush along the edge of the field as it flashed past his wing tip. As he approaches the end of the run the pilot doesn't wonder how close he can fly to the barn and trees before pulling up. He flies right to them and the plane rotates skyward.

When the pilot of a crop duster goes to work, he does not think of flying the plane, he is a part of the plane. It is an extension of his body. All the pilot's conscious thought is on the application of the chemicals to the crops, not the flying. He thinks of the wind. Which direction is it from? How strong is it? Look at the grass, smoke, ripples on the ponds or the movement of the grain for a sign of the wind. He thinks of the field. Are there any hidden obstacles waiting to trap him? Where are the telephone and power lines that serve the house and barn? Do they cut across the corner of the field or do they follow the drive? Do any guy wires stick into the field from the polls? Are there any obstacles in the field, irrigation equipment, anything?

He thinks of the area around the filed. Are there any trees to avoid? Antennas? Towers? Are there any houses to stay clear of? Are there any places to make an emergency landing? A hay field or road?

He thinks of the spray system. Are all the nozzles working? Are there any leakers to fix? Is the chemical coming out right? Is the rate of chemical per acre correct?

These are the things the crop duster consciously thinks about. Flying the airplane, he never thinks of. There is no need the plane just responds.

MY FIRST JOB

JULY 16, 1970

My first actual crop-dusting job was in Baraboo Wisconsin. I flew there in a Pawnee 150 along with two other pilots, John and Jack. We were working on a very large muck farm. (Muck is a type of soil that is very high in organic material. It is swamp land that has been drained and is now farmed.) It was several thousand acres and some of the spray runs, we call them swaths, were over a mile long. The only problem is that there was no airstrip. We landed on a north-south farm road. Calling it a road was giving it the benefit of the doubt. What it really was is where the tractors and pickup trucks drove enough to keep the weeds down. This "airstrip" was about 1,200 feet long and just wide enough for my landing gear to ride in the ruts made by

17

the trucks and tractors. On the east side a foot or two from the tire ruts was the soft dirt of a plowed field. If I drifted that way the airplane would be pulled into the field and wrecked. On the west side of the strip about three feet from the edge of the rut was a drop off of about six feet into a ditch used for drainage. To top it off the road was not level. It sloped to the east so when I was taking off, I had to hold left stick and right rudder to keep from sliding off the road to the east. The take-offs were very strange. I would add full power and hold the Pawnee strait with the stick and rudder. As the speed built up the tail would come off the ground. A little more speed and the right wheel would lift off. The Pawnee was now level running down the road on just the left wheel. Shortly after that the left wheel would come off the ground the Pawnee would be flying and I would gently ease back on the stick and stagger into the air just as the post on the end of the road would pass under my wing.

All of the modern Ag-planes have dump levers so if you get into a situation you might not be able to get out of you can hit the dump and jettison the whole load in about 5 seconds. This always gave me piece of mind to know if I did get into trouble, I could lighten up fast and probably get out of it. The only problem is that all of the chemicals are expensive, and some are toxic in high concentrations. Dumping a load or part of a load was only done if the alternative was to lose the whole airplane.

Landing was just as difficult as taking-off. After our first landing the three of us discussed how we were going to fly the fields. The loading area was very small. It would be a tight fit for two airplanes. We would have problems with three but at least one would be in the air at all times so we would be able to manage it O.K.

We decided to land to the west right toward the tractor shed. We would come in from the east low with full flaps and as soon as we were over the small bridge chop the power brake hard and then release the left brake to pivot to the right and stop at the loading tank. The landing area was only about 700 feet long.

John loaded up first and took-off. He needed all the length that road had but he made it over the post at the end by a few feet. Jack was next, he got toward the end and I saw him dump some of the load so did the farmer we were working for. Each load was worth $1,100 so this didn't go over to well. I was next off. Jack and John had 235h.p. Pawnees, mine was a 150 h.p. Pawnee. I taxied across the bridge doing a mag check along the way. I straightened out and gave her full power. The muck is soft, almost like a sponge. I accelerated slowly with my 100-gallon load. Left stick, right rudder as I slowly accelerated. I was continually fighting with the rudder to keep straight on this tilted take-off. The tail came up and it was a little easier to keep straight. The post at the end was getting bigger and bigger. The right gear was next, then the left and I was airborne. The post passed safely under my left wing as I slowly gained altitude. A fully loaded Pawnee didn't climb very fast. Sometimes 500 feet over the ground was all anyone would be able to get.

I dropped in behind Jack leaving enough room for him to pull up and start his turn before I pulled up. The flying was easy once I was off the ground. John was empty and landed to re-load and Jack soon ran out. John was back in the air and fell in behind me as Jack landed and re-loaded. I was getting lined up for landing when Jack took-off. I saw him dump part of his second load. I was down level with the bridge with full flaps and just enough power to keep it flying until I was on top of the bridge then I chopped the power and touched down immediately. I was pressing hard on the toe brakes. The tractor shed sure looked big and strong as I was landing toward it at what looked like jet speed. The

19

Pawnee slowed quickly, and I released the left brake and swung to the right into positions to load. It only took about four minutes to load a hundred gallons of chemical and dump in five gallons of gas then I was off again. The second take-off wasn't as bad as the first. I knew what to expect, the danger was still there but the unknown was not.

I dropped into position behind Jack and followed him as before. Jack emptied out and landed. I saw him take-off, but he didn't drop into position. He headed back north to Antigo. I think the farmer and Jack mutually decided that Jack had had enough. John and I finished on the 18th and headed home.

I was tired from the early get ups and long days, but it was with a sense of satisfaction that I flew home along side John. I had successfully completed my first job as a crop-duster. Something I had so long watched and wanted to do was mine. I was a crop-duster

CRANBERRIES

My fifth day on the job as a crop-duster I will log 18 hours and 30 minutes.

We were scheduled to spray the cranberry marshes.   I was to work with Jack. He had sprayed them several times before and knew where they all were. I had   flown over them in the Cessna 172 with my dad John and Jack a week

or so before. The bogs were spread out from Tomahawk, WI to Manitowish Waters and Land-O-Lakes in the Upper Peninsula of Michigan. The marshes are located in some pretty sparsely populated areas. Most of them have only pine trees
and lakes for neighbors. Navigation is hard enough, (this was before GPS), when you are in an airplane   at a couple thousand feet and can see for a good distance but when you are on the deck it is next to impossible.

My Pawnee 150

Jack and I left before sun up so we would be on the ground at the Tomahawk airport by first light. The people we were supposed to meet to load us would be waiting. I filled the gas tank on my 150 Pawnee, it held 40 gallons, and I had 20 gallons of gas in 5-gallon plastic jugs in the hopper. The June morning was cold in the pre-dawn hours. I was wearing my usual shirt, army fatigue shirt, and sweat shirt and nylon jacket. I could see my breath as I did my pre-flight. I always enjoyed this time of day, once my feet hit the floor and I was awake. Everything is so quiet so still. It was cold sitting in the cockpit of my 150 Pawnee as I started the engine. I wobbled the throttle a couple times then let it cracked open. Mags on, master on. Clear! Then press the starter. The engine rotated half a turn then stopped on the compression stroke. I released the starter button and the prop moved back slightly, I quickly pushed it again. This time it made it through the compression stroke and spun a few rotations before roaring to life. I checked the oil pressure gauge to see it coming into the green. The oil temp. was on the bottom peg, cold. I sat there with the engine at idle, cold, not really thinking of anything, just glad to be alive and here. Jack had started his 235 H.P. Pawnee C and was ready to go. The oil temp. was coming up and I was ready. I ran up the engine to 1500 r.p.m. as I taxied out, the mags checked good. Carb heat on, r.p.m. dropped then came back up, the air was cold and moist I had picked up a little carb ice. My navigation lights were on, I didn't have any instrument lights or landing lights. I followed Jack as we took off in formation. He was on the left side of the runway and I was on the right. We broke ground and headed for Tomahawk.

The airport at Tomahawk* is a strange one. It has a railroad track running across it and a sign warning that trains have the right of way. We were met just as planned by the loaders from the cranberry marshes. I filled my gas tank from the cans I brought as they loaded 100 gallons of insecticide into the hopper (the hopper is the tank that holds the chemicals). It had been a couple of weeks since I flew over the marshes in the 172 so I asked the foreman to show me on the sectional chart, (The sectional chart is the standard map used in navigation for light airplanes.), just where the bogs were that I was to spray. He had never seen a sectional before and couldn't point out the bogs. He pulled out a road map and showed me on there. It was the best he could do and it was ok. If I got lost, I could always drop down and read the road signs.

Jack had split up the work and given me some of the farthest bogs to spray. We got paid by the acre so the more you did the more you earned. I didn't complain. I started with the closest bog on Jack's list and worked my way out.

It started out as a smooth calm day and the work went well. It was now just before noon and the wind was up to about 10 m.p.h. That was usually just about our limit. It caused turbulence close to the ground and also drifted the chemicals. I loaded my last load from the Tomahawk airport and headed north to spray a bog on my way to Manitowish Waters. With a hundred gallons of chemical and 40 gallons of gas I was over loaded. I could only get up to about 500 feet over the trees which made navigation difficult. The air was getting rough from the heating the sun had been doing so far that day. I had put away my jacket and fatigue shirt and was down to just my shirt. The bog I was looking for was set in the forest and I was having trouble finding it. I had flown back to the highway and dropped down to read the signs. I was in the right area. I followed the road north until I found the junction to the left on the road map the foreman gave me. I followed it west for several miles and found the bog. I recognized it once I was there from the scouting trip in the 172 a couple weeks before. I circled it twice looking for obstructions. There was no place to make an emergency landing. The wind was from the northwest at 10 m.p.h. or so but it was very rough air. It had warmed up to about 75 degrees and between the wind and thermals it was getting uncomfortable. I dropped in on the southeast side of the group of bogs. Just over the top of the bog I hit the spray handle to the on position. I was making money. The Pawnee was heavy and was easy to push down into the bog and I knew it was going to be equally hard to pull it out on the other side. About half way through the swath I added full power so I would accelerate to help with my pull out at the end of the run. The Pawnee started up grudgingly and as I got to the tree tops I started my procedure turn to the right, down wind. Just then a gust of wind hit me hard and started to roll me over. I didn't have much momentum left, I was just barely over the trees and I was running out or airspeed fast! I put the stick over hard left and forward. I hung on and hoped it wouldn't roll inverted. My chances of surviving an inverted crash into the trees was about nil. The Pawnee was just short of 90 degrees of bank when the aileron started to take hold and level me out. I rolled level just about 50feet over the trees. I climbed a little higher and finished my turn. I dove back in and finished the bog, but I was very careful of starting any turns to soon in those conditions. Once I lightened up it was no problem. I had all the power and speed I needed to keep control. I finished the bog and continued on to Manitowish Waters. I had a crop-dusters lunch

of some crackers and a candy bar from the vending machine when I got there. I finished up at Manitowish Waters and Land-O- Lakes just before dark. I fueled up and left for home as soon as I was finished. I made it home after dark at about 10 p.m. My dad was worried about me and was at the airport waiting when

I arrived. I guess the sound of that 150 h.p. Lycoming engine and the sight of my navigation lights looked as good to him as the runway lights looked to me. Jack was back by noon. I logged over 18 hours that day. I was exhausted and my hands were shaking from lack of food and fatigue. I left Antigo at 3:30 A.M. and returned at 10:30 P.M. The days were usually long   but you normally got a lunch break when the wind came up, and a couple of hours of rest. I had neither that day. I was still young and eager. I got a quick meal and a few hours of sleep and I was back at it the next day.

* The Tomahawk airport I described in this story was closed a year or two after this incident took place. I understand they built a new airport, without the rail road tracks running through it, but I haven't been there.

WIRE

Crop dusting is an inherently dangerous occupation. When you are flying an airplane at a hundred miles an hour only two feet over the ground you have to be alert for every possible obstruction. Things that you would normally not even pay attention to can become a deadly trap.

Joe Kapusta stopped out at the airstrip one fine afternoon in June to get on the schedule to have his oat field sprayed. We took his order, and since it was my first year spraying and I didn't know where all the fields were, John, Jack and I rode with Joe to look at the field on the ground before we sprayed it. Jack and John were experienced spray pilots and I listened carefully as they discussed the field and how they would spray it.

Along the road, on the north side of the field, was a set of telephone wires about fifteen feet high and a fence below them. Jack and John said the wires were high enough to fly under while doing the field. I didn't agree. It didn't look big enough for a Pawnee, with me at the controls, to fit under those wires. To the south, about one hundred yards from the end of the field, were some trees. There were no other obstructions close to the field. It looked like an average difficulty field to spray for Northern Wisconsin.

The following day, as things worked out, I was to spray Joe's field. I was applying MCP for week control. It was a clear, calm morning and the air was cool and solid. I had sprayed several other fields already that morning and my Pawnee 150 was performing very well.

I loaded up and took off for Joe's field. When I arrived over the field, I circled it once, as usual, checking again for any obstructions. I dropped down from the trees on the south side of the field for my first pass. This would give me two passes to lighten up before I would have to pull up and fly over the trees again. I was starting on the east side of the field and was going to work toward the west side. As I came over the edge of the oat field, I turned on the spray. A quick glance at the right and left booms showed that the nozzles were working properly. As I   approached the wire on the north side of the field, I could see it was above the windshield, which meant that I could go under it. This was not the time to be changing my mind, so I shut off the spray and pulled up. The Pawnee was heavy and started to climb grudgingly. Once over the wires I banked right, starting my procedure turn.

A glance at the booms assured me that no nozzles were leaking. I looked behind, over my right shoulder; to see the field to be sure the MCP wasn't drifting. Everything was okay so I banked left to reenter the field. When I was once again lined up with the field and spaced over forty-five feet for my next swath, I dropped down level with the wires again to check them out. It would be tight, but I could make it. I dropped lower. Just clearing the road, I was under the wire with the spray on.

I don't know why but every time I go under a wire I always duck and grit my teeth. It doesn't do any good, I'm in an enclosed cockpit with a wire cutter across the windshield and a wire deflector running from the back of the canopy to the top of the tail, but I duck anyway.

One hundred yards from the south end of the field I eased the throttle full forward. Those trees looked mighty big and I wanted all the speed I could get to convert into altitude (I didn't have any "tree" cutters or deflectors on the Pawnee).

I pulled up and started my procedure turn to the left. I saw some kids running through a hay field about a quarter mile away from the field that I was spraying. They were waving at me and jumping up and down. I waved back and they kept running to watch me spray.

27

It takes a lot of concentration to fly a spray plane. There isn't any time to really relax until you are empty and heading back for another load. You never think of flying the airplane that is automatic. You develop a direct link from your brain to the controls; the plane goes where your brain wills it to go. Your conscience concentration is on spraying.

I start the right turn; engine gauges green; no "leakers"; line up on the third pass; power back passed the trees; push her down; at five feet break descent; spray on; pressure 30 psi.

I am getting toward the middle of the wires; keep the power down so the tail doesn't come up. These wires sure do seem to droop a lot. Duck down, spray off under the wire, full power pull up, turn right, and bend it around for the next swath. That was the lowest part of the wire. The next pass will be easier, not so close. Relax a little.

Line up, power back; push her down, check for cars, here comes the wire. BANG! Full power! There is no question as to what just happened. I hit the wire but it didn't break. The airplane is slowing down; the wire is stretching like a rubber band. The Pawnee's nose is coming up close to a stall. Finally, I feel a snap and the Pawnee starts to accelerate then slows again. The wire didn't break; it only popped off the insulator. I am still tethered to the ground. Please break! I feel the Pawnee slow again, the nose is up. A stall is only a second away. The wire pops again but still doesn't break. I am just pulling it off the insulators.

Now I know what it is like to land on an aircraft carrier. The Pawnee slows again, how long can this go on? Just before it stalls I feel a pop again, airplane starts to accelerate. This time the wire must have broken. I am accelerating but very close to a stall. The trees are coming up fast. I need to get some speed and altitude. I can't turn left; the kids are there and I don't know how much wire is trailing behind me. If I dump the load, I will damage a lot of oats and pasture. Some of the spray could get on the kids. I have to fly straight ahead and hope for the best. Trees sure do grow tall around here.

The trees were approaching fast; too fast. My Pawnee is climbing better now. I think I will make it over the trees. If it looks like I can't, I'll have to dump the load. I'll be past the kids with only pasture below me.

The Pawnee clears the trees, but I can feel the wire dragging through the branches. I continue climbing until I get to 1,000 feet as I headed back to the airstrip. Looking out the back window, I could see the wire draped from the canopy over the stabilizer brace wires, but I didn't know how much wire there is. There didn't appear to be any damage. I moved the rudders hard left and then hard right to check for freedom of movement. It was okay but the tail kept swaying like a pendulum. There must be a lot of wire down there. Once I knew the airplane was not damaged, I played around with the controls trying to shake the wire loose. It didn't work.
I approached the airport high and about 400 feet over the end of the runway. I chopped the power, pulled full flaps and pushed down hard. I didn't want to drag the wire over everything.

After I landed, I inspected the airplane and I was amazed. The wire caught on the small air vent on the top of the canopy. One inch lower when flying under the wire and I would have never caught it. I simply lifted the wire off the air vent to set my Pawnee free. The metal hood over the vent plates had a quarter inch dent in it. That was all the damage the airplane sustained. I was curious to see just how much wire I had been dragging around. When I paced it off and rolled it up, I figured there was 300 feet on each side. That was a lot of copper.

NO PARKING

It was early spring 1970. I had come home from college in Oshkosh, Wisconsin for the weekend to find my dad was working at the Riverview Country Club, in Antigo, spreading fertilizer. I drove out to see how everything was going and to see if maybe he needed any help. Spring fever was setting in and I was anxious to start flying again. It was about 3 hours until sunset and Dad said he could use the help to finish before dark. I raced back to the airport and, as quickly as I could, put the spreader on one of the 150 Pawnees. It was a short hop from the airport to the golf course. As there was no runway for us to use at the golf course, we were just using the fairway near the club house for take off and landing. The chemical company had a truck there with the 50-pound bags of fertilizer on it. We didn't do much fertilizer work, so we didn't have any mechanical loading devices. We had to load each bag by hand.

For the 150 Pawnee, the loaders would set out 15 bags on the ground with the tops cut open. When the airplane landed it would taxi as close as possible to the waiting bags because the loaders didn't want to carry the heavy bags any further than they had to. The pilot would set the brakes, jump out on the wing and open the hopper lid. As the loader tossed the heavy bags up to the pilot, he'd catch them and dump the chemicals into the hopper.

That is how the 1970 crop dusting season started for me.

I flew over the landing area checking it out before committing for a landing. On final I pulled carb heat, cut the power, pulled full flaps and landed over the road to the club house, clearing the power wires that ran along the road. The fairway was smooth, so it made a good runway even though it was short.

Some of the regular patrons were starting to show up at the country club for the Friday night fish fry. I guess we were providing the entertainment that evening.

As I taxied up to the loaders, they were out and ready to toss me the bags. I saw the 235 Pawnee make a pull-up around the 9th hole. When I was loaded, I would go there and join in. It only took a couple of minutes to load the fertilizer into the hopper, so I jumped back into the cockpit. I had left the engine idling because the time on the ground was only a couple of minutes and I didn't want any problems with a hot start. I buckled up did a quick check of the gauges and hit the power. As I said, the fairway was a little short for my takeoff with a full load and clearing that wire by the road was going to be close. Although, it wasn't a problem if I couldn't get over the wire, I would just go under it. There was plenty of room for that.

I was already half way down the fairway, and by the way the Pawnee was accelerating, I knew that I wouldn't make it over the wire. Okay, so I would go under it. No problem, until I saw that there was a car driving on the road to the club house. He started to slow, then came to a STOP right in front of me! I think he was going to park there to watch the show! I didn't have anywhere to go and I couldn't stop as there wasn't enough fairway left. I couldn't dump the load of fertilizer because it wouldn't dump fast enough to help in time. The only thing that I could do was to keep going. I had decided that if I couldn't scare him into moving, I would have to pull up into the wire and crash on the other side of the road. The tail was up and the main gear was just breaking ground. I didn't have enough speed to maneuver. I was about 75 yards from the car. I could see the man's face. 50 yards. His eyes were getting bigger by the micro second. 25 yards. His mouth dropped and he finally realized I was not going to make it over the wire. He hit the gas and the car jumped clear just as I got to the wire. I flashed underneath it, gaining speed to start a climb on the other side. I could finally exhale, and then take a deep breath to clear my mind and get on with work.

Next load I think maybe 4 bags less and I'll clear that wire.

TIGHT SPOT

SAM BAGINSKI'S

Crop dusting, like most businesses, is often very competitive. The farmer is always looking for the best price for getting his fields sprayed, but he also wants to be sure he gets good coverage so that the entire field is protected from insects and disease. No one can blame them for that but sometimes the farmers don't take into consideration just how difficult and dangerous it is to spray some of the land that they plant.

Sam Baginski certainly didn't when he planted this particular field. The east side was bordered by a road with telephone lines running north and south along it. The west and south sides bordered woods that had several tall pine trees poking out well above the other trees. The north side was also bordered by woods, except for about 1 75-foot-wide strip on the east side running to the road. To top it off, a set of power lines that we called "H" poles because they were made up of two poles tied together by a cross poll (which made it look like a capitol "H") ran along the north end and over that 75-foot-wide strip of field.

Sam planted his potatoes in this entire 20-acre field, including under the power line and the little jog that was in the northeast corner under the power line. We had been spraying for Sam for several years and he would use a ground rig to spray that little section under the power line.

This year we had a new competitor in the area and he was eager for all the business he could get. He told Sam that he would spray the whole field, including the part under the highline and the jog on the northeast corner. Sam was no fool. Using that ground machine was a pain in the butt he could do without. He called us to see if we would match the offer made by our new competitor. We had three pilots working for us at the time and we all drove out there to look at it on the ground with Sam.

The only way that northeast jog could be sprayed was from the northeast toward the southwest. It is hard to describe in words what it would be like to fly this little jog, but I will try. Flying at 100 mph, the pilot would have to nearly have his wheels on the road to make it under the telephone wires just a few feet from the poll. Then fly under the "H" poll power lines before pulling up over the trees. Any miscalculation would mean a crash and maybe death. It could be done, but we were in the crop-dusting business, not the stunt flying business. We declined. Sam, with this field and 250 acres of other fields, went with our competitor. It was work that would be sorely missed but I was satisfied in my own mind that our decision was correct, even though the loss of work was a financial blow as well as a blow to our morale.

Our competitor was a good pilot but he was not any better than we were. He was hungry for the work and was willing to take the risks to get it.

Later in the season I was spraying a field near that confined little 20-acre patch of Sam's. When I was finished, I circled Sam's field, like I would any field I was going to spray, checking for obstructions and planning how I would spray it. I lined up for a pass on that little jog. I checked for traffic on the road. I got low, over the road, under the telephone wires, past the telephone poll two feet off the left, then between the "H" poll and the trees, as I went under the high-tension power lines, before pulling up over the woods.

From the time I crossed the road until I was pulling up on the other side of the high-tension lines was 3-4 seconds. It was a very tight fit, but I handled it without incident.

I really don't know why I made that run. There was no one watching. I wasn't trying to prove anything to anybody. I never thought I had anything to prove to anyone else. I suppose it was just to prove to myself that I could do it even though I (we) chose not to.

I flew back to the airport and got my next load and kept on working. I had never mentioned to any of the other pilots that I had flown through that little wire trap. I doubt they would care one way or the other if I had mentioned it. I forgot about it and just kept doing my job.

Near the end of the season we were all doing some hangar flying, waiting for the weather to clear and the subject of that little field of Sam Baginski's came up. I found out that we had all flown through that tight little corner at some time or another during the season.

FLY LIKE A BIRD

ED VOIT

Ed Voit was in his second-year crop dusting and I was in my first. We were both flying 150 Pawnees and often worked together. Today it was to be at William's Farms near Suring, Wisconsin. No one liked to work at "the farm" for several reasons. It was about a 30-minute flight from Antigo so you would lose that time while you ferried to the farm and it was dirty work, with the wind and prop kicking up the light dry black dirt. It was what we called a muck farm. It was a drained swamp, which meant the soil was dark black, very high in organic matter (in fact it could burn), and when the wind blew, or an airplane propeller passed over it would easily become airborne and get into everything. Add a warm day and a little sweat and by the end of the day a person would be covered in this black soil. Given that and the fact that, Al, the manager of the farm, had a habit of putting plastic stakes at random spots in the field to check our spray patterns, he was very particular. He complained if the coverage was not to his liking. He was generally hard to get along with and was abrasive. You can see why the junior pilots were the ones to work the farm.

We were spraying potatoes and carrots that day. As usual it was hot and sticky. By the time the wind came up we had finished the last load. It was time to head for home. Ed and I put in another 10 gallons of fuel for the trip back home and took off. Ed led the way and, as soon as the dust cloud from his takeoff had dissipated, I throttled up and followed him. We joined up a few miles west of the farm and, as was our custom, flew formation back to Antigo.

It was unusually hot and the ventilation in the 150 Pawnee was not very good, so I backed off on the throttle, pulled up a little on the stick and undid the locks on the doors. With the doors open and being held down on the side of the fuselage by the force of the wind I increased the power and moved into a little tighter formation. Ed and I could see each other well but we had no radio, so the only communication was with hand signals. I had the Pawnee trimmed for hands-off. I stuck my arms through the open doorway on both sides, straight out like they were my wings. I was turning my hands left and right as if I was trying to turn the airplane. Of course, it didn't turn, but it did start a very slow decent. I looked over at Ed with a faint look of surprise and started to flap my arms like a bird as the Pawnee continued it's decent for five to ten feet. Ed started to laugh so hard he told me he could barely fly. When we landed, he said the look on my face when the Pawnee started down and my arms flapping away frantically was the funniest thing he ever saw in an airplane. We have fun where we find it.

RACE WITH THE WIND

It was early summer. I was spraying around Shiocton, WI using a gravel road for a runway. One of the farmers that I was spraying for was nice enough to let me move his mail box out from in front of his driveway, so I could park my airplane in his yard when I wasn't flying.

It was about 10 o'clock in the morning. The wind was up and I had stopped spraying until evening when the wind would calm down again. I taxied my Pawnee into the yard and shut it down, setting the parking brakes and locking the controls. The weather was good. The plane would be all right for a few hours until evening and I once again began to work. I lived about ten miles away and my loader dropped me off at home then he went home for a short break before beginning to prepare for the evening's work.

I was tired, so after breakfast, at 11:00, I laid down and quickly went to sleep. About an hour and a half later, I awoke with a start. What was it? What had awakened me? Then I heard it. Thunder! I went to the door and saw a huge black cell moving fast, right toward where my airplane was parked. I ran for my car keys and quickly put on my boots. The cell was fast moving and I had to get to the Pawnee before it was torn apart by the gust front that I knew would be in front of a cell that size. I started the engine of my Datsun 240Z and sped off. It would be a race with the wind and right now it was a toss up on who would win.

If I was to make it, I had to go all out. The cell was moving from west to east, and I was southbound on Highway 45, doing 90 mph. The cell was about to over-take me and I was still about four miles away from my Pawnee. All I could think of was what I was going to do when I reached the airplane. I caught a break. The only traffic light in town was green. No traffic. I took the turn, east, onto Highway 54, doing 60 mph. and using the whole road. I could feel the wind. The cell had overtaken me. Rain was beginning to spot my windshield and the temperature had dropped.

There was only seven gallons of gas in my plane, but that would have to do. I was racing east, now, doing 95 mph. I had out run the storm cell, for now, but it wasn't far behind me. I still had a chance to get to my airplane before the storm did.

I knew the starter on the Pawnee wasn't working and I would have to prop it to get it started. My plan was that I would take off and head for Clintonville. It was the only place that I could get to with the limited fuel that I had in the plane. I was about a half mile away when I could see the Pawnee sitting in the farmer's driveway. The storm was nipping at my heels. I could see the farmer was walking out of his house. He had seen the storm, too, and he was moving his car out from behind the Pawnee. He knew what the wind would do to it.

I hit the brakes hard and turned left onto the gravel road I was using for a runway and then right into the driveway. I didn't have much time. I cleared the driveway, turned off the car's engine, pulled on the emergency brake, and jumped out all at the same time. I ran to the Pawnee, opened the door and got in. The parking brakes were on.

I flipped on the master switch and mags on. I set the mixture full forward, pumped the throttle twice, and jumped out. I ran around the wing and propped the engine. It started on the first pull.

The storm was almost upon me. I ran back around the wing, jumped into the cockpit, buckled up, and hit the power. But it was too late. The gust front hit. The Pawnee rocked from side to side and almost became airborne. It took more than half power to fight the wind and hold the plane on the ground.

The rain started soon after the gust front hit. It rained so hard visibility was totally obscured. Like most thunder storms, it didn't last long. In twenty minutes, it was all over. I hadn't beaten the wind, but at least I tied it. My airplane was safe.

SURPRISE

I have known Jim all of his life. His family lived next to mine in Racine. I remember his mother bringing him home from the hospital, I was 8. My family moved to Antigo, Wisconsin while Jim was in junior high school, but he would come and work with us in the spraying business during the summers.

When Jim got his driver's license, he would drive a mix rig for us. The mix rig was a 3/4-ton pickup truck with a 300-gallon fuel tank in the back pulling a 1000-gallon water tank with pumps and hoses for loading the airplanes when we operated away from base, what we called remote operations. Jim and I have shared many adventures together, some of which are chronicled here. It would be fair to say we knew each other well. He knew to be on his toes and alert when I was flying. I liked to sneak up on him and surprise him by buzzing the truck.

We had just finished spraying at William's farms for the day and were heading back to Antigo. Jim left first in the truck and I left a few minutes latter in the 235 Pawnee. I knew he would be watching for me. Highway 64 was a great place for an ambush. The roadway was lined by trees on both sides. The clearing for the road way was about one hundred feet wide.

I flew over the road a few hundred feet high. I wiggled my wings at Jim as I passed overhead and flew off to the west, climbing as I went. I figured by doing that Jim would relax and not expect me to try and sneak up on him. Once I had flown out of sight, I dropped down low and circled back. I was just over the trees. Jim would not be able to see me coming. I would get a glimpse of the truck every once and a while. I was nearly on top of it now and just off to the right. The timing was perfect! I roared over the trees and dropped down to a couple of feet over the road, just in front of the truck. I popped off an auto flag * and pulled up. As I was climbing away, I looked out the rear window and saw the auto flag caught on the grill of the truck and whipping back and forth across the windshield. A perfect strike!

When Jim made it back to Antigo, I was waiting to here his side of the story. He said he saw me fly by and wiggle my wings and then continue west. That was the last he saw of me. A little while later he was just coming around a slight curve when all of a sudden, he heard this huge roar and the windshield went white. He said he didn't have any idea what happened, first the roar then the windshield went white! He slammed on the brakes and was nearly stopped when he caught a glimpse of the airplane and instantly knew I got him. Surprise!

* An auto flag is a strip of thin white tissue paper, about 10 feet long, attached to a trapezoidal piece of cardboard used to mark your position in a field. There is a long thin box that will hold over a hundred of them attached along the cord of the right wing. When the pilot pulls the trigger on the stick a solenoid will eject one of the flags.

TAKEOFF AT COUNTRY GARDENS

The runway used by the Country Gardens Cannery near Peshtigo, Wisconsin is only about 50 feet wide so if you are driving past it and blink you will miss it. If you are flying by and don't know where it is you will never see it.

It is bordered on the east and west sides by the cornfield it was cut from. The north side is bordered by Hwy 64 with a set of wires running along with the highway. The south side has one big tree sticking up perfectly aligned with the center of the runway. The runway also has a large dip in it that makes takeoffs interesting.

We would often work two airplanes from this strip at the same time. It was quite challenging since the runway wasn't wide enough for the airplanes to taxi past one another in the normal way. The airplane that just finished loading and the one waiting to load would have to rotate like gears with their teeth passing each other. Only in this case the gear teeth were wings. The airplanes would line up facing opposite directions with the right wing of each almost touching the right wing of the other. Then each pilot would add power while holding the right brake and pump the left brake as needed to rotate the aircraft to the right until the wings were clear of each other and the loading pad was open. The loaded airplane would takeoff while the other was loading.

The takeoffs were far from normal even for a crop-duster. Once clear of the other plane I would add full power and head down the runway with the cornstalks just a few feet from my wing tips. The corn was taller than the airplane, so it appeared I was in a gully. When I got to the large dip in the airstrip the airplane was not ready to fly but because of its speed would be launched into the air. I would hold the stick full back to cushion the "arrival" as much as possible as the airplane fell back to the ground. The airplane goes negative G (negative gravity), as it falls back to the ground and the white chalky chemical in the tank comes out around the tank lid and coat the windshield in an opaque white. It is like flying inside a bottle of milk. I would have to keep the airplane straight using just my peripheral vision while I waited for the chemical to be blown clear of the windshield. Even then it left a white semitransparent haze that was hard to see through. As the airplane accelerated more, the tail would come up on its own, indicating it was ready to fly. I would pull a little back-pressure on the stick to clear the corn then slide to the side to avoid the tree and continue the climb enroute to the field. Once clear of the tree I would take the windshield rag I was sitting on and stick my arms out through the vent windows in the doors to wipe the chemical residue from the windshield. The procedure was the same for every takeoff all day long. It just became routine.

Jack, one of our pilots, failed to hold the stick full back once. The hard impact caused the landing gear to collapse. He crashed on takeoff careening on his belly into the corn field. He was uninjured but the airplane had substantial damage.

CHAMBERS ISLAND

Crop spraying isn't all long hours of hard work, interspersed by moments of shear terror, as the saying goes. Occasionally, very occasionally, there is time for some pure fun.

I was spraying for Country Gardens Canning Company out of a small airstrip near Peshtigo, Wisconsin. The morning wind had come up early and there was nothing to do but wait until early evening when the wind would set before continuing to work. I had often looked at the Sectional Charts of the area, studying the airports and general lay of the land. One particular feature kept drawing my attention to it. Chambers Island. It was in the middle of the bay of Green Bay. To me it was mysterious and inaccessible. I knew I was close and this might be my only chance to go for it.

I told my loaders, Jim and Tom, of my plan to go to the island and land there if possible. They asked if they could go along with me. Now, the Pawnee has only one seat but we weren't going to let a little thing like that stop us. Jim had accompanied me all over the state that summer, sharing that one cockpit seat with me. It was crowded, but I was able to fly okay. Tom would have to sit outside the cockpit in the hopper (the tank where the chemicals were loaded).

I took the lid off and scrubbed the hopper while Tom and Jim went to pack a lunch and get Tom's coveralls, motorcycle helmet, goggles and camera. Tom had been asking for a ride for a long time. He had flagged for me all season and wanted to see what crop dusting looked like from my view point. It didn't take more than an hour before we were loaded up and rolling down the airstrip.

Tom wanted to experience a crop-dusting run and take some pictures. That sounded good to me. I dropped into a familiar field that was just under a half mile in length with trees on the far end. Even though Jim was sitting right next to me I had to shout at the top of my lungs for him to hear me because of the air and engine noise. I told him I was going to stay down on the spray run until Tom ducked down into the hopper.

So, there we were, three men in a single seat Pawnee, just two feet over the tops of the corn, doing one hundred miles an hour, heading straight at a line of trees on the other end of the field. Tom's head and shoulders were sticking out of the top of the tank. It made it hard to see straight ahead, but I was able to manage. Tom was excited and was looking around, taking pictures. He looked straight ahead and noticed the trees for the first time. He stared at them for a few seconds then turned around to face me behind the windshield. He pointed towards the trees. I smiled and nodded that I saw them. Tom kept looking around; however he would stop his scan to look at that line of trees coming closer and closer. We were less than a quarter mile away now and the trees were looking bigger and we seemed to be approaching them faster. We were coming up on two hundred yards from the trees.

The wind blew onto Tom's face unobstructed, distorting it into grotesque shapes. It made me laugh. He was now fixed on the trees that were only 100 yards away. Tom turned around again to look at me as he pointed vigorously at the fast approaching tree line. I can only imagine what he thought. I returned his distorted look of panic with a simple smile and a nod of my head. At fifty yards from the trees, Tom's head snapped from looking at the trees to looking at me. His eyes wide open in panic, filling his distorted face. He looked me in the eyes for only a second; sure, he was seeing a mad man hell bent on killing him. He whipped back around, and then pulled his whole body down into the spray tank. The scene was so hilarious. Jim and I were laughing so hard, that I almost didn't have the strength to pull the stick back. As we zoomed up over the trees, I looked back over my shoulder to see a sprig of three leaves falling from one of the trees. I climbed to cruise at 1000 feet and set course for Chambers Island. Tom, realizing we hadn't crashed slowly brought his head out of the hopper and looked around. Seeing no more trees and feeling safe, he once again wiggled his shoulders out of the small round opening at the top of the tank. He was pale and moved slowly. The wind making his cheeks ripple like ocean waves. I was still laughing, and this new scene was almost as funny as the previous one.

As we headed out across Green Bay, Tom's enthusiasm returned. The camera came back out as Chambers Island came into view. We made a low circle of the island, finding a spot suitable for landing on the northeast end near a small lake on the island. I could see where a vehicle, probably a pickup truck, had made a pair of ruts in the grassy flat land leading back to a dump. There were no roads on the island other than that trail and only a few cottages and a big brick building that I had later found out was a Catholic retreat house.

I made a low pass over that trail and I saw that it looked okay to land on. I didn't see any rocks or big pot holes. I pulled up and swung around for a landing. I kicked the tank to get Tom's attention. He turned around and I motioned for him to get down so I could see for landing. His head quickly disappeared. I loosened the seat belt a little so Jim could squeeze over to the right as much as possible. The landing was going to be difficult enough and I would need as much freedom of movement as I could get.

Carb heat on, full flaps, my main gear lined up on the ruts. Touchdown! It was rough, but nothing the Pawnee couldn't handle. I rolled out, turned the airplane around and cut the engine. We were all glad to leave the cramped confines of the Pawnee.

When we were all standing on firm ground, Tom looked at me and asked what the hell I was doing flying right up to those trees like that? My response was simple, "You wanted to know what it was like from my view point to spray a field. Now you know." I think the experience gave Tom a really good understanding of exactly what I do.

We had lunch, waded in the clear water of the lake and explored the island for the rest of the afternoon. It was a gorgeous day and a pleasant break from the daily routine. I hated to see 4 o'clock come around, but it did, and we had to leave. I have never been back to Chambers Island. I have been over it a few times, and twice one summer I tried to sail to it on my boat. However, I was forced to turn back by threatening weather.

I'll make it back some day.

FATIGUE

I was a crop duster for 10 years. I was a loader, a mixer, and a flagman for five years before that. I often look back, longingly, at those years. I miss that kind of flying. Single seat airplanes, no radios, no instruments, just myself, my airplane, and my work. I miss the fast pace, the excitement, the sense of urgency to get the job finished before the insects toke over or blight infected our fields, the team work. I miss all that and more, but when I reflect on it, I never forget the fatigue. The fatigue manifested itself in many different ways, but it was always brought on the same way, hours and hours of work with little sleep. Who had the time to sleep? I would wake at 3:30 am, with the buzz of the alarm clock, to be at the airport before the sun came up. If you have ever wondered who wakes the roosters to wake the farmers, I can tell you. It is the crop-dusters.

While the mixers were mixing the first load of the morning, I would be untying my airplane, checking the oil and getting it ready to start the day's work.

With the first hint of morning light showing over the eastern hill, I would start my engine and sit in the cockpit shivering as the propeller blasted the cold morning air over me. When my engine had warmed up, I taxi over to the loading pumps to load and be ready for take-off at first light. I would continue flying load after load, hour after hour, day after day.

One of the ways the fatigue manifested itself came when I was staying at a motel in Coleman, Wisconsin. I had finished spraying for the day. I had no ground transportation, so the cannery man dropped me at the local cheep motel. I was showering before bed. I filled my palm with shampoo and instead of putting it on my head; somehow, I put it directly into my open right eye. The burning was incredible. I rinsed and rinsed my eye trying to get all of the shampoo out. I did the best I could and when the burning subsided, I dried off and turned in for the night.

The next morning my eye still burned. I washed it out some more and got ready for work. It was still dark when the cannery truck pulled in to pick me up for the drive to the airfield. While the cannery people mixed the first load, I got my Pawnee ready for the days work. My eye hurt so much I couldn't keep it open. I was taking off from the narrow strip in the corn field with the dip in it and the tree at the end (it seams many of my adventures started there). I forced my eye open for takeoff and then closed it until I was getting ready to dive into a field to start my spray run. I quickly opened it long enough to get my depth perception back to dive in and level off then closed it again until I was getting close to the end of the field and needed it again to judge my pull up point. Once I pulled up, I would again close my eye until I needed it for my depth perception.

Thankfully for me the wind came up early and we closed down the operation after just a few loads. We would start again in the evening when the wind usually went down.

 I got a ride into Menominee to see an eye doctor. He cleaned out my eye and gave me some drops to use for a couple of days. By evening I was ready to go.

Another time flying from the same airstrip the fatigue manifested itself again in a very different and much more dangerous way. As usual I had been working long hours for many days. It was afternoon and I just finished spraying the last field on schedule for the canning company. I was fueled up and ready for the flight home to Antigo. It was hot and after 2:00 in the afternoon. I hadn't had breakfast or lunch, not even a bottle of water (bottled water was not readily available at that time).

I picked a couple of ears of sweet corn, put them on the shelf just behind my seat and took off for home. I climbed to a good cruising altitude for a crop-duster of about 2,000 feet. I don't know exactly how high because the set knob on my altimeter was broken off. The doors on the Pawnee are more like windows. They are a metal frame filled with Plexiglas. You could fly with them open in flight and I often did for the extra ventilation. If you takeoff with the doors down no problem they just stay there but if you want to open them in flight you have to pull the nose up almost to a stall so when you release the latch on the top of the door they could hinge down without the air flow slamming them down into the fuselage with such force they could break. Once the doors were down they stayed next to the fuselage.

The noise inside a crop-duster is incredible and with the doors down it is even worse. The earplugs and helmet I wore helped, but only a little. All that noise also brings on fatigue.

It was a beautiful hot clear day. I was at a comfortable altitude with the airplane trimmed up perfectly. I raised my hands from the stick and throttle and grasped the cross bar forming the top of the cockpit roll cage. I leaned my head forward to rest against my arms and I was instantly asleep. I was asleep but dreaming I was awake and flying the airplane! While I was asleep in a deeper layer of my subconscious, I could hear the engine noise getting louder and louder. Somehow this deeper subconscious made me realize I was not flying the airplane, but I was asleep just thinking I was flying! I snapped to and found the airplane in a left spiraling decent. The adrenaline kicked in and I quickly righted the Pawnee and got back on course for home. I didn't have any further problem with falling asleep on that trip! I don't know how long I was asleep, but it couldn't have been long as the airplane hadn't quite made a 180 degree turn. I was lucky once again!

There was another time when I was flying from New Richmond, Wisconsin for a cannery. The weather had been bad for a couple of days and I was just hanging around waiting for it to clear. The morning of the third day was perfect. I started spraying at first light, about 4:45 a.m. that time of year. Once again, I didn't get breakfast; no one was open that early. I had been flying load after load all morning and putting a good dent into the number of acres I had to spray. It was after 2:00 in the afternoon and I still hadn't eaten or had anything to drink. I was tired and hungry but the wind, which usually starts to blow by 10AM causing us to stop spraying, was still calm. So I kept working.

Spraying is not boring, but it is routine. I would power back and drop into the field, stop the descent with power and a little back stick, take my left hand from the throttle and turn on the spray lever. We called it the "money lever" because we were paid by the number of acres we sprayed, so when the lever was on, we were making money. I would move up and down slightly in altitude following the contour of the field at 1 foot doing 100mph. Nearing the end of the field I would move the throttle foreword to full power to gain enough energy in the form of speed to make it up over the trees. Just as I started to pull up, I would take my hand from the throttle and move it to the spray lever and pull it back to turn off the spray, then back to the throttle. Once clear of the obstacles it would be a hard turn downwind. After about 60 degrees of turn I would reverse to a hard turn upwind moving over 45 feet for my next pass, (much like the pattern when mowing a lawn). Again, throttle back and dive down. Stop the descent with power and a little back stick, again and again and again all day long.

Hot, tired, thirsty, I powered back and dropped into the field for another pass, stopped the descent with power and a little back stick, left hand from the throttle to the spray lever pushing it forward to turn it on. I would move up and down slightly following the contour of the field. Nearing the end of the field I moved the throttle forward to full power, then, just as I started to pull up, I took my hand from the throttle and moved it to the spray lever and pulled it back to turn off the spray. The roar of the engine suddenly went soft at idle and the trees were coming up fast! I was shaken from the routine and instantly realized that I hadn't moved my hand from the throttle to the spray lever. My hand was still on the throttle and I had closed it! I instantly moved the throttle forward to full power, continued my pull up and cleared the trees. Somewhere in that sequence I turned off the real spray lever. I leveled out and took a few seconds to process what just happened. I didn't finish the load. I just flew back to the airport, landed and shut down the operation. It was time for some food and rest. Fatigue is insidious and can be lethal.

After a few hours rest I continued working. I sprayed 1,100 acres that day and earned over $300 dollars. That was a lot for 1972. I also used up one of my nine lives and hopefully learned a lesson.

THINGS AREN'T ALWAYS WHAT YOU THINK

Bob came over to help me with the Country Gardens cannery work. I had been spraying the same fields for several years and I knew where they were and what obstructions were around them so Bob just followed me. We worked the fields as a team. In team flying the first airplane would drop into the field and start its spray run. The second airplane would delay dropping in until the first airplane was part way down the field. The object was for the second airplane to pull up and start its procedure turn just before the first airplane was ready to drop back into the field. The airplanes would be approaching nearly head on so the timing was critical. The pilot waiting to drop into the field would carefully watch the airplane in the field and adjust his turn to avoid a collision. In this way it was easy to mark your progress through the field because the spray from the airplane just pulling up was still visible. You just spaced over 45 feet and started your run.

Bob and I had flown together in this way a lot and even though I was flying a 235 Pawnee and he was flying a Cessna Ag-Truck we had no problem staying coordinated as we worked a field together.

The next two fields we were going to work were separated by a road and a set of power lines. I maneuvered to the downwind side of the field and dropped in to start my first pass. Spray on. Approaching the road, spray off jump the road and wires, spray back on. I came to the end of the field pulled up and started my turn. Bob was approaching the end of his spray run and I was ready to drop back in. Spray on, approaching the road spray off, jump the road and wires, spray back on. At the end of the field I pulled up and started my turn. I could see Bob wasn't as far down the field as I expected so I widened my turn waiting for him to pull up before I could drop back in. For some reason Bob just wasn't keeping up. His turns were wide and slow. We finished our loads and landed at the Crivitz airport. I shut down and started to walk over to Bob's plane to ask what had happened, why he was so slow? Before I got to his airplane I saw what the problem was. The top quarter of his rudder was missing!

I asked Bob what had happened and he said that on the first pass of the last two fields we sprayed he lost sight of me for a moment and thought I went under the wire separating them, so he decide he would go under the wire too. As he got close to the wire he saw a second double strand under the "T" on top of the pole. He was too close to pull up so he chopped the power to lower the tail and tried to squeeze under the wire. There wasn't enough room and the wire deflector running from the top of the cockpit to the top of the tail hit the wire. The wire rode along the deflector until it came to the top of the rudder. There it snagged on the rudder and pealed it off just above the top rudder hinge. Bob knew something was wrong but he didn't know part of the rudder was missing.

We drove back to the field and found the missing piece of the rudder. We inspected the remaining parts of the rudder and found they were not damaged. Bob flew the Ag- Truck for over a week before we could get a new rudder installed.

WHAT ARE THE ODDS?

I was just finishing up the days work at Williams Farms. It was after noon and I hadn't had breakfast yet. I was hot, tired, and hungry and ready to head back to base at Antigo.

I fueled my Pawnee and started the engine. I checked the oil pressure and temp then did a mag check. The left magneto (mag) was dead. All airplanes have a dual ignition system so that if one fails the other will keep the engine running for a safe flight and landing.

I sat there for a minute figuring the odds. I wanted to leave. I was tired, hot, and hungry and I wanted to leave. What were the odds that the right mag would fail before I could get back to base and fix the left one?

The terrain was mostly trees and lakes, few spots to make a good emergency landing. I wanted to go but I just couldn't. I called home base and informed them of the problem. A spare mag was loaded into the Super Cub with the mechanic and flown to me. It took a couple of hours to get the mag and install it. I was satisfied that I had made the right decision even if I didn't like the consequences.

With the new mag installed I took off for Antigo. Over the woods between White Lake and Antigo, no where to land, the right mag quit! What were the odds? I guess taking the time to do it right and fix my mag problem before departure just paid big dividends.

THE CONCAVE TREE

As any pilot can tell you, there are many kinds of air and they all affect an airplane's performance differently. Cold, dry air is the best. It makes an airplane really perform well. Hot, humid air is the worst. It turns an airplane into a ground loving machine that won't do anything, especially fly. The kinds of air go beyond density, altitude, and humidity. It also is affected by stability, wind and other factors that have no name. It is important for all pilots to be aware of these facts, especially if the pilot is a crop duster. The performance of a spray plane in different kinds of

air and differing load conditions is one thing he must
know. If you have a chance, listen to a crop duster
pilot discussing air.

....."Boy, that air was solid this morning. I had 150
gallons in that Pawnee, full fuel, and it flew like it was
empty."

....."It sure is rough out there. Hardly any wind, but
my head has been bouncing off the windows all
morning."

....."That's some bad air. I rolled 2500 feet before I
could get her off the ground. After I did, it wouldn't turn
worth a damn and I only had 125 gallons in the hopper and
10 gallons of fuel."

I started my second year of crop dusting, just as I did
my first, flying a 150 Pawnee. It was a good airplane to
start in, but no matter what airplane you are flying, there
is always something bigger and better that you would
like to be flying. I soon got a chance to upgrade to a
235 Pawnee. The 235 Pawnee is a little bigger than a
150, although they look almost identical. The 235 is
also heavier than the 150, and it takes a little more lead
to clear obstacles on the pull up, than the 150.

The early spring work in potato country consists mostly
of herbicide applications on the potato fields for weed
control. That was my mission that particular day.

It was 5 o'clock in the morning, and I was getting ready
to take out my first load of the day. I would be applying
a combination of Lorox and Dowpon, for weed control,
to one of Wendt Farms' potato fields. It hadn't been
foggy, but it was very humid and unusually warm for

that time of the morning. The field I was to spray ran north and south, with some short rows on the east side, where a creek cut into the field. On the northern border of the field, there where a few small trees, maybe 20 feet tall. On the east side, following the creek around to the south, were some taller trees that were probably 45 to 50 feet tall. The field was about 100 yards long on the east side, and expanding just over a quarter mile further to the west.

I finished loading my 235 Pawnee with 150 gallons of spray and about 15 gallons of fuel. It sure felt nice to be flying the 235. Pulling out of the loading area, I made a circular motion with my hand, to the loader - the man who loads the chemical into the airplane's hopper. It was the standard signal to ask if the fan brake on the Air driven pump, between the landing gear, had released. The loader made the same motion back to me, indicating the pump was indeed turning. If the brake was stuck the pump would not work to pump the chemicals and I would have to land and release the brake. A landing with a full hopper was always a little tricky because the chemical could start to slosh around and move the airplane in unplanned ways possibly causing loss of control on the ground.

I checked the mags, carb-heat, and controls. Take-off was beautiful. The prop was beating a tube of moisture out of the air that surrounded my airplane. It was like taking off through a white tunnel of cloud vapor. The Pawnee rolled a little longer than usual. I had expected that because of the warm, super moist air.

My climb to 500 feet was normal, as I went around the south side of town. It was calm when I took off, but I still checked for any signs of a breeze. As I passed the town, the leaves on the trees were not moving and the smoke from the cheese factory's boiler was going straight up into the air.

When I got to the field, I circled, still checking for any wind. It was still calm. I knew I would need a little more room than normal for my pull-out, and the short rows on the east edge of the field looked long enough, even with the full load and the high humidity. I lined up or my first pass, heading south along the east edge of the field. As soon as I cleared the trees on the north end of the field, I pushed the nose down the last 20 feet to start my spray run. Immediately I knew I was in trouble. The Pawnee dropped like a brick. It felt as though I had entered a void with no air at all to support my plane. I jammed the throttle full foreword and pulled back on the stick as hard as I dared. I started climbing, but I could see that I wasn't going to clear the trees on the south end. As I reached for the dump lever, I could already imagine my airplane lying smashed to pieces in the woods. I knew I wouldn't clear the trees, but I hesitated to dump the load to lighten up enough to be able climb out of the trap I had gotten myself into. I knew if I dumped all that herbicide, the ground would be sterile for a long time. I was also afraid it would wash into the creek and do a lot of damage down stream.

During a crisis, its funny how many thoughts go through your mind in only a hundredth of a second. However, the thought of being hurt didn't even enter my mind. All I could think of was the damage I was about to do to my airplane and to the land.

When I hit the tops of the trees, it looked and sounded like two dozen of those wood chippers, that cities use to clean up all the downed branches after a wind storm, were all working at once in front of me. All I saw was a blur of green, shrouding my whole airplane. I held the stick steady. I knew it would only be a second before I would hit something hard! I didn't feel the Pawnee pitch down. I had expected it to at any instant, but it didn't. To my amazement, I broke out the other side of the tree, still flying! I wasn't going to crash! I kept the Pawnee climbing and quickly checked for damage. The wings looked okay, but the spray booms were covered with leaves and small branches. I still had a full load of chemical on board, which made a landing dangerous. My Pawnee didn't appear to be damaged, so I elected to try and spray out part of the load to lighten up before attempting a landing. This time I went to the west side of the field on the long rows where I would have no problem climbing back out.

I dropped into the field and turned on the spray valve, but the nozzles on the boom did not come on. The leaves were so thickly packed around the nozzles that the nozzles were unable to work. I would not be able to lighten the load enough to safely land. There was nothing to do but to head back to the airport.

The runway was 3,000 feet long and open on the south end. I came in low with lots of power. Over the end of the runway, I pulled full flaps, keeping the power up, and set down carefully on the main landing gear, slowly reducing the power until the tail wheel touched down. I was careful not to get the liquid sloshing around as I rolled out. When I shut the engine down to check my airplane and clean off the leaves, the only damage to the airplane was a one-inch tear in the bottom of the fabric on the right flap. However, the tree didn't fare as well. It now is a tree with a concave top. I often wonder if, one day, some arborist will look at that tree and wonder if it was a genetic defect. They would never guess the truth.

FOG

Early morning flying is always the best. Cool smooth air and quiet. It is also a time for fog. There are many kinds of fog. There is thick dense fog that covers large areas and will take hours to burn off. There is thin fog that you can see the sun through. There is patchy ground fog that hangs in low spots while the higher ground near it is clear. There is fog that you can easily see the ground through when looking down from an airplane even though on the ground the visibility is near zero.

I departed Antigo for an airstrip west of Pound, Wisconsin to spray some corn for Country Gardens cannery. This strip, like the one I previously described, has a large hump in the middle of it. This hump is bigger but more elongated. When landing on this strip you have to fly the contour of the hump while landing. The slope of the hump is your reference, not the horizon, to judge your landing flair.

This morning there was patchy ground fog enroute and as I arrived over the strip it was covered in fog. I could see through it from above but I knew I could not descend into it and land.

A technique I had used in the past would make it possible for me to get in for landing this time too. I lined up with the runway just above the fog and maybe 30 feet over the ground. I pull full flaps and added full power to make as large a wake as possible. As I flew over the runway the fog was swirled up in the wing tip vortices and left the runway clear. I pulled up 60 degrees into a modified wing over, kicked in some left rudder, chopped the power and headed quickly back down, leveling out just over the runway and landed. As the vortices lost their energy the fog came tumbling back over the runway and me. I taxied slowly toward the loading truck and shut down my engine. When I approached the canning company men they said with wide eyes, "How the hell did you get in here?" I said, "I just blew the fog away and landed." They were amazed an airplane could do that. It took a little while before the fog cleared enough to go to work.

THREE OUT OF FOUR

Bernard's Spraying Service was located south of Stevens Point. He needed some work done on one of his Stearman sprayers. I went there to pick it up and fly it to Antigo for the maintenance. It was a work airplane and it looked like it was worked hard. It had high lift wings with squared off tips and four ailerons. The high lift wings had a flat bottom and curved top to produce more lift than the standard symmetrical (curved on top and bottom) wing. I did a preflight, checked the oil and filled it with gas for the flight. It flew ok but I noticed it turned better to the right than it did to the left.

I didn't get a chance to fly a Stearman often. My dad exclusively flew the one we had and that was his baby. I snuck it out a few times to spray with it but not often. The tank on my dad's Stearman held 180 gallons and it handled the weight well. It had standard Stearman wings with a symmetrical airfoil. Bernard's had a 215 gallon tank and high lift wings. I wanted to see how it compared so when I got to Antigo I pulled up to the loading pad and filled it with water so I could test it out. It took off ok but I could tell it was heave and it took some left stick to fly level, much more than on the flight to Antigo. I did a couple of turns to the left and right to feel it out. The turns to the right were much easier. I made a few passed with the water then dumped it. It's quite exciting to dump a load. The airplane losses 1,600 pounds in about 5 seconds. You have to push forward on the stick to keep the nose from pitching up too much.

When I landed I started studding the airplane to see if I could figure out why I had to hold so much left stick, especially when It was heavy. At first glance everything looked normal. I took a close and careful look at the wings then I saw it. It did not have a set of high lift wings. It had three high lift wings and the bottom right wing had a standard symmetrical wing with a squared off wing tip.

Mystery solved. The lower right wing is the one that usually gets damaged in a ground loop so my guess is that's what happened. There were probably no high lift wings available so Bernard just put on the standard wing because that's all he had.

T-CRAFT GLIDER

Like most airports ours had a derelict airplane on it owned by someone who wouldn't fly it and wouldn't sell it. Some were just left to rot away on a tie-down with grass and weeds, untouched, growing around it. Ours was a T-Craft tucked away in an old T-hanger. The story was that it had been recovered some 14 years ago and never quite finished. It sat with no propeller on its engine and no carburetor. It actually looked pretty nice, especially with all the years of neglect it had endured. It had caught my father's eye and he had started to track down the owner. As it turned out it was a partnership and my father did business with one of them. After a few weeks of negotiations my father acquired the T-Craft. My best recollection is that it was built in 1939. It was a pale orange and cream color. It looked quite nice.

The first order of business was to do an inspection on the T-Craft to see what kind of shape it was in. As it turned out the airframe was in good shape. The fabric was grade A cotton, not used anymore, and after 14 years or so it was in marginal condition, even though it had never been flown. The engine, on the other hand, needed an overhaul after sitting so long.

It was a rare, slow, summer day. All of our spraying was done for the morning and I was looking for something fun to do. I had been looking at the T-Craft and I remembered how everyone always talked about how much of a glider a T-Craft was. I was a glider pilot so I decided to find out if a T-Craft really was a good glider.

I mounted a glider tow hook to the bumper of a pickup truck. I was going to tow the T-Craft into the air with the truck. I took off the left-hand door for easy egress, incase things didn't go well and I needed to get out quickly. With help I walked the T-Craft to the end of the runway. I had a length of tow rope we used for towing banners that had a tow ring on one end and nothing on the other end. I hooked the ring to the tow release that was attached to the truck. I had one of our other pilots sit in the back with a hammer to hit the release if I got into trouble. The other end of the rope I threaded through the hole in the cowling where the carburetor was supposed to be and through the fire wall where the heater hose was supposed to be. I wrapped the rope twice around the tubing that the landing gear was attached to and held on to the loose end. All I had to do was let go of the rope and the truck would pull it away and I could land.

My plan was to have the truck driver accelerate to about 45mph. That should be enough to get me airborne. I would fly straight down the runway at about 10 feet and release when I needed to land. Including myself, there were about 10 people plus my wife, Nancy, there to watch the fun.

I put on my stars and stripes "Easy Rider" crop-dusting helmet and prepared for takeoff. I signaled the truck to go and it quickly accelerated. At about 40mph indicated airspeed the T-Craft lifted off and flew smoothly and stably down the runway. About 800 feet from the end of the runway I released the rope and it was pulled out just as planned. I brought the plane in for a nice smooth landing. I did another two solo flights. It flew so well that I began to give rides to almost everyone, including Nancy. This was fun but the flying time was too short. I wanted to extend the flying time and the only way I could think of was with an aero-tow behind our Super Cub.

Bob, had towed banners but he had never towed a glider. I gave him a quick briefing on what I wanted him to do and what to expect. We hooked the tow rope to the Super Cub this time and put the other end through the T-Craft cowling and firewall as before, but this time I tied it to the inside gear support. I put my hunting knife under my leg so I could cut the rope for my release. The door was still off from the left side of the T-Craft. I leaned out and motioned to take up the slack in the line. With that done and Bob in the Super Cub idling, waiting for my signal to go, I made one last check to see that everyone was clear, then wagged my rudder full left then full right as the signal to go.

The Super Cub started to accelerate at what seemed to be a good pace. If you have ever seen a glider being towed into the air, the glider quickly gains flying speed and flies along just off the runway waiting for the tow plane to get airborne. That is what I had expected but not what happened. The Super Cub accelerated and got airborne before me. Nothing to panic about, I just waited and expected the T- Craft to be airborne any moment, but that isn't what happened either. The Super Cub kept climbing steeply and I was still on the ground. I thought of cutting the tow rope, but I was so far down the runway I was afraid I couldn't stop before rolling into the potato field and flipping over. I didn't cut the rope. I continued to accelerate as the Super Cub climbed and eventually dragged me off the runway. The T- Craft had flown so nicely behind the truck but now I was at 50mph indicated, and not flying, but being dragged aloft.

With the door off, the T-Craft was buffeting from the disturbed airflow. It hadn't done that either behind the truck. I could see that Bob knew something wasn't right but with no radio communications he did as I had briefed him and circled over the airport. We had gained enough altitude for me to try to improve my situation.

I was in what glider pilots call a low tow position. The Super Cub was well above me pulling me up. I thought I would try to move to the high-tow position by banking and turning left to accelerate like you do in playing "crack the whip." The turn would make the T-Craft go faster relative to the Super

67

Cub and I thought I might be able to climb into the normal tow position behind the Super Cub. As I started the turn the T-Craft buffeted even more, and, as I pulled back on the wheel and started to climb, I got caught in the wing tip vortices, (horizontal tornadoes), coming off the Super Cub. There I was, tethered to the Super Cub and starting to do a slow roll on the end of the rope without enough energy to climb above it! I pushed the wheel forward to gain some speed then started a hard turn to the right, hoping to gain energy to pull up into the normal tow position. As I got to the right side I pulled back again hoping to power through the vortices. As I climbed, I once again got caught in the vortices and started to do another slow roll on the end of the tow line. I pushed down and centered the T-Craft behind the Super Cub. This was not a good ride but a lot better then doing slow rolls on the end of the tow rope.

Bob had kept me over the airport. We were now at 900 feet heading south. I was getting ready to cut the tow rope when it occurred to me. I wondered how the C.G. (center of gravity) was affected by the missing propeller and carburetor. Well it was too late to think about that now. I took my knife out from under my leg and cut the rope. I was later told by the observers on the ground that it looked like I just fell out of the sky.

I pushed the wheel forward to try and gain flying speed. As I did so the T-Craft started to buffet violently. I could not focus on the airspeed indicator because it was buffeting so badly. I pulled back some and the buffeting got better, but only by a little. I only had time and altitude enough to make a left 270 degree turn from directly over the airport and just clear the road on the east side as I landed on the grass runway facing west. I just sat there for a moment, drained, and feeling very lucky. As I sat there my left leg started to hop up and down with the release of adrenalin and tension.

I know a cat is supposed to have nine lives. I don't know how many lives a pilot is supposed to have, but I know I used one of them that day. I pushed that T-Craft back into the hanger, closed the door and never looked at it again.

Editor's note:

Nancy didn't tell me until many years later that my father had seen from home what was happening with the Super Cub towing the T-Craft and came racing to the airport and onto the runway. He had gotten out of his car and just stood there next to Nancy. He didn't say a word, just watched. She said after I landed safely he got back in his car and drove home, not a word was ever said.

TEMPERATURE DEW POINT

August. Warm days, cool nights and mornings filled with solid, smooth, dense air for crop dusting. August is another thing too. August is fog.

This morning was very cool. Dew covered my Pawnee. My feet were soaked by the wet grass as I walked around the airplane removing the tie downs and doing the pre-flight. Twenty eight gallons of fuel in the tank, that's one hour and thirty-five minutes, plus 3 five gallon cans in the hopper. Oil is at 10 quarts. The pre-flight is complete.

It will be light soon. The first orange rays of sun are showing in the east. It's time to get rolling. I have thirty minutes flying to get to Coleman, where I'll be working today. The 235 Lycoming engine kicks right off. I love the smell of the burned 80 octane fuel. As I sit in the cockpit with the doors open, I listen to the low, throaty music of the Lycoming O-540 engine while I let it warm up.

It is a short, bumpy taxi to the end of the north-south grass strip at Nicollet Airport in DePere Wisconsin. Mags; check. Carb heat; check. The r.p.m. drops more than expected and the engine runs rough then smoothes out as the carburetor ice melts and the r.p.m. increase. I'll have to keep an eye on it. Controls; free. Trim; set. Flaps; up. The check list is complete. The Pawnee is ready for takeoff.

As the engine comes up to takeoff power, the propeller starts to beat the moisture out of the air. For a few seconds during takeoff, I am sitting inside a white tube of clouds. As the airplane accelerates, the moisture stops forming its shroud. The Pawnee is not equipped with anything but the essential instruments; a sensitive altimeter with a broken set knob, airspeed, oil temperature and pressure, and a compass. There are no gyro instruments or radios. Not even a turn and bank indicator. But why would they be needed? This is a work airplane, a crop duster.

The serenity of early morning flight can be very hypnotic, too hypnotic. When you are flying an airplane, any airplane you must stay alert. I wasn't. I don't know exactly when it happened. One minute everything was fine, the next it wasn't. The ground had disappeared. I never saw anything like it before. All I can figure out is that a wind must have come up out of the northeast and blew the warm, moist air off the bay of Green Bay and onto the cooler ground. The air was already saturated as evidenced by my takeoff. Stupid idiot! If I had been more alert, maybe I would have seen it coming. Maybe I could have landed in a field and waited it out. I have only been flying for about ten minutes and I have one hour and twenty-five minutes of fuel left until the engine quits. That is a lot of time. I just hope it is enough.

I don't know how far the fog extends, but I am going to find out. The only way I can go is west. North follows the Bay. It is likely to be foggy all along it. East is over the Bay, no place to land there. To the south is Austin Straubel Airport at Green Bay. It's a controlled field and I don't want to get tangled up with any of their IFR traffic.

There is a lot of desolate country around here. I sure am glad that my compass works. I have always made sure it was accurate. It is the only navigational aid that I have. On a heading of west, I checked my watch. In seven minutes I should be over Pulaski. There is a church there with a tall spire that should be sticking out of the fog. It will tell me how thick the fog is, and I know the Pulaski Airport is just a few miles south, and a little eats of there. My seven minutes were up and still there is nothing below me except fog. Even the church spire remained hidden. I pressed on another twenty minutes but still there was nothing but fog. Further west there was only more fog and rough country. I decided to turn back toward the east.

I was following a four lane highway toward the north before the fog hid it from me. If I went back, I might see some car lights, something by which to navigate. Twenty-eight minutes went by. I should be over the highway, but still I couldn't see anything. I turned the Pawnee north to see if it gets any better up there. It didn't. That far north there aren't many fields good enough to land in. In fact, there aren't many fields at all. Near the Bay there are a lot swamps and trees. There are at least as many woods as farm fields in most of this area. Much further north and there would be even fewer places to land. I had better turn south. At least there would be better odds of finding a field to land in if the fog clears in time.

By my estimate I was over the highway. I knew the country pretty well. It had been an hour and ten minutes and I'd had twenty-five minutes of fuel left. Twenty-five minutes of hope. I decided to try to take it down through the fog. There might be enough visibility to land, or at least confirm my location.

I trimmed the Pawnee as well as I could. Just a little nose down, maybe 300 to 400 feet per minute. What I wouldn't give for an attitude indicator or even a turn and bank instrument. I didn't have my hand on the stick. Instead, it was resting on my knee. I'd hoped this would help keep me from turning. Carb heat is on for the descent. The clouds came up to meet me. It was just like flying around in a glass of milk. The altimeter reads 1,800 feet when I enter the fog. I have no idea how far that is above the ground since the set knob is broken and I was unable to adjust it to the field elevation when I departed. What was that reading? I'd wished I'd remembered. At least it will tell me how far I have to go to get back on top. Seconds passed like minutes. No change in airspeed. The altimeter is unwinding slowly. I have gone down about two hundred feet. My whole body is tense. The wind shield is misted over with water picked up from the fog. Out the side, I see it is getting darker and darker and darker. Suddenly I see just below me, in the darkness, is a woods mere feet away. Full power!, start the climb. Stay calm, don't move anything. Up I go the woods disappears. Now it is just milk all around me. The altimeter shows I'm climbing. I wait to see the sun.

Thank God it doesn't take long to climb the three hundred feet back into the clear. The adrenaline is really pumping. I know there is no choice but to try again. I will wait for five minutes and then try to go down through the fog again while I still have fuel. In a few minutes I will run out of fuel and I will be going down anyway, better to do it while the engine is still running and under control.

I turn back north over where I hope the four lane highway is. There are still no lights visible through the fog. The decent last time was well controlled. I'll do it the same way this time.

Power back.
Carb heat on.
Box the stick with my knees and try to keep her from turning.
In the fog again.
Concentrate, but do NOTHING!
I look out the side window, nothing.
Check the airspeed; steady at 80 mph.
Altimeter going down slowly.
Compass is north and steady.
Back outside still nothing.
Keep relaxed, do nothing.
The darkness starts to close in again.
Suddenly I see the washed-out form of a group of trees. Grey on grey.
The visibility is a little better. That is I have some.
I can make out a hay field next to the trees.
I circle the field at about 75 feet to check for wires and other obstacles while making sure it is big enough to land in.
The visibility is low, not even an eighth of a mile. The field looks big enough to land in, I hope, but there is no other option, I'm landing here.

Throttle back.
Full flaps.
Push down easy.
No obstructions visible.
Flair, touchdown!

I didn't notice if the field was bumpy or not. I'm just glad to be on the ground and safe. The taxi to the south end of the pasture is a short one. I shut the engine down, open the doors and just sit there, as the tension drains from my body. After a few minutes I unbuckle my seat belt ant take off my helmet. I pour the three five gallon cans of fuel I carried in the hopper into the fuel tank so I will be ready to leave when the fog cleared. I climb on top of the fuselage, over the spray tank and lay down. I figure since I'm not going anywhere for a while I might as well get some sleep.

At 9:30 it appears clear enough to fly. I'm not going to get caught in the fog twice in one day, I'll wait. At 10:00 I can't see any trace of fog anywhere. I can leave now. As I'm getting down onto the wing I notice a pickup truck coming down the lane toward me. It must be the farmer who owns this land. He drives up to me and my plane and stops. He calls out through the window, "You all right? Need any help?" I call back, "Everything's okay. I'm just getting ready to leave" The farmer waives and drives off. I climb into my Pawnee 235, fire up the engine and takeoff. Everything is "okay" now that is.

Editor's note:

The field I landed in was about 1 mile west and 1 ½ miles south of where I thought I was. Not bad for unplanned dead reckoning navigation!

JUST A SECOND

I was spraying a large potato field with my Cessna Ag-Truck, one of those 160 acre fields with the center point irrigation system. It was located several miles southeast of Nekoosa, Wisconsin, bordering a military restricted area (R-6904B) used for bombing and gunnery practice.
We had permanent marker flags set across the middle of the field so we could keep our proper spacing while we sprayed the field. The flags were set up so we would fly over one, then in between that one and the next one, then over the second flag, and so on. Every fifth flag we would put in a double flag to make the counting easier. When you finished a pass you would pull up and start your procedure turn* to line up for the next pass. As soon as the flags became visible you would count over to the next flag in sequence, line up on a row, and start your spray run.

On big fields like this we would often fly a race track pattern. We would start the first pass in the middle of the field and at the end we would pull up and start a down-wind turn to the far end of the field and lay a pass in there. At the end of the pass we would pull up and turn up-wind and line up for the second pass moving over from the center. All turns would be in the same direction, flying a big oval. It was much faster flying a field in the race track pattern but it made counting the flags more difficult because you had less time and two sets of numbers to remember.

As in all phases of ag-flying it took a lot of concentration and there was no room for distraction. I was nearly finished with my first load so the airplane was handling quite well. I pulled up from my pass and started a turn to set up my next pass, when I did something I never did. I turned my head away from the field and looked out the small window in the top of the canopy on the high side where all you could see was sky and there, looking down on me from about 100 feet above, was an F-4. He was banking along with me so he could see me and what I was doing. I could see him in the cockpit with his visor down giving me a thumbs–up sign. I gave him a quick nod of recognition and dove back into the field.

It was only a second but one I have remembered through time.

procedure turn: First you would pull up out of the field, turn 45-60 degrees down-wind then reverse the turn to up-wind to line up the next pass or swath.

ILL TIMING

I arrived at the airstrip near Pound, Wisconsin early in the morning. The loaders for Country Gardens cannery were there and ready to go. I filled the tank and started to work my first field. I was feeling a little ill but thought I would try working. When I landed after my first load I used the field manager's new mobile phone (the kind that was bolted to the truck and weighed 20 pounds) to call back to base and ask for someone else to come out and finish up because I wasn't feeling well. There wasn't anyone to help because we were behind as usual. I was told to finish if I could or come back if I had to.

I wasn't feeling that bad so I decided to try another load. I was spraying a field I had sprayed many times before. It was boarded by Highway 41 on the east side and a set of "H" pole high lines ran from the west side to the east side cutting the field in half. Just to the south of the high lines there was a cutout for a house and a few small buildings bordered by medium sized fruit trees.

After a few passes under the high lines and pulling up over the house, I pushed back down on the other side to the end of the field. On my next pass I reached the west end of the lot the house was on. I was heading south. I went under the high lines and it looked like I was clear of the trees behind the house. Just before I cleared the last of the trees I heard a terrible loud bang. The airplane yawed hard left. I pulled back on the stick to climb and put in full right rudder just to straighten out the plane. Instead of flying south I was now heading east with full right rudder just to hold my heading. I looked at the left wing and saw that about three to four feet of the leading edge had been flattened out. I must have misjudged my distance from the trees and hit one.

Except for having to hold full right rudder to go straight the airplane was in good shape. The engine was running normally no other damage noted on the left or right side. I decided to head back for the airstrip. I had to make a 180 degree turn to the left to head back to the west. When I got over the airstrip I had to make a 270 degree turn to the left to line up on the runway. The airplane still would not turn to the right. I matched my landing flare to the rolling hill of the runway and landed without incident.

I got out and checked for damage. The last three or four feet of the left leading edge was smashed in but I couldn't believe that that was the reason I couldn't turn right. I looked down the runway and found the reason for the problem. There was a large bush-like part of a tree lying on the runway. It must have been ripped off of a tree and caught on the leading edge. It was stuck to the wing until I slowed down after landing when it fell off. The top of the wing covered all of it so I couldn't see it from the cockpit. A branch that size with all those leaves certainly was enough to cause the drag I experienced.

I figured I needed to get some aluminum to patch the wing, but it was too early for the stores to be open. So I had the guys take me to town for breakfast, I felt better after that, and then we went to the local HVAC shop where I bought a length of aluminum and a couple of rolls of what we called 100 mile an hour tape, more commonly known as duct tape. Back at the airstrip I taped the aluminum over the damaged area and went back to work.

There was no damage to the wing except for the leading edge. I flew that airplane with my patch on it the rest of the season.

ONE LONE TREE

It was late September and the crop- dusting season was all but over. One of our pilots had already left for the season. and I had unofficially retired from crop dusting to pursue a career in commercial aviation. I was in Sturgeon Bay packing some household items to move to our new apartment in Illinois when I got a call from Al Rushton, one of my partners in Ag-Air. He told me they were behind in the spraying because of some bad weather and needed some help if I could. I had a few days before starting my new job, and I had missed crop dusting that summer, I said I would be able to help out for a few days.

I went to Clintonville where I had run one of our spraying operations for several years. Bob Taylor had been based there that summer but he had just left for the season. One of our 235 Pawnees was in the hanger waiting for me. Clyde, one of our pilots from Antigo, was there with a Pawnee Brave. We were going to work together for the next day or two. We each loaded our planes with Paraquat. We were going to
spray sunflower fields to defoliate them so they could be harvested. Clyde took off first. The Brave was a bigger plane than the D model 235 Pawnee I was flying so Clyde could carry more chemical and do more acres with each load. (and make more money) I pulled out onto the runway as soon as Clyde started his takeoff roll. I checked the mags and carb heat everything was good. I had a hundred and fifty gallons of mix on board. That was a normal load for the 235 Pawnee. The day was cool and calm. The runway was 4600 feet of blacktop, much more than was normally required. I hadn't flown a Pawnee for three months, but it seemed to be accelerating slower than normal. It took a long time for the tail to come up, indicating the Pawnee was nearly ready to fly. I eased in a little back pressure and the Pawnee staggered into the air. Something was wrong but I didn't know what. There just wasn't any power. I was climbing but just barely. Clyde was getting further away and I didn't know where the field was that we were to spray other than it was east of

New London. I had my hands full just trying to keep this airplane in the air. Paraquat is a hazardous chemical. My airplane had a dump system where I could get rid of the whole load or just part of it, but if I did that it would certainly sterilize the soil and be a hazard to people on the ground.

I hung on and kept the Pawnee headed south. I could only climb to 300 feet above the ground. I couldn't see Clyde anymore. In all the tight spots I have ever been in one thing has always been the same, time slows to a crawl. What takes only seconds seems to take minutes and minutes seem to take hours. This was no different. I kept heading south. I was scanning the horizon for Clyde. I spotted him ahead and to my left as he pulled up over some trees at the end of the field as he turned around. My Pawnee was just above stalling speed. I wasn't able to make any tight turns or abrupt maneuvers. I circled the field Clyde was spraying and checked it for obstructions and emergency landing areas. I knew Clyde had seen me and I planned my turn so I could follow him into the field for my first pass. Instead of bringing the power to idle, as I usually did when I dropped into a field, I keep it wide open. I would need all the speed and power I could get to pull up at the end of the field and clear the trees. I was making my spray run at a little over 100 miles per hour. It's amazing how quickly you can cover a half mile field when you are doing a hundred miles an hour. It's amazing how quickly the trees at the end of that field can fill your windshield at a hundred miles per hour too, especially when you're not sure you'll be able to clear them when you pull back on the stick asking, imploring, begging, your airplane to climb. My airplane did climb. It didn't give me much extra, but we did clear the trees. Clyde had dropped back into the field just as I pulled up and started my procedure turn. I was again just a little above stall speed. I had dissipated all my energy pulling up over the trees. Clyde was finished with

his pass and procedure turn before I was able to get turned around. I extended my turn to let him make another pass toward me then I dropped in for my second pass. The trees came up to fill my windshield just as fast but I was getting lighter and the pull up wasn't as hard. I had a little more energy. The turn was not quit as long or difficult. It took several more passes before I lightened up enough for the Pawnee to start to perform the way it should. When I was down to about 100 gallons in the
hopper the Pawnee was doing pretty good. I didn't need the help of prayers to climb over the trees any more. I was able to keep up with Clyde in the turns now and we finished the field together.

On the way back to the Clintonville airport I flew formation on Clyde's left wing. I didn't have my normal crop dusting helmet; it was in Illinois. I hadn't intended to do any crop dusting on this trip, I was just packing up some things and tying up loose ends. My crop-dusting helmet had a communications headset and microphone in it. It also had a sun visor so I could hide from that bright ball on first light flights and in the evening when the sun could blind you. All I had was my old motorcycle helmet. It was a stars and stripes helmet like the one Peter Fonda wore in "Easy Rider." It didn't matter. It was nice to be flying again. Clyde and I didn't need a radio to communicate anyway.

When we shut down in Clintonville to reload, I told Clyde that something was wrong with my airplane. He said he could tell I wasn't turning very well at first, but he didn't know anything was wrong. The engine checked out all right, but it just didn't seem to have any power. I told Clyde I was only going to take one hundred gallons a load and when we quit for the morning I was going to take the airplane to Pulaski and have Ted, our mechanic, take a look at it.

With the lighter loads it was no problem flying the Pawnee, I just wasn't getting as much work done or making as much money, although the money was always secondary to getting the work done with me.

Ted pulled the spark plugs out and found they were in bad shape. They were all fouled with lead deposits. I set to work cleaning them. Ted also thought the mags were a little weak, so we took the mags off one of our other Pawnees. That Pawnee had an unfortunate "navy landing" when the tail wheel caught on a telephone wire during a takeoff, and made a landing from about 20 feet in the air. Its repairs won't be finished until next season, so the mags won't be missed. Ted and I finished that afternoon. When I test flew it it was very evident that
 we had cured the problem. It had a lot more power then when I brought it into the shop. I flew the Pawnee to William's Farms near Suring where I would be working the next morning.

One thing I always liked about the early fall spraying is that first light isn't as early as it is in the spring. I never really got used to getting up that early. It was part of the job so I did it without complaint, but I never liked it. Once my feet hit the floor I was O.K. When I got out into the pre-dawn cold for the short ride to the airport I was awake. This morning was the same. A short night followed by an early get up. I stayed in a motel that night and it was too early for the restaurants to be open. Nothing new there either. It was too early to eat anyway. We usually stopped for breakfast around 10:00 or 11:00 when the wind came up and it was too windy or turbulent to spray anymore. The ride to the airport took about 20 minutes. I had the heater on full. That along with my usual array of shirt, sweat shirt, and jacket was enough to keep me warm for the ride to the airstrip, but not when I started the engine on the Pawnee and stood in the prop blast while I loaded the hopper.

It was still dark out with just a hint of light showing to the east. Donnie, my loader, was already there, waiting in his truck, with the engine running and the heater on full. He was half asleep when I rapped on his window. He popped up awake and gave me the plat maps and list of fields we had to spray. I had sprayed most of them before when they were planted in corn. I looked at the list and the maps and batched them into loads for Donnie to mix for me. The first group of fields was about six or seven miles away, between our airstrip at William's Farms and Pound Wisconsin. Donnie was mixing my first load while I did the pre-flight on the Pawnee and filled both the wing tanks with fuel. This was a "D" model Pawnee with one 18 gal. fuel tank on the end of each wing. I didn't like that arrangement as

well as the "C" model with one 36 gallon tank in the nose. I guess it was safer then the "C" model but the "D" was a lot harder to turn with the fuel so far out on the wing tips. I took off for a quick flight around the airstrip to warm up the engine and oil as well a to make sure the rest of the airplane was working ok. The morning was chilly, almost cold, which made the air dense and solid as a rock. I touched down near the north end of the strip where the water tank and mix rig were parked. The Pawnee came almost to a stop just short of the loading area. I applied a little right brake and rudder as I hit just a little power to spin the Pawnee around 180 degrees, coming to a stop right at the end of the loading hose. I let the engine run while Donnie pumped in the chemical through the side load connection, on the left side of the airplane, just behind the cockpit. I watched the tank fill through the translucent fiberglass hopper as the mixture quickly reached the 130 gallon mark.

I signaled Donnie to close the loader valve. He did and put the cap over the coupler to prevent any leaks. He gave me the thumbs up sign to let me know he was clear and everything was ready to go. I eased the power up to 1500 R.P.M. and checked the mags again then pulled the carb heat. The R.P.M. dropped about 300 then came back a 100. I had a little ice, I'll have to keep checking that this morning to make sure it doesn't build up and kill the engine during flight. Oil temp. and pressure check good. I check once more to make sure Donnie was clear and everything was O.K., then brought the power up to the stop. I started to roll. Even with a near full load on the soft muck strip the Pawnee accelerates quickly, much better than yesterday. The strip is a little rough from a long hard summer

of use. The Pawnee bounced around a little during the takeoff roll, but as soon as I got it airborne the ride was as smooth as glass. The sun is just below the horizon with its light spilling onto the fields below. The trees have the first hints of fall color and the air was cold, dense and smooth. Times like this make all the rest worth while.

When you are crop dusting all your concentration is on Crop-dusting. You don't have time for distractions. You are constantly looking for obstructions hidden in and around the field. You are checking for wind and any signs of drift. You are checking your nozzles to make sure they are all working properly while you are in the field spraying and to be sure they are off and not leaking while you are in the turns. You sneak a quick peak at your engine gauges during the turn to make sure they are all in the green. When you are in the field spraying you check your primary flight gauge, the spray pressure gauge, to make sure the pressure is correct for the rate of application you are using. You continuously check your chemical and your progress though the field to make sure you are not running long or short on chemical. This is where your conscious thoughts are. The airplane almost flies itself. Your brain thinks something, usually subconsciously, and the airplane just reacts. You are the central flight computer and you are plugged into the airplane through the cockpit seat and flight controls. This is where your thoughts must be. Anything that distracts you from that is putting you in danger. At 2 feet and 100 miles per hour it doesn't take much of a distraction to put you into the ground.

It only took a few minutes to fly to the first field I was going to spray. I circled it once and saw the white flag marking it as the right field, but there was a fence line separating it from another field of sunflowers. I wasn't sure if both of the fields were to be sprayed or not. I circled again checking the map and looking for a second flag. The rule was that if there is a fence line separating two fields to be sprayed that both fields need to have flags in them to prevent the kind of problem I was having now. I checked the map and the list of acreages and decided that both the fields were to be sprayed. The one didn't look big enough by itself. I had sprayed in this area many times before. The field without the flag in it was one I had sprayed when it was planted in corn. It had a row of pine trees on the northern border. The west was open but about 3/4 of a mile away was a string of high-line wires. The south was open as was the east with the exception of one tree near the northeast end of the field, right on the fence line.

I started spraying on the south side going east and west. The sun was just above the horizon making it hard to see when I was east bound. It's hard to think of crop dusting as being routine, perhaps rhythmic is a better term, but it is. Once you start working a field you set up a rhythm. Power back, slight push forward, at about 10 feet power to three quarters, spray on, hold at 2 feet. Nearing the other end power full, spray off, pull back clear the obstructions, hard right bank about 50 degrees then back to the left, check the nozzles for leaks, engine in the green, keep the turn tight, see the auto-flag, space over for the next pass, line looks good, pick a row and track it, power idle, slow, clear obstacles, push down, spray on... rhythm. I crossed the fence and kept going. The chemical looked about right I'm sure this was supposed to be part of the other field. I should have just not sprayed it but I was behind on work and I didn't want to waste time coming back for this little bit of work. It gnawed at me as I continued to spray. The full disk of the sun was now over the horizon. It was so bright I could hardly see in front of me. I glanced to the side and used peripheral vision to keep track of my position in the field. I wish I had my regular helmet with the sun visor. I'd be able to block out that lovely orb and be able to see where I was going. I was nearly finished with this field, only a couple of passes to go. The chemical was coming out right, both of these fields must have been figured together. I was headed east right into the sun and approaching the end of the field. Power full, spray off, pull up, BANG! Damn! My mind went into overdrive. I hit one of those electric fence wires that was on a pole over the gate! I was only about 10 feet above the ground and I expected the wire to brake and I'd be on my way, but I started to roll hard right. I was past 90 degrees in an instant. I threw the stick into the upper right corner to keep it rolling and push the nose up. I was inverted now and I knew if I went in upside down I probably wouldn't make it. The Pawnee keep rolling back right side up. I was only about 20 feet in the air and I had two choices. If I pulled back on the stick and the Pawnee was not badly damaged I would fly away wondering what the heck happened. If I pulled back and It was seriously damaged it would probably roll again. If it did, I would probably die. My other choice was to push it into the ground while I was right side up. The Pawnee was made to take a crash. I was setting in an energy absorbing roll cage wearing a helmet, seat belt and shoulder harness. The engine and an empty area where the fuel tank was on the "C" model, I'll never bitch about the fuel being way out there on the end of the wing again, along with the hopper were all in front of me to absorb the impact. It is something like modern stock cars. I've seen them make terrible crashes and the driver walks away.

I was hoping for the same kind of luck. I pushed forward on the stick and drove the Pawnee into the ground. I remember seeing the engine hit the ground, bend to the right and start to collapse back as the front of the Pawnee started to collapse inward. Then the empty area where the fuel was on the "C" model, began to collapse, and the hopper started to move backwards into the cockpit. The whole fuselage was crushing toward ME! I put my hand on the instrument panel and said that's enough and the collapsing stopped. I slid to a stop facing backward from my original direction of flight. When the airplane stopped sliding I checked right then left. There wasn't much left. All the glass was gone, and the Pawnee was setting flat on the ground. There was dust in the air. The left wing was just a lot of shredded aluminum and fabric. I looked down on the left side of the cockpit and saw a stream of gas as big as my thumb pouring out of the mangled fuel line. It dawned on me that I needed to get the hell out of there. I tried to get up but I couldn't move. Oh yeah, I pulled the seat belt release and took off running to the right side of the mangled remnants of what moments ago was a perfectly good airplane. I stood about 75 yards away for a while and took inventory. I had some scraped knuckles on my right hand and my right knee was a little sore. Thanks Mr. Piper for designing such a crashworthy airplane. What seemed like a minute or two later a pickup came driving through the field toward the wreck. It was the farmer who owned the field I was spraying. He was looking at the wreck then he spotted me. He drove up to me with an astonished look on his face. He looked at the wreck again then at me and asked what I was doing walking around. His implication and astonishment were understandable when I looked back at the pile of junk that had once been an airplane. I asked if I could use his phone. He took me to his house and I called the

office at William's Farms. Al answered the phone and I told him what had happened, then I put the farmer on the phone so he could tell Al how to find me. As I washed my hands and put a couple of Band-Aids on my
skinned knuckles, the farmer, (I never did get his name), told me he was just out the door on his way to his pickup when he heard me hit the tree (It was a tree not a wire). He said when he looked up, he saw the airplane roll through the air with pieces coming off of it. The ground was a little hilly right there, luckily for me because he said the wing wouldn't have cleared the ground if it wasn't for a little depression right where I needed it. He watched it crash and kind of cart wheel. (I don't remember any of that, but I was facing
backward when I stopped.) He told me he didn't know if he should call the ambulance, the coroner or first check to see how I was. (I took that to mean dead or alive. No sense calling the volunteer ambulance if all I needed was the coroner.)

While I was waiting for Al to pick me up a steady
stream of pickups started pulling into the driveway. They all had heard the Pawnee fly over and start working, but they didn't hear it fly away. They thought something might have

happened and they wanted to see if they could help. They were right, something had happened and thankfully I didn't need any help. Like the proverbial tree in the forest, I had always wondered if anyone would ever notice if I had a problem and went down. It was nice to know that there would be help if I needed it.

Back at William's Farm I told Al the story and called the FAA to report the accident. I told them the truth, I

screwed up and hit a tree. The airplane was working fine up to that point. I wasn't injured and no property on the ground was damaged. That was that, they gave me permission to move the wreckage. We were able to salvage the engine, the elevators, rudder, seat and the rotating beacon, that was about it, except for me.

I sometimes still wonder what would have happened if I had pulled up and tried to fly away. I'm at ease with the choice I made but, I still wonder.

That was my last time crop-dusting. A sad way to end an era in my life.

BRENNAN AIR FREIGHT

It was fall of 1974. Crop dusting season was almost over and I needed a job for the winter. Brennan Air fright was located in Clintonville, Wisconsin, which was the same airport where I was crop dusting, so I walked over and asked if they needed any pilots for the winter. As it turned out they did and I was hired. The fleet consisted of 3 Cessna 207s and a BN-2 Brittan Norman Islander.

The pay was $200 a week. At the time I was living in a 14'x70' mobile home that my mother-in-law helped buy. I had a wife and two daughters and I remember thinking, "man maybe I really can make a living in aviation."

The job consisted of flying one of several routes from Clintonville to Milwaukee Mitchell Field to drop off and pick up freight. The freight would be kept in a step van at each of the airports where we stopped. If the load was too heavy or bulky to fit in the airplane we would have to unload the airplane into the truck and drive the rest of the route, picking up the airplane on the reverse trip.

In the beginning all the flying was done VFR (Visual Flight Rules) because the company didn't have a Part 135 (Commercial) IFR operating certificate, only VFR.

I got very familiar with all of the routes and with that familiarity came a willingness to fly in some weather that was quite marginal. I made it in and out of Milwaukee many nights on a special VFR clearance that allowed flying in a control zone with weather below normal ceiling and visibility requirements.

On one such night I departed Milwaukee, in light snow, for the eastern run, along the western shore of Lake Michigan, to Manitowoc, Green Bay and Clintonville. I off-loaded a few packages in Manitowoc and departed for Green Bay. The light snow had become moderate and forward visibility was restricted, although visibility straight down was good making ground contact possible. I contacted Green Bay approach for flight following and a weather update. I would usually contact approach not so much for traffic advisories, I was the only one flying that late at night, but to have someone to talk to. It helped both of us stay awake.

This night I didn't need help to stay awake. The poor weather made it easy to keep awake and concentrating on the job at hand. The flight from Manitowoc to Green Bay is only 28 miles, or 14 minutes, on a course of about 320 degrees and lying along that course was a pair of towers topping out at 2,045 feet m.s.l. or 1,055 feet above ground level. I was below that and couldn't fly higher and still maintain ground contact.

I knew those towers well. In fact I knew the family upon whose land those towers are built, but this night I couldn't see those towers.

Controller: "Cessna 123, do you have the towers at 12 o'clock and 5 miles (2½ minutes)?"

Me: "Cessna 123, negative, looking".

I turned a few degrees right squirming in my seat a little and leaning forward intensely scanning ahead for the lights to identify the towers, still nothing.

Controller: "Cessna 123, towers about 12 o'clock and 3 miles."

Me: "Cessna 123, still no contact, looking"

I turned a few more degrees right and still straining to see forward. The towers were still invisible. I remembered a few years before when a small plane hit the tall TV tower at Rhinelander, Wisconsin. The tower collapsed and everyone on the airplane was killed.

Controller (with concern in his voice): "Cessna 123, towers 12 o'clock and 1 mile."

I had pressed my luck far enough. Still not seeing the towers and knowing I could be only seconds from taking one of these towers down myself, I called the approach controller.

"Cessna 123, still no contact, turning right and heading back to Manitowoc."

This night just got a lot longer. Instead of a few more minuets of flight to Green Bay and a short hop to Clintonville, I would be driving for several hours in the dark and snow. At least I was safe and would make it home that night. I don't know how close I came to the towers but maybe ignorance is bliss.

WHAT'S MY ALTITUDE?

Some nights I would not have any return freight. In that case I would just fly straight home to Clintonville. This particular night Bert, one of the other pilots also had no return freight. We decided to depart Milwaukee as a flight of two. When you do that the flight leader would do all of the radio calls and the number two would monitor the radio and just follow the leader. My altimeter had been sticking on the flight down so I told Bert to lead and I would follow him. It was a short taxi from Mitchell Aero to runway 7L. Bert got clearance from the tower to depart northwest. We both taxied onto the runway and Bert powered up and started his takeoff. Just as he broke ground I powered up and followed him out.

It was dark with overcast ceilings and some light snow enroute. After we both were airborne I closed up to about 50 yards behind Bert and we set course for home. Just south of Fond du Lac I was watching Bert's plane and poof, it just disappeared. A few seconds later poof I was IMC (instrument meteorological conditions) in the clouds and snow with no operating altimeter and no Bert. I called Bert on the radio and told him I was going to head for Fond du Lac airport and land if I could find it. I asked him to come back and get me.

I watched my attitude indicator and vertical speed indicator closely to prevent any change in altitude. I flew on for a few minutes in the dark. As I got close to Fond du Lac I could see straight down and the lights of the Mercury Outboard factory became visible. I knew the airport was just about a mile north west of there. I turned toward the airport and started a slow decent using my vertical speed indicator. The lights of the runway popped out from the snow and into my view. I lined up on runway 36 and I landed. Bert followed in a few minutes and we flew home together.

The next day the mechanics went to fix the altimeter but they said it was working just fine. A few days later it failed again on someone else. They finally decided to fix it.

IT WASN'T ALL WORK

One of the airplanes was left in Milwaukee overnight because there was no returning freight for it. The next day I flew with another pilot who would pick it up for the return run to Clintonville. We were empty on the first leg to Manitowoc so I decided to have some fun. We were going to play astronaut. I had the other pilot get out of his seat and go into the cargo area. I put the plane into a decent and sped up to redline, and then I pulled back on the wheel and started a steep climb. By pushing the nose down again the airplane would experience Zero-G and you can float like an astronaut. It was great fun and we did it several times.

One uneventful night enroute to Milwaukee I was just west of West Bend on top of an overcast. I saw a streak of light coming down from the sky. It was a meteor. I watched it burn through the clouds just about a mile off my right wing. A close miss.

PART TWO

THE AIRLINES

GETTING A JOB WITH THE AIRLINES

As I am sitting here in the cabin on an American Airlines 737 heading to Seattle then continuing on Alaska Airlines to Ketchikan, Alaska, I can't help but think of my airline career. It happened quite by chance. A number of factors all lining up to present me with the opportunity that would shape my life and career.

It started at the end of the crop-dusting season in 1977. My father had moved to Marathon Florida and Nancy (my wife and partner) decided we needed to visit for a short vacation before looking for a winter job. My father told me that Air Sunshine in Key West was hiring, and I should apply. I never wanted to fly for an airline. It looked too boring. I was used to flying an airplane 2 feet off the ground at 100 miles an hour dodging trees and flying under wires. Every time I looked up at an airliner it would just be flying a straight-line way up in the sky, but I didn't have a job lined up and Air Sunshine flew DC-3's, one of my favorite airplanes. I went to Key West and was hired.

Nancy and I went back to Wisconsin, picked up our 2 daughters from Nana, loaded everything we owned into the back of a pickup truck, hitched our Datsun B-210 to the back and headed to Key West!

After a week or so in ground school my two classmates, Carlos, Tom and I moved on to flight training. The DC-3 was the largest plane I had flown to date. It was love at first flight! The DC-3, or the "3" as we referred to it, was big but the controls were well balanced and nice to fly. It took a little while for it to react to the control inputs, so you had to be thinking well ahead of it especially on takeoff and landing. Sitting way up in the nose, by the time you noticed it start to sway one way or the other, the tail had already moved 3 feet. It wasn't hard to keep straight even in the constant crosswinds of Key West as long as you stayed alert (and carried a little power on the up-wind engine).

After flying the line a couple of months back and forth between Key West (EYW), Marathon and Miami and experiencing an engine failure on takeoff and a precautionary shutdown over the Everglades, it dawned on me that this was not such a bad gig. Push a button and a pretty young thing came to the cockpit and brought you a Coke. I wore a white shirt with epaulets to work even though it was oil stained from pre-fighting the Greasy-3 (as I began to call it) and wet with sweat while on the ground because the only air-conditioning was opening the side window. This wasn't bad! If I got a job with a real airline, I would make enough money to afford my own airplane for fun and have enough time off to enjoy it. Yeah, I was going to have to pursue this.

I knew I would be leaving Air Sunshine soon, so I decided to beef up my resume by getting an ATP rating in the DC-3. I was as current as I would ever be in a DC-3 and I thought a type rating in a large airplane would be helpful when I applied to the major airlines.

I went to Turse Air at Opa-locka Airport near Miami for the rating. They had a DC-3 for type ratings but it was a little different than what I was used to. It had Wright engines instead of the Pratt & Whitney engines I had been flying. It also had a horizontal situation indicator instead of a gyro compass and VOR. I had never seen one before and I learned about it as I was flying my first approach! Once I saw how it worked, I loved it but I learned about it while paying $300 an hour in the DC-3.

After a couple of hours of prep, I was ready for the check ride. All went well including the V1 engine cut, where the examiner pulls the power to idle on one engine just before liftoff. It makes it quite difficult to control the airplane with one engine at full power and the other at idle as I continued the takeoff and came around for a single engine landing. I was now a newly minted Airline Transport Pilot with a DC-3 type rating!

AIR SUNSHINE AND THE DC-3

My first engine failure came while flying as Co-Pilot on the DC-3 for Air Sunshine based in Key West, Florida. I was on a trip from Miami (MIA) back to Key West (EYW). We had a full load of thirty-one passengers and baggage. Our checklists were completed and the tower cleared us to take off on runway 27L. The DC-3 didn't have a pilot intercom system and it was too loud to communicate by voice so we used hand signals. The captain lined up and locked the tail

wheel in place and started to push the throttles up to takeoff power. The co-pilot monitored the engine instruments and gave the okay hand signal. When the captain approached full takeoff power the co-pilot tapped his wrist. The captain stopped pushing the throttles up and the co-pilot set final takeoff power of 48 inches of manifold pressure. As the aircraft accelerated to V2 the co-pilot held up two fingers in front of the captain's face indicating this speed. The tail would already be in the air, the captain pulled back gently on the wheel, and the aircraft lifted off. At about 400 feet the airplane began to vibrate heavily. I instinctively looked out my side window at the right engine. It was shaking so much I thought it might break away. We had no intercom so all communication at takeoff power was at a yell. I yelled over to the captain that I thought we blew a cylinder on the right engine. He quickly verified it and feathered the right engine. At this weight we could barely hold our altitude. We declared an emergency and slowly turned around for a landing on the runway we just left. I completed the emergency checklists and the before-landing checklist. The captain lined up with the runway and as he reduced power for landing, he also reduced the amount of left rudder he was using to keep us straight and overcome the loss of power from the right engine. The touchdown was smooth and normal. We made one of the turnoffs and had enough energy to turn back toward the terminal. I expected we would stop and get a tug to tow us back to the gate area. When the tower asked if we needed assistance the captain said no. He would taxi back to the gate.

The DC-3's engine and landing gear are both mounted in the same nacelle. With the engine in line with the main landing gear. With only one engine running I had no idea how the captain expected to get us back the gate. With the tail wheel unlocked he added power on the left engine and we started a right turn just as I expected. What I didn't expect is that when we nearly completed our 360 degree turn the captain locked the tail wheel. The airplane suddenly stopped its turn and lurched ahead. While holding full left rudder and using this method several more times we made it back to the gate. I was surprised the tail wheel locking pin didn't shear and I can only guess what it felt like to our passengers as the captain played crack the whip with them.

When the mechanics took off the cowling it was easy to find the offending cylinder. The cylinder head was completely broken off. The only thing keeping it attached to the airplane was the two sparkplug wires and the cowling itself.

ENGINE FAILURE NUMBER TWO

I was on a trip to MIA with Del as the captain. I liked flying with him. He reminds me of the character John from American Graffiti, a gear head with the same slicked back hair and attitude right out of the fifties.

We departed Key West enroute to Miami. When we leveled off I set cruise power of 2230 rpm and 33" of manifold pressure. I noticed the cylinder head temperature on the right engine was a little high. I pointed this out to Del and he said to keep an eye on it. As we proceeded up the Keys to Miami the cylinder head temperature continued to slowly climb and the oil pressure started to slowly decrease. Something was developing but as long as everything stayed within limits we would continue to MIA.

We were over the Everglades when we hit the limit on cylinder head temperature of 260 degrees centigrade. As Del prepared to shutdown the right engine I got on the intercom and told our flight attendant what was about to happen. Del informed Air Traffic Control of our plan to make a precautionary shutdown and divert to Homestead Airport. Then Del got on the P.A. and in his nonchalant way told the passengers we were going to make a precautionary shut down of the right engine and land at Homestead.

The weather was good VFR and we made a long slow decent from our cruising altitude. Del lined up on the center line and reduced the power on the left engine. We were just inches above the runway but Del was holding it off waiting for a perfect touchdown. He said he always made his single engine landings his best. Meanwhile we were nearly halfway down the runway. Finally I yelled out, "just put in on the ground!" The touchdown was perfect and we were able to taxi to the terminal without incident.

ENGINE FAILURE NUMBER TWO; PART TWO

The company flew in another DC-3 with a couple of mechanics and some spare parts. Our passengers and flight attendant flew on to MIA on that airplane. Del and I had to hang out and wait for our plane to be fixed. Things were not all bad. My dad kept a car at Homestead Airport, an old Pinto. I got the key from the office and Del and I went into town for some dinner.

It was near midnight when the mechanics finished with our airplane. They said it had three cracked cylinders and they replaced them all. Del and I started her up and with all of our checks done we called the tower for clearance to MIA.

Takeoff power set. V2 rotate. Positive rate gear up.
The empty airplane jumped off the runway and climbed well. I could feel the gear start up then the nose slowly pitched down slightly as the gear didn't fully retract and started to fall back down. My mind raced through the hydraulic system for what could be wrong. I got it! I turned the cowl flaps from the trail position to off. The mechanics had failed to connect one of the cowl flap hydraulic lines and with them in the trail position the fluid was free to flow overboard. We declared our second emergency of the day.

We carried a spare gallon of hydraulic fluid in the cockpit so I got up and opened the filler cap. Fluid was spitting all around as I emptied the gallon of fluid into the reservoir. The gear was down and latched and we had some hydraulic pressure to operate the flaps. Del made another smooth landing at MIA.

ENGINE FAILURE/SHUTDOWN NUMBER THREE

It was the last departure of the day from MIA to EYW. Our takeoff and climb was normal. As we left the lights of Miami behind us and headed over the Everglades, the Keys stretched out before us like a string of pearls. The Everglades were void of light and the Keys seemed to be suspended in the sky. The world looked upside down. The sky was lit by the stars and the ground was black as coal. We leveled off at our cruising altitude and went from auto-rich to auto-lean on the engine mixture. I was absorbed in the beauty of the night and the surreal look of the Keys floating in air with their lights twinkling in the distance. In my peripheral vision I thought I caught a reflection of blue flashes of lightning. I looked to my right and saw that it was not lightning. It was blue flashes of electrical sparks coming from inside the nacelle of the right engine (why is it always my engine?). With that broken wire flopping around inside the nacelle it wouldn't take much time for it to ignite something and we would be a shooting star in the night sky. I yelled over to the captain telling him what I saw. Almost instantly he pulled the right throttle to idle and the mixture to cut-off then pushed the propeller's feather button. The right engine quickly stopped and the blue sparks stopped along with it.

The engine starters are also the generators. There is no way to stop the generator from turning and making electricity except to stop the engine and that is what we did. I nicknamed the DC-3 the Greasy 3 because I couldn't get

104

close to it without getting grease or oil on me somewhere and most of that oil comes from the engine nacelle.

We declared an emergency and returned to MIA without incident.

The scariest part of the incident was the flight back to Key West on a chartered Piper Navajo flown by a young pilot inexperienced pilot. I'm a nervous flyer when I'm not at the controls so I took the co-pilots seat. My Captain and the flight attendant sat in back. Climbing out of Miami we were approaching a cloud deck and I could see the pilot was getting nervous. I asked him if he would like me to fly while he got the Instrument clearance to Key West. He thought that was a good idea and he gave me the controls.

Our landing at Key West was with the normal crosswind and the pilot wasn't correcting for it. We touched down in a crab and the tires screeched and squealed as the plane straightened out. We were home and safe.

IS YOUR ENGINE OK?

I was flying as co-pilot on the Key West to Tampa flight. We would cruise at six thousand feet and the temperature would decrease at a rate of about 3 degrees per thousand feet. That means if the temperature on the ground was 78 degrees the temperature at six thousand feet was only 60. As we flew north to Tampa the temperature would decrease even more. The DC-3's that Air Sunshine was flying did not have heaters in them so the flight attendants would hand out blankets to the passengers. The captain and I both picked up one on our way to the cockpit.

It was a smooth flight to Tampa. We were flying on top of an overcast that would require us to make an ILS (instrument landing system) approach into the Tampa airport.

We descended into the clouds and were vectored on to the final approach course where we were cleared for the ILS approach. Just outside the outer marked (a radio beacon that marks the beginning of the final approach segment) the captain called verbally for landing gear down and used the thumbs down signal. I moved the gear to the down position, checked the down indicator and latched the gear pins. As we got closer to the runway the captain indicated he wanted ¼ flaps by holding one finger up in front of me and calling flap one. I reached the flap lever and moved the flaps to the ¼ position. The captain looked at me and shouted over the engine noise. "How's your engine?" I looked out the window, the engine was shaking normally. A quick check of the gauges verified everything was ok.

A short time later the captain called for flaps to the ½ position by holding up two fingers and calling flaps 2. Again I reached for the flap lever and moved them to the ½ position. The captain again looked at me and asked if I was sure my engine was ok. I checked again and said yes it's fine. The captain then said "Ok flaps up." I retracted the flaps. We continued the approach and broke out of the clouds about 400 feet above the runway. The captain made a no flap landing. As we were leaving the runway and taxing to the gate someone radioed us saying our flaps were down on the right side.

The flaps are mechanically tied together. One side can't be down unless both sides are down, that is unless the mechanical torque link connecting them is broken, and that is what happened. Every time the captain called for flaps down, only the left side went down. That makes the airplane feel like the right engine wasn't making power. By the time we moved the flaps to half the captain figured out what was happening and he retracted the flaps. That put the airplane back in a balanced condition where he could make a normal landing.

BACK TO CROP-DUSTING

As May approached, I knew I was going to have to quit and go back to crop-dusting. I couldn't afford to live in Key West, the most expensive place in Florida, on my salary of $500/month. So, with my savings nearly gone, I loaded up the pickup and headed back to Wisconsin. My wife says there are still claw marks on US Hwy 1 from her holding on as I dragged her back up north.

As we approached Illinois, I was down to my last few dollars. We couldn't take the Toll Way because I couldn't afford it. Luckily, I had a credit card for gas. When we arrived in Clintonville, I got an advance on my pay and found a place for us to live. It was a nice little white two story on a corner in town. Unfortunately, the previous occupant had just passed away in it and hadn't quite left yet, but that is another story.

I hired a helper to load the plane and get chemical etc. and made sure the Cessna Ag –Truck I would be flying was ready to go.

I also started filling out job applications to all the major airlines, many of which don't exist today because of mergers and bankruptcies. I sent applications to United, American, Delta, Continental, Braniff, North Central, Ozark, Northwest, Eastern, National, Pan-Am and all the rest. I got back a very nice form letter thanking me for applying but they were not hiring however they would keep my application on file. After that I would send monthly updates and get the same response until a letter arrived from Delta Airlines offering me a ticket to Atlanta for an interview.

Delta had started as a crop-dusting company and my father had worked for them in the 60's. He had gotten us a pass to go to Texas to visit him. My first ride on an airliner was from Chicago to Atlanta on a Delta DC-8 jet. From Atlanta we flew to Dallas Texas on a Delta DC-7 prop plane.

My father, at that time, had never been on a jet and he wanted us to experience it, which is why we went to Atlanta before going on to Dallas. The jet was so smooth and quiet it spoiled me because the DC-7 was noisy and bumpy. I knew then jets were the way to go. I hoped this would give me an edge in the interview.

The interview process went well until I got to see the shrink. Remember Delta started as a crop-dusting company and some of their senior pilots started that way. After I sat down he picked up my file and scanned it briefly. He then leaned forward in his chair with a stern look on his face and said, "I see here you are a crop-duster. Isn't that dangerous?" I looked at him and answered, "The accident rate is slightly higher than general aviation, but the fatality rate is lower than general aviation. If you know your limitations and those of your airplane and stay within them then, no, I don't think it is dangerous.
.
That was the end of the interview. I don't think he liked my answer, I didn't get a call back from Delta and I kept on crop-dusting

A few weeks later, Ozark Airlines offered me an interview in Saint Louis. I picked up a round-trip ticket in Milwaukee and flew on a DC-9 to Saint Louis for my interview. I had been flying a lot and was fatigued from that and didn't get much sleep the night before the interview. To make a long story short I flunked the eye test. 20/20 was required and I didn't quite make it. I appealed but it was no use. I went back to finish the season crop-dusting and, with my wife's help, filling out updates and applications. I also started to apply to commuter airlines.

MIDSTATE AIRLINES

As luck would have it a local commuter, Midstate Airlines in Marshfield Wisconsin was hiring. I interviewed and got a job flying a Swearingen Metroliner. It was a twin-engine turboprop 19 seat airplane. Wow! That was a cool airplane. The DC-3 was big but the Metroliner was fast! After training in Marshfield, I was based in Sturgeon Bay, Wisconsin. It was a tourist town and many wealthy people from Chicago kept summer homes there. Our main business was flying them between Chicago and Sturgeon Bay. The route was from Sturgeon Bay to Sheboygan and then on to O'Hare.

Sturgeon Bay only had an NDB approach so getting back home in some of the winter weather got challenging.

Sheboygan had a VOR approach which was a little easier with lower minimums and O'Hare had a full ILS approach system. Needless to say, I got a LOT of instrument experience. The Metroliners we had did not have autopilots, so we hand flew every trip and every approach. After a winter of that I was the best instrument pilot I ever was.

Things were moving fast at Midstate. The major airlines were hiring, and a lot of our Captains were getting hired by North Central and Northwest. I moved up to Captain after about 5 months. I joined an organization called FAPA, Future Airline Pilots Association. They would give you information on who was hiring and what they were looking for along with information on HOW to interview and what to wear. It was very helpful.

After reading, **Dress For Success** I went out and bought a new three-piece suit. I called it my get a job with the airline suit. It was a blue suit and vest along with a white shirt, Ivy League tie and of course gold watch. It was funny to sit waiting for my turn to interview and see everyone wearing the same suit. Of course, there were slight variations, but they were all the same thing. Evidently, we all read the same book.

I kept sending in my updates and applications monthly even though the airlines said they would keep my application on file. I thought it was a good idea to keep them opening that file and updating it. Maybe they went by weight or thickness or persistence to give out interviews.

THE METROLINER

After crop-dusting season was over in the fall of 1978 I was lucky enough to get a job with Midstate Airlines. They flew three SWIV Metroliners and a Beach 99. I was trained on the Metroliner and based at Sturgeon Bay, Wisconsin. I moved my wife and two small girls to a townhouse a short drive from the airport. Sturgeon Bay was so small all drives were short.

Midstate was located there because it was the summer home to a lot of Chicago businessmen. They would fly to Chicago on Monday morning and back again on Thursday or Friday. That coupled with an intermediary stop in Sheboygan, a base for a lot of manufacturing in Wisconsin, made the operation profitable, at least in the summer time.

I spent the early fall adjusting to the Metroliner and the life of a commuter airline pilot. Our home base at Sturgeon Bay had an ADF (auto direction finder, non-precision approach). Our intermediary stop at Sheboygan had a VOR approach. It was still a non-precision approach, but it had a lower MDA (minimum decent altitude) than Sturgeon Bay. Our destination, Chicago's O'Hare International Airport had several ILS approaches that would let us descend to 200 feet with a ½ mile visibility.

Because of the location of Sturgeon Bay on the Door County Peninsula between the bay of Green Bay and Lake Michigan it had mild summers and extended falls. But when winter hit it was notorious for low ceilings and ice laden clouds. It was on one of these days that I was flying as co-pilot from Sturgeon Bay to Sheboygan. It was cold and windy. The weather reports were acceptable with ceilings above minimums at Sheboygan and O'Hare. The heater in the hanger was broken and the airplane was cold soaked when I arrived to do the preflight checks. We had to keep our coats and gloves on for the first leg until the bleed air heating system could warm up the interior enough to keep from freezing. The Captains and co-pilots alternated who actually flew the airplane. The pilot flying would operate the flight controls taking off, flying the approach and landing. The pilot not flying would work the radios doing all the communications and operating the other systems on board.

It was my turn to fly. We were empty on the leg to Sheboygan. Just a few hundred feet after takeoff we were in the clouds. As forecasted the clouds indeed produced icing. I verified with the Captain that the anti-icing and de-icing systems were on. It was a short flight to Sheboygan and all of it was in the clouds. We were cleared for the VOR- approach. I flew the approach as charted. I didn't have a lot of actual instrument flying time at that point in my career and it was always satisfying to fly the approach and break out of the clouds with the runway centered in the windshield. All was going normal. The landing gear was down and green, landing flaps were set. We were about a half mile from touchdown when the right engine quit. The airplane yawed to the right and I corrected with left rudder. I looked at the Captain and he looked at me and we said nearly in unison, "What did you do!" The Captain feathered the right engine and I continued to a normal landing, (except for the fact that the right engine was not running).

We were able to taxi clear of the runway to where we could examine the right engine. Everything looked normal. There was no damage to the compressor or any other part that we could tell. There were no oil leaks or indication of a fire. It just stopped. It was a mystery, a mystery that was solved when we looked at the left engine. That engine had kept running but with a little less luck could have quit too.

On the tip of the spinner on the left engine was a piece of ice protruding about 2 inches in front of the spinner. Evidently the right spinner also had a similar size piece of ice that had broken off and because the engine air inlets are on top of the nacelles and we were in a nose high attitude for landing that ice was ingested into the compressor, ground up, and flamed out the engine. Our million-dollar engine had turned into a snow cone machine. We took the ice off the spinner on the left engine, started both engines and took the airplane up for a quick check flight to make sure everything was working properly before our next flight to Chicago O'Hare.

Most if not all jet and turbo-prop engines have a continuous ignition system to prevent this from happening. The Metroliner at this time did not. They have since been modified.

METROLINER SURPRISE

I had been flying the Metroliner for over 6 months and was feeling comfortable with it. I had been recently checked out as Captain on it. It was the highest performing aircraft I had flown to that point. To me it was big, powerful and fast. I enjoyed flying it even with all its little quirks.

It was a warm sunny spring day, a day that promised easy flying. What could go wrong on a day like this?

The plane had been parked on the ramp near the fuel pump. There was a slight slope to the right at the ramp but not enough to make the fuel gauges inaccurate. I was scheduled for two round trips to Sheboygan and O'Hare that day. I got the cockpit ready while my co-pilot for the day, Paul, did the walk around inspection. I reviewed the log book to make sure there were no discrepancies to be fixed. There were none. We were empty on this leg to Sheboygan except for one of our pilots deadheading to see his girlfriend.

With everyone on board we closed the door, started the engines and began to taxi for takeoff. While we were taxiing Paul and I went through the checklist. Flight controls checked; engines checked; fuel quantity; checked. It was a clear day and I decided to takeoff VFR and pick up our IFR clearance once we were in the air.

At the end of the runway with the before takeoff checklist completed I called for, "bleeds and speeds", the takeoff items of the bleed air valves to be turned off for maximum power and the speed levers to be advanced for full takeoff RPM, to be completed. We were light and accelerated quickly. Paul called power set, V1, rotate. As I pulled back on the control wheel the left side became airborne and started to roll the airplane to the right. I countered with full left aileron and some left rudder. It was all I could do to keep the airplane from rolling over and crashing. Paul could see what was going on and knew we were in trouble but what was wrong? We were airborne, both engines were running normally. The controls were operating normally. The propellers were both in forward thrust and operating normally. Then I found it. We had checked the fuel quantity, but I missed the fuel cross flow switch. The Metroliner didn't have a fuel cross-feed system where one fuel tank could directly feed fuel to either engine but what it did have was a cross flow valve. With that valve open fuel can flow between tanks. With the airplane parked on the ramp sloping to the right side and the cross-flow valve open about a thousand pounds more fuel was in the right tank than in the left tank. I had checked the quantity but not the distribution! We never used that valve. I wasn't used to checking it and that could end up costing me my life and my crew's life.

I had the control wheel as far as possible to the left and along with rudder I was able to keep the airplane from rolling over and crashing. As I climbed and increased airspeed I gained a little more effectiveness from the controls. It was a little easier to hold. I moved my right hand from the wheel to the power levers, (throttles), and reduced power on the left engine. This induced a yaw to the left helping me go from a right bank to a left bank. With the airplane in an uncoordinated left turn the fuel started to flow from the right tank to the left tank. It took a couple of turns, but I was able to get the fuel imbalance fixed. During this process our deadheading pilot came to the cockpit and asked why we were circling. I told him we were waiting for our IFR clearance from Green Bay Approach. We proceeded to Sheboygan.

I retrospect I should have fessed up to the mistake. It would have possibly changed procedures and prevented this from happening to anyone else. I never overlooked that switch again and I have always checked fuel quantity AND distribution ever since.

To paraphrase a famous aviation quote; Aviation, more so than the sea, is terribly unforgiving (intolerant) of any carelessness, incapacity, or neglect.

I got lucky, I was forgiven.

AIRLINE INTERVIEWS CONTINUED

I got an interview with United Airlines. At the time their process was a 5-part interview. You would go to Chicago, take a few tests, talk to a few people and repeat on five separate trips. After my first interview of talking to one of their interviewers and taking some tests I walked away scratching my head wondering what kind of an operation they were running and what kind of pilots they were looking for? I guess they didn't think much of me either because they didn't give me a call back and that was ok with me.

I think it was March when a letter arrived from American Airlines inviting me to Dallas for an interview. I liked American a lot and was happy to get the interview. I was flying the day before the interview and got caught in a snow storm and had to spend the night in Chicago. By the time I flew back to Sturgeon Bay, packed and got back to Chicago I had missed my flight. I called to American to see about another flight, but they said no they needed me all day for the tests and medical exam. They said they would reschedule and send me another letter.

They did send me another letter and this time I made the flight. The Flight Academy in Arlington, TX was a very impressive place and it was bustling with activity. American was in the midst of a hiring spree and there were new recruits everywhere. Those of us in the interview process were herded from one place to the next getting prodded, poked and tested. Because of the information I got from FAPA I knew what to expect, what to wear and what some of the questions might be.

I noticed a different attitude at American as opposed to the other airlines I had interviewed with. The others kind of treated you as an outsider they had to scrutinize to see if you were good enough to join them. At American you were treated with respect, as part of the team unless you proved otherwise. It was very different and comfortable. The first interview went well, and I was invited back for the next in American's three part interview process and again for the last interview.

The last step in the interview process was an evaluation ride in a simulator and a Captain's review board. For the simulator ride a group of about four of us at a time were given a flight profile briefing and then put in the simulator with an American Airlines captain to act as co-pilot. As I recall the profile was to take off from LAX fly to Seal Beach VOR, hold and then be vectored to an ILS back at LAX. This was usually done in a Boeing 707 simulator; way bigger than any airplane I ever flew. However, for my check the 707 was busy and I did the test in the Cessna Citation simulator. During the briefing the Captain check-airman said he would act as a good first officer but would not do anything he was not briefed or asked to do.

When we entered the small cockpit, I sat in the left seat, the captain's seat. I had never been in a full motion simulator before, in fact I had never been in any simulator before and my whole career rested on my performance. I buckled my seatbelt and the check airman gave me a cockpit familiarization briefing before he started the engines. We were at the end of the runway waiting for takeoff. The briefing said to treat the simulator just as you would a real airplane, so I did.

Before takeoff I briefed my "co-pilot" to make the standard callouts (V1, Vr, V2, etc.). If we had to abort takeoff I would abort. He responded, "Yes sir." That was unexpected, the check airman evaluating me calling me sir. I brought the throttled up to takeoff power and I could hear the whine of the engines behind me. As the "jet" accelerated I could hear the thump of the tar strips in the runway coming faster and faster. My co-pilot called V1, we were committed to takeoff, quickly followed by rotate. As I pulled back on the yoke and the nose wheel lifted, the sound of the tar strips changed making only a single thump instead of the quick double thump it made when the nose was on the ground. As we lifted into the air all I could hear was the whine of the engines. I called positive rate gear up. The co-pilot responded, "yes sir gear coming up." After takeoff now in the "clouds" with only darkness filling the windshield I was given a turn and climb. I asked my co-pilot to set the heading bug and the new altitude, his response was, "yes sir." I could get used to this.

I continued flying the profile, entering the hold at Seal Beach then being vectored to the ILS at LAX. I continued to ask my co-pilot to set altitudes, headings and frequencies while all I concentrated on was flying the plane. His answer to every request was, "yes sir." I flew the ILS down to the 200'DH, (decision Height), where you would break out of the clouds and land or if you didn't break out you would go around. I had it wired with the ILS perfectly centered.

The check airman briefed me to fly to the DH then he would take over. We would not be able to use the visual and land the simulator because it was being used by another simulator. At the DH (decision Height) the check airman called, "I've got it," and he took the controls. He continued flying the approach to the ground and landed all on instruments. I was impressed.

After the simulator check there was a break before being called in to the Captain's Review Board. The setup was like being a defendant at a hearing with me sitting in the defendant's chair facing five or six American Captains who would ask questions some of which had no good answers. It was intimidating and I am sure it was meant to be so they could see me work under pressure. When I sat down the first statement was, "I see here you are a crop-duster. We like you guys when you have the experience to get here." I smiled to myself and knew the interview would go well. I departed feeling good about the interview and was hopeful I would get the job.

In the mean time Northwest Airlines sent me an interview request. Most of the pilots that were hired from Midstate Airlines went to North Central or Northwest. Not knowing what would happen at American I went to Minneapolis for that interview.

The days passed at Midstate while I waited to hear from an airline, any airline. I came home from a trip one day and saw all kinds of decorations on the balcony of what I thought was the townhouse next to mine. I thought, "Oh Carol was having a party". As I got closer, I could see it was my balcony, but we were not planning a party. As I pulled in, I could see it was red white and blue streamers and a big red and blue AA in the middle! Nancy ran out to meet me and excitedly said she had gotten a call from American Airlines asking for me. I asked, "What did they say?" "He couldn't tell me, but he said it was good news and you should call him back!" As I dialed the phone my hands had a slight shake to them.

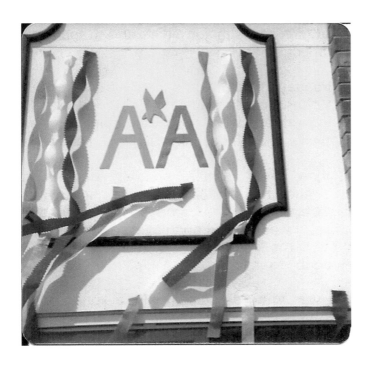

"Hello, American Airlines"

"Hello this is Alvin Johnson returning your call"

"Yes Mr. Johnson, (the pleasantries out of the way) American Airlines would like to offer you a position as Flight Officer"

"Yes of course, ………does anyone say no?"

"Not often. Congratulations, I will be sending you a packet of information explaining everything."

Nancy threw one of the biggest and best parties ever to celebrate the culmination of a long and concerted effort by us both to get hired by a major airline and to top it off the one I wanted most!

Ever since graduating from high school I had moved a lot, first for school then chasing my next job, and now I saw where I would work and what I would be doing for the next 31 years of my life. I can't describe the feeling adequately.

Previously there was always another step to take, something to reach for, to plan for, now I had it. I would start as a flight engineer then upgrade to first officer, then in time to captain. I was excited and satisfied in achieving my goal but at the same time there was a little sadness. What would there be to reach for?

Years later I was flying as captain with a young new hire first officer. She was in her mid-twenties and confided that she was a little depressed. She had worked hard to reach her goal of being an airline pilot and now that she had it, there were no challenges left. I looked at her and said that wasn't true. Now the challenge is to be the best airline pilot, to fly the perfect trip. I told her I had flown two. Maybe that was my answer too, to always strive to be the best, always look forward.

I spent the rest of my airline career with American Airlines flying based at O'Hare Airport.

THE FLIGHT ACADEMY

FLIGHT ENGINEER TRAINING

New hire picture 1979

When I arrived at the Flight Academy at Fort Worth in June 1979 for training, I found every other pilot in my class had a last name beginning with "P". Missing that first interview moved me from being hired with the "J's" to the "P's". That loss in seniority would be significant in the near future.

I started training in June of 1979. I was 29 years old. That was near the top of the age range that the airlines were hiring at that time and it made me number one in my group of four new hires.

At that time about eighty percent of all new hires were ex-military. I felt lucky to have been able to make the cut. Two of my classmates were C-130 pilots and the third was an F-4 pilot. I was a crop-duster and commuter pilot. All of us have been aircraft captains before being hired at American. Now we all started back at he bottom as Flight Engineers on the Boeing 727 or as it was called at American the seven two.

The training was intense. Four students and two instructors per class and we proceeded to study every system, switch, circuit breaker and dial in that airplane. We learned every operating limit, normal procedure, abnormal procedure and emergency procedure and checklist by heart. We were in class all day and studied after class until we couldn't fit anything else in to our heads, then we would go to the bar and discuss our class work and flying. I think that was a very important time.

I learned a lot in those bull sessions. We would discuss systems and procedures and worked out areas we were having problems with. Of course, we also talked about what we had done before getting to American. I didn't say too much preferring to listen to the stories of my class mates. Stories about flying the F-4 and the C-130 especially the airborne cargo drops from the C-130. I thought the military lingo was cool and the airline industry was permeated with it. Once they pressed me for what I did before getting hired by American. I had had a few beers and felt talkative, so I said I started crop-dusting when I was 19 and did that for ten years. They stopped me right there. You crop-dusted for 10 years and you're not dead?

I told them what I told the shrink at Delta, if you know your limitations and those of your airplane and stay within them, I didn't think it was dangerous. They demanded some stories and I recounted many of the same ones I have set down here for you.

American was expanding under deregulation like most airlines and was not only hiring record numbers of pilots but also a lot of flight attendants. The flight academy, where the pilots trained, was just across the street from the flight attendants Learning Center. They had their own pool and bar and their cafeteria stayed open for dinner. The flight academy was running 24/7 but the cafeteria was only open from 6:00AM to 2:00PM. We got the idea of going over to the learning center and hanging out at the pool and having a beer while we were studying, besides the scenery wasn't bad either.

We had been at the pool for a while when a very pretty, young, redheaded flight attendant trainee came up to us and in her sweet little southern drawl, asked if we all were pilots. We all perked up and said, "Why yes we are," all puffed up with ourselves. She asked, "How long do all y'all have to go to training to be a pilot?" We told her 10 weeks. She said, "ten weeks, we go for eight weeks, y'all mean if we went for two more weeks we could be pilots too?" We looked at each other with puzzled expressions then back at her thinking she was kidding. She wasn't. We realized the futility of any attempt at an explanation and just answered yep! That was the last time we went to the Learning Center.

Our training went from the books to the paper trainer. The paper trainer was a grouping of plywood panels roughly laid out to simulate the B727 cockpit with cardboard printed with the switches, dials, lights, levers and circuit breakers all placed where they would be in the real airplane. From there we moved on to the Procedures Trainer, a mockup of the B727 cockpit. It had all of the switches, lights, knobs, dials, circuit breakers, levers and controls that the real plane had. We practiced the preflight inspection and all of the tests of all of the systems associated with it.

After a few days of training in the procedures trainer we moved to a full motion simulator. We would practice with a flight crew of pilots upgrading to first officer and captain. Once we got airborne the simulator instructor would segregate us from the pilots and while they did their flying thing we would work on abnormal and emergency procedures. When training was completed, we had to take an oral exam on all the systems and procedures, then a simulator check where the examiner would put us through our paces by failing systems and giving us emergencies that we would have to handle.

The oral would be conducted at the paper trainer. This oral would last from 3 to 4 hours depending on how good you were doing and the examiner's mood.

When I did my oral the examiner started by asking me to go through the pre-flight inspection. As I proceeded, he would ask what I was looking for in a particular test or what the limits were for a particular gauge or system. I would answer his questions making sure not to ramble on beyond the question asked me.

Flight Engineer Station Preparation

Battery Switch (22 volts minimum)..............ON
Pack Switches ....OFF
B Pumps ....OFF
APU ....Start/ON
APU Fire Warning ....Check

Examiner, "Explain the fire warning check."

Me, "On the first APU start of the day the fire system must be checked. After APU start turn off the APU Fire Shutdown Switch. Hold the Fire Test Switch until warning devices are activated. If there is no warning within 60 seconds make an E-6 write-up and notify maintenance."

Examiner, "What is a good test?"

Me, "The Fire Warning Bell in the cockpit should ring. The Fire Horn in the nose wheel well should sound and the APU Fire Light should illuminate."

The oral went on for about three hours. It seemed at the same time to be both interminably long and yet it went quickly. At the end the examiner said, good job, I had passed!

I had the simulator check a day or two later. The check starts out just like you arrive at a cold dead airplane, no external power plugged in and the APU not running. The procedure was to start the APU and get the airplane ready for its first flight of the day.
Normally once I had the airplane powered up a captain and first officer that were also going through a check ride would come aboard and "fly" the simulator and I would do part of the test working with them, and part of it segregated from

them. As it turned out there were no pilots available so two engineer trainees occupied the pilot seats. They got clearance to pushback from the gate and I worked with them to start the engines. As each engine was started I synchronized the generators and put them on line and checked all of the other associated systems looking for a problem.

I expected the examiner to make his mischief at every turn but there was nothing. The engines all started with no problems. The hydraulics were all good. The generators all worked properly. This is not what I expected. All during training it never went like this. Something was always out of limits or failing. I was beginning to wonder if I had missed something.

I went through everything again but I could find nothing wrong. We were cleared for takeoff. Still nothing was wrong. I prepared for an engine failure on takeoff but there was none. I prepared for a flap failure when they were retracted, but there was none. I checked the air-conditioning packs expecting a failure, there was none. Pressurization was ok. I was wondering when the test was going to start and hoped I hadn't missed it.

Once we leveled off at cruise the number one generator tripped off line. I told the pilots and worked the problem. I check the frequency and volts. They were out of limits and the procedure called for disconnecting the CSD (constant speed drive). I informed the pilots we were operating on two generators and they should let me know before they extended the flaps. That was because when the flaps were lowered electric fans would automatically turn on causing a large electrical draw that might be more than the two remaining generators could handle. I then disconnected the CSD. As part of the procedure I would have to turn off one of the A/C packs before the flaps were lowered to prevent the fan from turning on. As the flight continued, I kept searching for problems but none were detected. The pilots were cleared for their approach and I continued searching for problems. I heard the outer marker beeping and looked to see if the pilots had extended the flaps without telling me. I checked the generator load finding it within limits. I hadn't been told by the pilots that they were going to extend the flaps, so I hadn't turned off one of the A/C packs. The electrical limits were not being exceeded so I let both packs run. Why, I don't know. If I had turned a pack off and chastised the pilots for not telling me they were extending the flaps as I had briefed them, I might have been able to salvage the check-ride but I didn't. I failed the check ride. The reason given was lack of crew coordination. The examiner said instead of flipping switches all the time I should have been paying attention to what was going on around me.

I was devastated. I had to undergo another training session and another check ride a couple of days later. I had the same examiner for the second check ride. Everything went well and I passed but I had lost six spots on the seniority list and more importantly to me, that black spot on my record.

Training at the Flight Academy was over for now. They gave me a couple of days off before reporting to the Chief Pilot at O'Hare Airport in Chicago. I would complete my ride along flights (just sitting in the cockpit jump-seat observing an Engineer) and dual flights with a Check Airman monitoring me before I would be cleared to go out on my own as a fully certified Flight Engineer.

After we took our check rides, we would get our seniority numbers and be on probation for a year. During that time every captain we flew with would get an evaluation report to fill out on us. After 6 month and again at 12 months we would be called into the Director of Operations office for our board examinations. He and several Chief pilots and Check airmen would grill us on procedures and discuss anything that came up in the evaluation reports. These review boards were taken seriously because if you screwed up your job was on the line. Our D.O. at the time was Captain Burkibile. He had a reputation as a tough but fair man. I had never met him, and I had never been in his office before. The saying was you wanted to finish your 30-year career and have the Chief Pilot not know who you were.

As I walked into his office there were several check airmen there, a union rep and Captain Burkibile. I looked around the office. It was bare of personal effects except for one photo on the wall behind his chair. It wasn't of his wife or family. It was of a Stearman crop-duster. I kind of chuckled inside and I knew everything would be just fine.

I worked for American airlines for 14 months before I was furloughed.

PART 3

CORPORATE FLYING

JOB SEARCH

June 1979, I started training at American Airlines. Until now I had been a gipsy, moving often, chasing the next job, but now this was it, no next job. I had reached my goal of flying for a major airline. I remember saying to myself, "this is where I will be for the next 31 years of my flying career."

(I was 29 years old and the mandatory retirement age was 60) Fourteen months later, after supplementing my meager probationary pay with the last of my savings I was furloughed, unemployed for an indefinite time. I was in the first batch of 500 to go. There would be many more behind me. Many of those who could, returned to the military. Others worked as FAA controllers and a few went into the business world.

I updated my resume and drove around to every airport in the Chicago area to personally deliver it to every corporate flight department that I could find. Most would not even take my resume. They said that they did not hire furloughed airline pilots. They didn't want to invest the time and money in training me because I would be returning to the airline as soon as they recalled me. I understood their position, but when I turned in my key and company flight manuals to American Airlines after I was furloughed, they told me not to expect to return.

The airline told me I wouldn't be coming back and the corporate flight departments wouldn't hire me because they thought I would be going back. In the mean time my family and I had to eat and pay rent. The next stop was the Unemployment Office.

I showed up at the unemployment office at 9:00 am and got in line. When I got to the counselor she looked up and asked me which airline I worked for. I was surprised and asked her how she knew I worked for an airline. She looked at me and rolled her eyes and looked around at the others in line. I looked too, then I understood. I was standing there in a clean white shirt, slacks, a gold watch, clean and shaved. I stood out like a sore thumb. She went over the procedures, gave me the paper work to fill out and I left.

I put an ad in Trade-A-Plane looking for a job and got a couple of interesting responses. One was from McAllen Texas. I had a DC-3 type rating and he was looking for a pilot to fly freight into Mexico. The pay was really good, too good. Red flags went off and I asked if it was legal. His response was that it was legal here. Evidentially he was flying consumer goods into Mexico and not going through Mexican customs thereby avoiding taxes. I told him thanks but that was more excitement than I was looking for.

Another response came from an operator in Alaska. He was operating DC-4's flying boxes of fish. My understanding was that they would takeoff from a beach near where the fishing fleet was and fly the fish to the cannery for processing. That sounded just like what I was after. My wife was ready to sell everything and move. We both thought Alaska would be a great adventure. When I called back to talk about the job the operator said he misread my add and thought I had a DC-4 type rating. I tried talking him into hiring me but he needed a pilot who already had the DC-4 rating. I went back to knocking on doors and handing out résumés.

I was driving around DuPage airport just west of Chicago handing out résumés when I spotted a hanger door open. Inside was a Cessna Citation business jet. I quickly stopped and got out. There was a man wiping the airplane down with a clean white towel. I asked if the chief pilot was available. He said no and asked what I wanted. I told him I was looking for a job and wanted to give him a résumé. He took the résumé and said he would pass it along. I thought that went well. Most corporate flight operations would not even accept my résumé because I was a furloughed airline pilot.

A week or two passed and the phone rang. He said his name was Jim Ireland Chief Pilot for Belden Corporation and he wanted to interview me for a pilot position. He picked a spot for lunch the next day. I was there early dressed in my get a job with the airline suit.

He was on the short side with graying hair, I would guess mid forties. We introduced ourselves and took a booth. He asked me some questions about my flying career, and I answered. I asked him some questions about the job and the outlook for the company. I had done some quick research and let him know I knew something about the company. When we ordered he let me go first. I ordered a burger and iced tea. During lunch we chitchatted, with him asking most of the questions. When lunch was over, he thanked me for coming and said he would let me know if he had any further questions.

A few days passed and Mr. Ireland called and asked me to meet him at their hanger the next day. When I arrived, he discussed the company and what he would expect from me. He asked what I wanted for pay. I was a horrible negotiator and desperate for a job. I started with my bottom line, $24,000 a year. He said he would pay $28,000 but if I worked out in two months, they would send me to school to get a Citation type rating. They would pay for the rating, but I would have to pay them back through payroll deductions. I agreed and we went to the main office in Batavia to make it official.

Some weeks later I had occasion to ask Jim why he hired me. He said when we went to lunch, I ordered an ice tea and didn't talk much. He said his co-pilot mechanic drank too much and his previous co-captain never shut up. I guess you never know what will get you the job!

BELDEN WIRE AND CABLE

FIRST FLIGHT IN THE CITATION

Mr. Ireland, Jim, he insisted, gave me the Citation operating manual to study for a few days before my first flight. I hadn't actually flown a jet. I had been a flight engineer on a Boeing 727 for American Airlines, but that job is operating all of the systems on the airplane not actually flying it. The closest thing to a jet I had flown was the SWIV Metroliner turboprop.

March 3rd, 1981, I showed up at the Belden hanger at 7:00 am. Jim and I were going to fly the Citation to give me a copilot checkout. The only airplane I had flown in the past year and a half had been a Cessna 150. He started the engines while I watched. Jim worked the radios while I taxied. When we finished the checklist and lined up on the runway for takeoff, I was a little nervous. When we were cleared for takeoff, I started to push the throttles toward takeoff power and Jim made the final power adjustments. The near empty Citation accelerated very quickly down the runway to rotation speed. I pulled back slightly, and we started to climb rapidly. We were at 10,000 feet and my brain was just off the runway. Things happened fast in a jet and I had to recalibrate my brain to keep up and then get ahead of it. We did some turns and approach to stalls and Jim showed me how the aircraft systems worked. We did several approaches and landings for about an hour. He considered me checked out and I would be flying a trip with him the following day.

We were to depart at 6:00 a.m. so I was up and out the door by 4:30 a.m. It was my job to pick up a dozen donuts before arriving at the airport. When I got there, I had to make coffee, fill the ice tray, and preflight the Citation while Jim got the weather and filed the flight plan. When our passengers arrived, Jim introduced me as the new copilot.

It was still dark out when we started the engines and called for our IFR clearance to Richmond Indiana. I soon found out this was our milk run 4 or 5 days a week. It dawned on me that Jim filed the flight plan and did the routing. I had no idea of how we were routed. The controller read the clearance so fast I missed most of it. Jim could see I was lost and he keyed his mike to read back the clearance. I was totally unprepared. I got out the map and found and set in the first fix. Jim was taxing and I was reading the checklist. We were cleared for takeoff and away we went. I was so far behind on that flight I thought this would be my first and last day of work at Belden. The flight lasted about an hour. I spent most of it just trying to catch up with the airplane. After our passengers left, I apologized to Jim for my poor performance. He let out a little chuckle and said, "I expected that, I've flown with airline pilots before."

The rust of not having flown a high-performance airplane for 14 months quickly faded and I enjoyed flying the Citation.

N962JC

It was the 80's and Cooper Industries, like many large corporations of the time, had been growing rapidly through mergers. Recently the company I worked for, Belden

Corporation had been purchased by Crouse-Hinds Corporation out of Syracuse New York and they were involved in a hostile takeover by another company. Cooper Industries ended up as a white knight, buying Crouse Hinds and, as was their practice, made the Chairman of Crouse Hinds a co-chairman of the board of Cooper Industries (more on that later). Because of all these mergers, Cooper Industries ended up with 16 corporate aircraft of different types. They decided their operations only required 7 aircraft. I was lucky that I flew the Cessna Citation because it was one of the aircraft Cooper decided to keep. The bad news was that they moved it, Jim and me from DuPage Airport in West Chicago, Illinois to Memphis, Tennessee. They also transferred Ron to Memphis from Dallas where he had been flying a Beach King Air.

Cooper decided to replace the early Citation 500 we had with a new Citation II. The Citation II, besides being new, could fly higher, farther, and faster with more passengers than the C500 we currently had. When the new Citation was ready for delivery Jim, Ron and I went to the factory in Wichita KS to pick it up.

It was beautiful, white with blue and grey trim and the company logo on the tail. Jim had me fly the airplane on the acceptance flight with the Cessna factory pilot in the right seat and Jim kneeling between us. I felt lucky to be the first one besides the Cessna test pilots to fly it. After about an hour we landed back at Wichita with a few discrepancies on our debrief sheet to be taken care of.

On our second flight I landed and went into reverse thrust on the rollout. When we slowed enough for brakes, I depressed the brake peddles and nothing happened! I pushed harder and still nothing. In my mind I quickly went through the systems diagram and figured out that the antiskid system failed and wouldn't let the brakes engage because it sensed a wheel lockup. I released the brake peddles reached down to the anti-skid switch, turned it off and tried the brakes again, this time they worked. We came to a stop and added that to our list of items to fix.

The whole process only lasted a couple of days and we were on our way back to Memphis with our brand-new Citation II and big smiles on our faces.

COOPER INDUSTRIES

BOB ARNHOLT, DIRECTOR OF FLIGHT OPERATIONS

As part of all this consolidation Bob Arnholt, Director of Flight and Chief Pilot, was visiting all of the crews at their different bases and doing a ride-along to get to know all the pilots and check on how they were performing.

Bob Arnholt had been with Cooper industries since they bought their first Beech Queen Air. He didn't fly much anymore but he was in charge of managing the pilots and aircraft owned by Cooper Industries. He was a friendly man in his early 60's.

Bob had come to Memphis to check out our operation and ride along on a trip to El Paso, Texas. During the flight he had come to the cockpit area to see how we were doing. He suggested that whoever was not flying that leg should go to the cabin and serve the passengers drinks and the food we had catered. My co-pilot Ron and I exchanged looks and told Bob we were unable to do that. Regulation required both pilots to be at the controls. The flight continued uneventfully.

We landed on runway 8R in ELP (El Paso, TX.) which put us about a mile from the FBO, (Fixed Base Operator), where we would be parking. I taxied at idle speed easing on the brakes occasionally to slow down, but because of the distance it was a little faster taxi than normal. When we got to the FBO we were guided to a parking spot where we shut down our engines and opened the door for our passengers. Ron went to the nose baggage compartment, unloaded the baggage and set it on the ground while I helped the passengers deplane. The passengers picked up their baggage and walked to the FBO terminal. Ron, Bob and I followed with our bags. There were cars waiting to take our passengers to their meeting. As we all would be spending the night and returning to Houston (Corporate Headquarters) in the morning, we called the hotel and waited for the curtsey van to pick us up. While we were waiting Bob took the opportunity to debrief the flight. He was disappointed that we did not go to the cabin and act as flight attendants and serve our passengers drinks and snacks. We defended ourselves quoting regulations, but he reiterated his position. After some discussion we left it by both Ron and me saying we understood what he wanted (we did not serve drinks).

Bob also said we should carry our passenger's bags for them. We told him that we always helped if a passenger had more than they could carry but didn't think it presented us in a professional light to our passengers and would degrade our captain's authority in making operational and emergency decisions if we looked and acted as servants to our passengers. He also said that I taxied in too fast, that each of the tar strips we went over on the runway while taxiing in made a bump in the cabin and was loud and uncomfortable. He said he understood that with my background of crop-dusting and flying for the airline it was ingrained in me to get the job done quickly and on schedule but he wanted us to give our passengers a nice smooth ride, even if it took a little longer. I said I would keep that in mind and try to comply with his suggestion.

When it was time to depart the following day, we helped our passengers as usual with their bags and loaded them in the baggage compartment. We had the airplane catered with drinks and snacks for the short trip to Houston, TX. I gave the normal safety briefing to the passengers and started the engines for taxi. The winds were out of the west meaning we would have to depart on runway 26L. The departure end of 26L was over a mile and a half taxi from where we were parked. Remembering Bob's comments from yesterday I taxied at an excruciatingly slow pace.

After an uneventful flight we landed in Houston and taxied, slowly, to the FBO where we said goodbye to our passengers and got their bags out for them. Bob was the last to leave and complimented me on my smooth taxi. We did not porter our passenger's bags or serve them drinks in flight. That was the last time I saw Bob until several years after I left the company. He did not press us further on carrying bags or serving drinks in flight. He retired some months after our check ride. Ron and I flew the airplane empty back to Memphis to wait for our next trip.

PART FOUR

THE AIRLINES AGAIN

I had been furloughed for three weeks short of four years. I remember being in the attic of our house in Memphis looking for something. I opened a tall wardrobe box and inside was an airline uniform and some white shirts, one with three stripes on its epaulets. I was a little surprised to see it and then said to myself, "Oh yeah, I did work for an airline once."

A few months later at 11:00 p.m. a cab pulled into my driveway. I had been in bed sleeping but the lights woke me up. I saw the door open and a man start walking to my door. I got up to answer it and the cab driver said he had a telegram for Alvin Johnson. Nothing good can come from a telegram delivered at that late hour. I opened it with some trepidation. When I read it and then re-read it, I was slow to fully understand it. It was from American Airlines and I was being recalled. I had not been keeping up with the airline news and the recall came out of the blue. Nancy and I discussed weather or not we should accept the recall. My job with Cooper Industries was good and we were making decent money, in fact I would be taking a pay cut for the first two years if I went back to American. The airline industry looked strong and poised for a big expansion. My corporate job depended on the whim of the CEO. If he liked having the airplanes and found them useful, I had a job. If the CEO changed or their attitude toward airplanes changed, I would be looking for a job again. At least the job of an airline is to have airplanes and fly passengers. There was no chance of an airline deciding to get rid of all of their airplanes although I knew they could shrink, and I could be furloughed again. We decided to tale a chance on the airlines again.

I reported to the Flight Academy for re-qualification training on Easter weekend 1984.

REQUALIFICATION TRAINING

On the first day of training they had us all assemble in a class room and briefed us on what we would be doing and getting all of the new paperwork filled out to re-join the company.

It all went well. Our original training was excellent with two instructors and four students to a class. All of the procedures, systems, and limitations came back quickly.

I was paired with Chick (Charles) Burlingame for the simulator check ride. We were scheduled for a fasting blood draw for the day of the check-ride after we completed the ride. That was unacceptable. We would be doing a check-ride without having eaten for more than 16 hours. We decided to go to Medical and have the blood draw done the day before the ride. When we arrived at Medical for the blood draw, without an appointment, the head nurse refused to do it. We explained the situation and she still refused to do the draw. We both told her we would not be there to do the blood draw as scheduled the following day then we left.

Chick and I did the simulator check-ride successfully the following day then immediately departed for Chicago. We shared a motel room for a week while we were on reserve and looking for a more permanent place to live. Two days after arriving in Chicago we both got a phone call from American Airline Medical office ordering us back to the Medical center in Dallas at the flight Academy for the mandatory blood work. The blood work was drug and alcohol testing required by the FAA and they wanted to know why we refused to take it. We gave a brief explanation and said we would be there as scheduled.

When we arrived, we were informed that the director of the Medical Department would be there in a few minutes to talk to us and do the blood draw. We looked at each other thinking we had really stepped in it this time. When the Doctor came in he asked us why we refused the blood draw. We told him the whole story about how we hadn't refused. We came in a day early for the test and the nurse refused to do it. We explained about the timing of our check-ride and how long we would have been without food etc. He listened to our explanation then apologized to us and said we did the right thing. He said the nurse was wrong to refuse to give us the test when we requested it. He said he would fix that problem.

The blood draw was done, and we were release to go back to Chicago.

HUNTSVILLE (HSV) 1984

It was the second day of a three-day trip. We spent the night in Huntsville, Alabama. I hadn't slept well. I felt like I was getting the stomach flu. I got up and met the rest of the crew in the lobby for our 6:30 am pickup and the ride to the airport. I was flying as the Flight Engineer on the Boeing 727. I told the Captain that I was not feeling well but I was able to do my job. When we arrived at the airport, I proceeded to the airplane and did the pre-flight inspection to ready the 727 for our flight. We were going to be flying to Birmingham and then onto DFW (Dallas, Fort Worth) before our destination, El Paso Texas, where we would be spending the night. It was a short flight to Birmingham with a quick turnaround and then we were on our way to DFW. When we got to cruise I told the Captain that I was getting a little worse and thought I should call in sick once we landed. He told me to make a radio call to dispatch and tell them I would be calling in sick and to have a reserve FE (Flight Engineer) meet the flight so there would not be any delays. I made the call as he requested. I continued to get worse on the flight and was glad I had decided not to continue on to El Paso. It would be much easier to replace me at DFW than it would have been in El Paso. Besides the Medical care, if I needed that, would be better in Dallas.

We landed at DFW and taxied to the gate. The Captain parked the brakes and shut off the engines. I was doing the parking checks as the agent positioned the jet bridge at the door. I could hear the door open and moments later two paramedics came rushing through the cockpit door asking in an excited tone who was sick. I looked at them in surprise and asked who they were and what the hell were they doing here. The lead EMT said they had gotten a call that one of the pilots was sick and needed help. I said I called in sick but did not request help. The EMT asked what the problem was and asked if he could do a preliminary exam. I agreed and told him how I felt and that it had been getting worse. He pushed on my lower right abdomen and asked if that hurt. I said it was uncomfortable but not too bad. He released the pressure and asked if that was any worse. I told him no, about the same.

By this time the passengers had started to de-plane. The EMT said they had a gurney outside and wanted to put me on it and take me to the hospital for an exam. I said no thanks, I could walk. The EMT said if I was embarrassed they could put a sheet over me so I wouldn't be seen. I said HELL NO! In retrospect it would have been funny to do that and then let my arm fall out with my uniform jacket on so my stripes would be visible. I can just imagine the reaction of some of the people in the terminal.

After I refused treatment the EMTs left and the Chief of Engineers came in. He introduced himself and said his car was just outside the terminal and he would be taking me to the hospital. I unlatched my seat and slid it back. As I got up I found the pain had gotten worse and maybe I should have taken the ride on the gurney. The chief took my suitcase and kit bag as I made a slow painful walk up the jet bridge and out to his waiting car.

I continued to get worse and was thankful that I had gotten off the flight. At the hospital they wheeled me into the ER and put me on a gurney. They did some blood work and other tests and found nothing conclusive. I stayed on that gurney under observation for most of the day. The chief stayed with me except for a lunch and dinner brake. Around 8:00 pm it became apparent that my appendix was the problem and they would operate in the morning. This was in the time before cell phones so the nurse wheeled me to a wall phone so I could call my wife Nancy and let her know what was going on. When she picked up the receiver on the other end of the line I said, "Hi guess where I am?" After I finished talking to her, the chief got on the phone and told her he would make arrangements for her to come to DFW on the first flight out in the morning.

I have always appreciated how American Airlines took care of me and my wife during this stressful time.

My recollection is a little hazy here, but things took a turn for the worse and the doctors decided they could not wait for morning. It was just before midnight and I was being prepped for the operation. The pain had gotten to the point where I had no fear of the operation, I just wanted the pain to stop. Live or die, I didn't care just stop the pain. The chief said he would stay until I was out of surgery. Later Nancy told me that he had kept calling her to keep her up to date on what was going on and then again when I was out of surgery.

The last thing I remember as I was going under was the anesthesiologist saying, "Where is that Hussein anyway?" I thought I was going to die!

I woke up in a hospital bed. It was light and I was alive. The chief brought Nancy to the hospital later that morning. I could see the concern in her face and I was very happy to see her. She was just like an additional private nurse taking excellent care of me. The nurses set up another bed in my room and Nancy stayed there looking after me. The doctor came in later in the day to examine me and explain what was going on. Evidently my appendix was wrapped around my intestine and had become infected. With it being wrapped around my intestine it masked the normal signs of appendicitis. The end of the appendix had been eaten away by the infection and started to poison my body, so they decided to operate immediately.

I was pretty much out of it the first day. The second day when the doctor came in to check on me he started to probe around the incision. This hurt so I grabbed the side of the bed and gritted my teeth. He kept pushing around the incision and obviously found something he didn't like. With no warning or preparation, he pulled open the wound and inserted his fingers in my abdomen and began probing around inside. The surprise and pain was incredible. Nancy and the nurse were standing in the doorway, their eyes got big as saucers and Nancy turned away. I griped the bed so tight I thought I might bend it. That is the moment I knew I would be able to endure torture. When the doctor finished and left the room the nurse told me tomorrow when they see the doctor coming they would delay him and bring me a shot for the pain.

The next morning we could hear the doctor coming and the nurse rushed out to get me the shot she had promised for the pain we expected to come with him. The doctor made it to the room before the nurse and when she came rushing in holding the hypodermic needle with the pain killer in it the doctor looked up at her and then back at me and asked if I was in pain. I looked him in the eyes and said not yet.

The infection was persistent and the wound was slow to heal. Nancy had left our 7 and 9 year old girls with our good friends and neighbor. Nancy would call every day but after about five days they became convinced I had died and mom just wouldn't tell them. Nancy called from my room so I could get on the phone with the girls to convince them I was still alive.

I was in the hospital for a total of 10 days. They wanted to keep me longer, but I begged them to release me. I promised to keep a follow up appointment with a doctor at home. They finally consented and I was on a plane home. I had lost almost 20 pounds in the hospital. My uniform just hung on my body. I could hardly walk but I made it on the plane to go home. Once I got home, I recovered quickly, however I was unable to go back to work for over a month.

COFFIN CORNER

Aircraft performance is affected by factors such as weight, altitude, temperature and speed. This data is displayed on a chart, in graphic form, with a solid border. Anything within the border, the airplane is capable of flying safely; anything outside the border; it is not capable of flying safely or maybe not even at all. The coffin corner is the top edge of the performance envelope that is just within the envelope with no room for error. An easy way of understanding the coffin corner that it is a point where the maximum performance an aircraft is capable of is the least performance that is required to maintain safe flight.

When I was recalled to American Airlines in 1984, I was in the front of the largest hiring boom in airline history. The airlines were buying hundreds of airplanes and hiring thousands of pilots. All of this expansion meant rapid promotion. I returned to American as a Boeing 727 flight engineer and in a year and a half I upgraded to MD80 copilot. I upgraded as quickly as I could. I wanted to be at the controls flying instead of just operating the systems. That meant my flying schedules wouldn't be as good as it would be if I stayed a flight engineer and gained seniority in that position. In the airline industry, seniority controls everything. But, making FO early meant a pay raise and I got to face forwards and have a window seat. Some pilots decided to stay flight engineers and move to the DC-10 to have better schedules and make more money than they would as engineer on the 727.

The airline pay system works on the seniority system. You start out in the lowest position. At this time, it was 727 flight engineer. The company published a list of flight schedules we called "lines of flying." All of the pilots in that category bid for the lines and were awarded those lines based on their seniority. The lines of flying control your days off, the number of days you work, where you go, and your pay, among other factors. The same position on a bigger airplane pays more than the same position on a smaller airplane. Copilot pays more than engineer and captain pays more than copilot. The pay system was developed in the early days of commercial aviation and based on the system used by railroads to pay railroad engineers.

I had been flying copilot on the McDonald Douglas Super 80 (MD80) for more than two years and had over 1,500 hours in the Super 80. I was very comfortable and competent in the airplane. The captain I was flying with that month was new to the Super 80. He had been a flight engineer for 14 years. Unlike many other engineers, he hadn't actually piloted an airplane while engineer, in fact he hadn't flown anything during that time. He chose to fly engineer on the DC-10 and defer promotion to first officer to get a better schedule. The pay for a DC-10 engineer was almost equal to a MD80 copilot and a senior engineer could get a lot better schedule than a junior copilot. When he could not defer his upgrade anymore, he became a 727 first officer for about a year before upgrading to captain on the Super 80.

I bid a good line that month. I would start out in the evening and fly to San Diego, spend the night, then on to DFW (Dallas/Fort Worth) and eventually back to Chicago.

This particular night, as usual, we were full of passengers and at max weight for takeoff. The captain would be flying the first leg. The normal practice is to alternate legs. The captain would start out flying. Then he would have the copilot fly the next leg. We were cleared into position on runway 4-Left to hold. Runway 4L and 9L at O'Hare intersected, and the controllers would assign a runway based on your direction of flight, 4L for west bound and 9L for east bound, then they would alternate takeoffs on those runways.

The controller cleared us for takeoff. We checked 9L for traffic, as the captain pushed the throttles part way up, waiting for the engines to come up from idle and stabilize at 1.4 EPR, (EPR is Engine Pressure Ratio, and is the reference used to set power on a jet engine).

Then the captain called, "Auto-throttles on."

The engines went smoothly to takeoff power. I checked the engine instruments for proper operation as the airplane accelerated. I called, "80 knots."

We checked that our flight instruments were operating normally, and we had the proper indications displayed. The airplane continued accelerating.

I called, "V1" followed quickly by, "Rotate."

The captain moved his right hand from the throttles to the control yoke and put a slight back pressure to rotate to liftoff attitude. The airplane's nose wheel lifted from the runway followed a short time later by the main gear.

I called" V2+10."

The captain pulled back on the wheel. The airplane rotated to flying attitude and lifted off the runway. The Captain called, "Positive rate gear up." Meaning the airplane had lifted off the runway and was climbing normally.

I pulled the gear lever out and up to retract the landing gear. The gear lights went from green to red as the gear cycled up. I disarmed the auto spoilers and auto brakes. I could feel the main gear clunk up into the up position, and I both heard and felt the nose gear clunk to the retracted position. I checked all gear lights were out indicating all three landing gear were properly retracted. We continued to accelerate to our best climb speed of 155 knots.

At 1,000 feet the captain called, "Half rate, flaps up, climb power."

I set the controls accordingly reducing our rate of climb to half of what it was currently indicating. I retracted the flaps and set climb power on the auto throttles.

The controller gave us a left turn and told us to expedite our climb. I acknowledged the turn as the captain set the heading bug on the DFGS, (Digital Flight Guidance System) and started the turn. I told the controller we were heavy and giving him all we had for climb. The captain began pulling back on the wheel to comply with the controller's expedite climb request. This maneuver startled me, because he should have known that at this weight, we were doing the best we could, and any increase in pitch would only decrease our climb rate and push us close to a stall. I instinctively put my right hand out to prevent the wheel from coming back. I looked at the captain and told him we were doing the best we could at this weight. This was the second time this month the captain had just pulled the wheel back, disregarding our speed, in an attempt to comply with a controller's instruction to expedite our climb.

After our three day trip, we had three days off, and then went to work to do it all over again. This time it was my turn to fly to San Diego. The weather was good, and the flight was smooth. The moon was bright enough to get a good view of the Rocky Mountains as we passed over. The marine layer hadn't come in yet at San Diego, so the approach would be an easy visual let down over the hill to the east of the airport. The airport was easy to pick out amongst all the bright lights of the city. It was the dark spot with the parallel rows of white lights along the runway and at the edge of the bay. As you get closer, the blue taxiway lights start to show up. I just followed the slope of the hill to the east of the runway and touched down on the white thousand foot mark on the runway.

The next morning, we departed SAN for DFW. The weather was good, and it should be a routine flight. Even though the San Diego departure is a busy one, I always have a few seconds to admire the view of the city, the ocean and the mountains. San Diego is one of my favorite cities.

A jet engine is more efficient as its altitude of operation increases; so in order to save fuel, the airlines plan cruise altitudes as high as possible within the performance constraints of the aircraft and the effect of wind direction on the cruise speed. Our flight plan had our initial cruise altitude set at flight level (FL) 330; (about 33,000 feet) then, as we burned fuel to lighten up, we would climb to a cruising altitude of FL 370.

With the captain at the flight controls, we burned off enough fuel, (6,000#/hour) that we were light enough to climb to FL370; so, at the captain's request, I called ATC (air traffic control) and asked what the ride reports were at 370. ATC reported smooth, so I requested FL 370. ATC replied with our call sign and a clearance to FL 370. I set 370 in the altitude select window of the DFGS control panel. As per normal procedure, we were on autopilot with the auto-throttles engaged. The captain rolled the pitch wheel on the autopilot to initiate the climb. When the engines reached climb power, he selected Mach climb so the aircraft would maintain its Mach speed during the climb. Just then the interphone chime rang, and I answered it. The flight attendants were cold and wanted more heat. While I was online with the flight attendants, ATC called on the radio. The captain answered.

After I hung up the interphone, I checked the flight instruments. I blinked and scanned them again. I couldn't believe what they were telling me. We were at 36,500 feet with an air speed of 188 knots and decreasing quickly. We were climbing in vertical speed at 1,000 feet per minute instead of a Mach climb. Mach- climb climbs the aircraft at a constant Mach speed and varies the rate of climb to maintain that speed. It protects you from getting too slow and stalling the wing which would result in plunging many thousands of feet before a recovery would be possible. Climbing in vertical speed mode eliminated that protection and held a constant rate of climb and let the speed decrease if the engines didn't have enough power to hold both the speed/Mach and rate of climb. That was way too fast of a rate of climb for this weight and altitude! The radio call that the captain answered while I was on the interphone was the controller asking him to expedite his climb. The captain rolled in a 1,000 foot per minute climb on the DFGS. The engines were at max power, and because the airplane was now in vertical speed mode instead of Mach airspeed mode, the airspeed began to bleed away to maintain the 1,000 foot per minute climb.

The air was smooth, but I could feel the fast rhythmic vibration of the air starting to separate from the wing, similar to a motor boat moving fast through small waves.

I called out "Initial buffet."

The airplane was too slow and getting ready to stall. The captain looked at me quizzically and did nothing. I knew he didn't realize that we were moments from falling out of the sky. I pushed the altitude hold button on the autopilot, then rolled in 1,000 foot per minute rate of decent, disconnected the auto-throttles and checked that the engines were set to max power. I told the captain to call ATC and tell them we could not maintain altitude and were descending. We could take a turn for traffic, if they needed it. He complied. We had descended below FL350 (35,000 feet) before the airplane was flying normally again. I reengaged the autopilot and auto-throttles and set our new cruise altitude of FL 330 into the altitude select window. It only took a minute or two to get everything squared away and back at normal cruise, heading to DFW. ATC had no problem with our descent, and nobody there knew what had been narrowly avoided. The interphone rang again, and it was the number one flight attendant. She asked what that shaking was as she hadn't felt anything like that before. I told her it was just turbulence, so we went to a smoother altitude.

En route to DFW, we briefly discussed what had happened. Once we were parked at the gate at DFW, I pulled out the performance manual and showed him what the stall speed was for our weight and altitude. He saw the numbers and knew what they meant.

He was a good guy and we got along well, but he wasn't as sharp as he needed to be on performance limits. I contacted the professional standards committee representative for Chicago and told him of the incident and the two other incidents where the captain was eager to comply with an ATC request without adequate understanding of the performance ramifications. The captain was already scheduled for recurrent training over the next week, and I strongly suggested he be put through extensive training in performance limits. Professional standards said they would make sure he would get that training.

I had always wondered what it would take for me to take control of an airplane from a captain, I found out that day.

767 INTERNATIONAL

I flew the Boeing 767 internationally for two and a half years while I waited to be senior enough to hold a captain's bid in either the B-727 or MD-80. I enjoyed the European destination. I had a lot of Paris and Munich layovers along with Manchester, U.K., Geneva, Switzerland, Frankfort, Germany and others. We would have about 24 hours off at our destination before we would fly back to Chicago. Paris was my favorite. I would spend hours just walking the streets and absorbing the atmosphere. I felt very comfortable in 1980's Paris.

On my first layover in Paris the Captain, F/O and I all went to a small sidewalk restaurant. It only had about 5 tables and all of them were covered in flowers. When we sat down the owner came over with menus. We asked if he had English menus. He didn't speak English and none of us spoke French. He asked if anyone spoke Italian, no, I asked if he spoke German, he said no. When he discovered, I assume through our accents, we were Americans he got very excited to have us in his restaurant and bought us all a glass of wine on him. Between the four of us we managed to order a delicious dinner and had a pleasant evening. That put to rest the myth of the snobbish French for me.

One of our trips was a 6 day Paris trip. We would leave Chicago in the evening and arrive in Paris the next morning, spend 24 hours there then fly to Raleigh Durham, spend 24 hours there, then fly back to Paris, spend 24 hours, then fly back to Chicago. We would be gone six days cross the Atlantic four times and sleep three nights. I still haven't figured out how that was possible. It took me two day at home to rest after those trips.

DACHAU GERMANY

On one of our Munich layovers the Captain, F/O and I decided to visit the Dachau death camp. It was only about 12 miles north of Munich. We checked into our hotel, changed our clothes and met in the lobby. We took the train to Dachau and walked to the main gate, there we saw a sign saying closed*. We had not checked for hours of operation. I never did get to go back and take the tour.

* Dachau is now open daily from 9AM to 5PM except December 24th.

MD-80 CAPTAIN

SAN JOSE, CA (SJC)

I was a relatively new captain and SJC was a relatively new hub for American Airlines. I was descending for approach to the north and as usual ATC had kept us high to clear the mountain ridge and now I had to make a quick decent to get on the arrival and approach to SJC. It was a dark night with some lights breaking through the low clouds beneath us. It was cold enough that I had the engine and airfoil anti-ice turned on and that made a quick decent harder because I had to carry some power to keep the bleed air used for the anti-ice systems operating properly.

The tower operator was busy with the general aviation (GA) aircraft using the parallel runway. There was a lot of continuous radio chatter. It was a little hectic in the cockpit with final checks and intercepting the approach but we were almost there. It was late and I was looking forward to the end of a long day.

We were cleared to land and I focused on the touchdown zone past the end of the displaced threshold line. The runway looked clear. Just as I flared for touchdown, I heard a radio call, "Tower did you clear that aircraft to land over us?" What aircraft? Who landed over whom?

We touched down and as we rolled out to exit the runway the tower controller came on the radio, "American 123 call the tower when you are able."

The co-pilot and I looked at each other and asked the same question, "Did you see another airplane?" "We did get a landing clearance, right?"

157

After we parked and finished shutting down the airplane, I called the tower. The tower controller verified he had cleared us to land and that we did land over another Super 80. He said he was removing himself from duty for the error.

How could I have missed an aircraft as big as a Super 80 on the runway? How did we avoid a disaster? I analyzed the situation for my report to the company of the incident.

There were a lot of blinking lights around because of the massive amount of construction going on. The runway we were landing on had a displaced threshold, which means the end of the runway was not the touchdown area. It was displaced 1,000 or more feet down the runway. So the airplane on the runway was over 1,000 from the part of the runway I was landing on which gave me enough clearance to miss the other airplane. But how did we not see the airplane on the runway waiting to take off?

The white "tail lights" on the Super 80 are not on the tail. One light is on each wing tip. They were roughly in line with the edge of the runway. The red strobe lights are on the top and bottom of the fuselage. The high "T" tail blocked the top light from our view and the bottom light was not visible. With all of the constant radio traffic the pilot on the runway missed the tower controller giving me clearance to land and I missed him giving the other Super 80 clearance into position and hold on the runway.
Some time after this incident FAA procedures and American Airline procedures changed. Anytime an aircraft is cleared onto a runway they turn on their landing lights to make them very visible and controllers don't have airplanes holding for extended times on the runway.

This was a disaster that due to luck and circumstances wasn't.

SYRACUSE, NY (SYR)

I was flying as captain in the Super 80 into Syracuse (SYR). Every time I flew there I thought of all the times I landed there and went into the Crouse-Hinds hanger on the south end of the field. But this day, I had other things on my mind. There was a thunderstorm just outside the outer marker on the approach.

I checked the storm on radar. It would be safe to continue the approach and landing, but I would have to make a tighter than normal turn to beat the storm and line up on the ILS[1] approach. I made it past the storm with just a bump or two and continued the landing. I was close to an on time arrival, but I would have to hurry to make it so I taxied faster than normal. As I approached the gate, I could see the guide men were there to meet the plane and get us parked. I followed the guide man's signals to the parking line. I set the brakes, and checked the time on the ACARS[2]. I made it on time.

---

[1] ILS instrument landing system

[2] ACARS is the avionics system that records aircraft specific data and reports it back to Operations

I continued with the parking checklist. When I was finished, I opened the cockpit door to say goodbye to the passengers. Near the end of the line was a man in his sixties. He looked at me and said, "Hello Dan." It was Bob Arnholt the Chief Pilot and Director of Operation for Cooper Industries, my boss when I worked for Cooper. I greeted him warmly and said goodbye as he stepped off the airplane and onto the jet bridge. I smiled to myself and thought back to El Paso. I wonder if he noticed the tight turn to final approach and fast taxi to the gate.

EL PASO, TX (ELP)

It was a 3 AM departure from El Paso to DFW. The wind was howling all night and it was cold even inside my room. When I got up to get ready I looked out and saw that it had snowed during the night. I turned on the Weather Channel and listened while I brushed my teeth.

On my way to the van for the ride to the airport with the flight crew, I was glad I had my coat. With the wind blowing and the moist air, the cold just ripped right through you. There wasn't much talking on the ride to the airport, we weren't fully awake yet. When we got to the terminal, I went to Operations to do the paperwork and the rest of the crew went to the gate to ready the aircraft for the flight.

In Operations, a dead-heading[3] FO (First Officer- three stripes) came up to me and asked if I was taking the flight to DFW. I said I was, and he asked if he could ride along in the jump seat. I checked his ID and said sure.

---

[3] Dead-heading is flying on a flight while you are not working that flight.

After I printed the flight plan and checked the weather, I got the aircraft logbook and started reviewing it. It seems that the MD-80 I would be flying had skidded sideways off the runway while landing because of the slush on the runway. Maintenance had changed two tires on the right side because of the side load and scuffing from the skid. They inspected the tires on the left side but didn't change them. The aircraft logbook was signed off as inspected and good for service. I looked at the FO who wanted to ride to DFW with us and said, half joking, he might want to wait for the next flight. This was going to take some more investigation.

I found the mechanic who changed the tires and did the inspection and asked him why he only changed two tires. He said that was because he only had two tires on hand. I told him I didn't care how many tires he had on hand, I wanted to know why he didn't change the other two. He said he had called Tulsa Tech (American keeps a 24-hour technical staff available in Tulsa to help with maintenance questions and problems over the phone) and they told him the other tires were within limits for operation. I decided to call Tulsa Tech myself and, with the El Paso mechanic beside me, have them explain what they did and why. I was satisfied with the explanation and preceded to the aircraft to get ready for departure. The FO already did the walk around, but I decided to check out the tires and landing gear myself. I turned on the landing gear wheel well lights and inspected all the tires and wheel wells. Everything looked normal.

Back in the cockpit, I tuned in the ATIS (Automated Terminal Information Service) frequency on the number 1 radio and got the current report. There was slush covering the ramp and runway, but the ATIS didn't report the depth. This was important, because we would have to adjust our takeoff performance for slush on the runway. If there was more than a half inch of slush, we would not be legal for departure. It was already departure time, and the agents were trying to get me to go, but I couldn't. I explained the situation to them and told them it would be a while before we would be ready.

The reason this is all so important it that snow or slush on the runway makes acceleration to takeoff speed slower due to the increased resistance. It also makes stopping take longer because of the slippery runway. Depending on the length of the runway, it may not be safe to takeoff at all under these conditions. In any case, it reduced the V1 (action speed) which is used to determine whether to stop or to continue your takeoff if you experience an engine failure or other severe problems.

I called the ground controller on the radio and asked if he had a report on the depth of the slush. He did not. I told him I needed one before I would be able to depart. He said he could get an airport car to pick me up and drive me down the runway to check, if I wanted. I told him that would work. I told the copilot to figure out new takeoff data for a half inch of slush on the runway. That was the maximum allowable. If we were good to go with a half inch, then any lesser amount would be good to go too.

I borrowed a ruler from the gate agent and met the airport grounds worker at the bottom of the jet bridge. He drove me to the runway, and I had him stop about every 100 yards so I could measure the depth of the slush. It was right at a half inch all the way down the runway.

Back in the cockpit, I also did the performance calculations for a half inch of slush on the runway. I compared the takeoff data that I calculated to the copilot's calculations. The figures both agreed, indicating we were legal for takeoff and what speeds we would use to set our airspeed bugs.[4] With the passengers loaded and all of the required preparation completed, I asked the number one flight attendant to give our jump seat rider a seat in the cabin. Then I called for pushback from the gate. I was an hour and a half late. I always looked at the captain's job as not to get the flight out on time, but to get it out when it was safe and ready while striving to make it on-time.

We taxied to runway 4 (040 degrees magnetic) with confidence we had done all we needed to do to make it a safe departure and flight to DFW. With a clearance to takeoff, I taxied onto the runway, lined the airplane up with the center of the runway and held the brakes on. I briefed the FO to make all the standard callouts on the takeoff roll and give the engine instruments a little more attention than usual because of the slush. All takeoff checks were completed. I pushed the throttles up checking for any warning horns indicating an important item needed for takeoff was not done. There were no warnings. I held the throttles at 1.4 EPR to let the engine anti-ice heat the engine nose bowl and inlet guide vanes before we started our takeoff roll through the slush.

I said, "OK let's go."

Auto-throttles on. I held the brakes while the engines spooled up to max takeoff power then released the brakes and started to roll. It was dark with only the runway edge lights and the reflection of my landing lights visible.

---

[4] The airspeed indicator has little movable markers or "bugs" that are used as markers for operational speeds such as V1, V2, flap retract speed, slat retract speed and clean minimum maneuvering speed.

The airplane accelerated down the runway with the copilot making all of his normal calls; power is set.... engines are good..... 80 knots.... V1.... BANG!

What was that?

We were past V1, so we would have to continue the takeoff. The airplane didn't yaw. Instead it stayed straight and continued to accelerate. The engines were good, still making max power. My mind instantly settled on a possible blown tire.

The copilot continued his callouts:" V2" ...."Rotate".......V2+10."

I called positive rate gear up by rote.

The copilot hesitated and asked, "you sure?"

I said yes and he retracted the landing gear. That was a mistake. I didn't process what the copilot was saying when he asked if I was sure about raising the gear. If we did blow a tire it could be shredded and damage the wheel well or even become stuck and not come down for landing. Too late to change that decision now. Luckily the gear retracted smoothly with no sign of a problem, so we continued flying the departure and headed to DFW. I told the copilot to tell the tower we might have blown a tire on takeoff so they could check the runway for any debris.

Climbing out of 10,000 feet, I pushed the chime one time indicating to the flight attendants the end of the sterile cockpit. Below 10,000 feet the flight attendants are not to call the cockpit except in an emergency. This is to cut down on distractions during critical phases of flight. As soon as my finger left the call button, I heard a "ding-ding" the signal that a flight attendant was calling the cockpit. I answered the interphone, and one of the flight attendants from the back was on the line. She said she heard a loud bang on takeoff. She said she talked to the deadheading FO and he said it sounded like a blown main tire. I told her we heard it too and asked to speak to him. The deadheading FO also flew the MD-80, and I asked him if he would be willing to check the main gear through the viewing ports in the cabin before we landed. He said he would. That way I wouldn't have to have my copilot go back into the cabin to do the check. It would take a little of the work load off of us. The view ports are in the floor of the main cabin.

Once we were at cruise altitude, I gave control of the aircraft and radios to the copilot while I called Tulsa Tech on the number one radio. I talked to the same maintenance technician I talked with when I was in El Paso. My bet was he wished the El Paso team had changed the other two tires now. I filled him in on everything and asked him to have a maintenance crew standing by with jacks and new tires at the end of the runway when we landed at DFW. I didn't want to tie up the runway any longer than necessary during the morning rush if the aircraft was disabled and I couldn't taxi off the runway.

When we reached the DFW approach area, I informed them of our situation and asked for a descent below 10,000 feet so we could depressurize the cabin and inspect our landing gear. Under the carpet in the main cabin there are two inspection covers that open to the landing gear wells that make it possible to inspect the landing gear in an abnormal situation such as we were having. In order to open the inspection covers, the airplane had to be depressurized because the landing gear wells are not pressurized. The access covers cannot be opened unless the cabin is depressurized. Approach cleared us for the descent. They gave us vectors to keep us clear of other traffic and still close to the airport so we would be able to land in a timely manor. I descended to under 10,000 feet and depressurized the cabin. The deadheading FO pulled up the carpet at the appropriate place and looked through the view ports. He said the right side looked good, but the light in the left wheel well was out and he couldn't see anything. I asked him to standby, and I would lower the gear for him to check again. The copilot and I had both inspected the wheel wells before takeoff and both of the lights were working at that time. We also knew that the tires on the left side were the ones that were not changed. This was more evidence that we had a blown tire, and that it was on the left side.

The moment of truth, I called for "gear down."

The "gear-door-unlocked" light illuminated along with all three red "gear-not-down" lights. This was the normal situation when the gear handle is first put to the down position. After what seemed an inordinately long time, all three landing gear clunked into place and the green "gear-down" lights came on.

I pushed the cabin chime two times. When the interphone was answered I asked the deadheading FO to check the gear one more time to see what he could see. He reported back that the right gear was down and the locked stripe was aligned, but it was dark, and he could not see anything on the left side. I thanked him for his help and asked him to seal the view ports as we would be landing soon.

I briefed the flight attendants on what I expected during the landing with two scenarios. One, if only one tire was blown and the other one held, and we stayed on the runway I did not expect an emergency evacuation. Under the second scenario, if both tires were blown and, depending on what damage, if any, I might not be able to keep the aircraft on the runway. One wing, I thought probably the left one, would be down and there would be the possibility of a fire in the area of the left landing gear so it would be a good idea not to use the front door on that side to make it easier for the fire fighters to get to that area and deal with any fires. I told them that I would give the standard "Easy Victor" signal if I thought we needed to evacuate. All the flight attendants checked in that they understood, and I hung up to let them start briefing the passengers for the possible evacuation while I prepared for landing.

I had called for the fire equipment to be standing by, and I could see them near the end of the runway with their red lights flashing, waiting. I could also see an American Airlines maintenance truck with jacks and tires waiting. I was lined up on runway 13-R with flaps set to 40 degrees for landing. I was coming in at as slow of an airspeed as I could, and descending flatter and slower than normal. I wanted as soft a touchdown as possible to put the least strain possible on the only tire I might have on the left gear. I would use reverse thrust to slow and not use brakes until I absolutely had to, and then as light as possible especially on the left side.

Landing checks were done and at 250 feet above the runway the copilot called "Brace" over the PA, the signal for the flight attendants and passengers to prepare for touchdown.

The copilot called out our altitude, "100" ...."50".."40".."30".."20".."10." The aircraft gently kissed the runway. We could hear the chirp of the tires as they touched. So far so good, the aircraft was in a normal landing attitude and tracking straight down the runway. The spoilers were deployed, and I had the engines in full reverse. As we approached the end of the runway, I stowed the reversers and added a little brake to come to a complete stop. I set the parking brakes and didn't touch anything. I got on the PA and announced that we would NOT, repeat NOT, need to evacuate.

I then got on the radio to the mechanics and asked what it looked like outside. He said he checked all of the tires and they were all good. I was shocked and asked him to check the tires again. He did and again reported everything was good. I asked for the mechanics to follow me to the gate and I released the fire trucks to return to their station. The copilot and I looked at each other in disbelief ("WTF, Over").

We called for clearance to the gate and did the After Landing and Taxi checklist as we started to taxi. Once we were parked at the gate, a mechanic came to the cockpit and said they took three 5 gallon buckets full of slush out of the rear baggage compartment.

The only thing I can think of is that we hit a hole, or dip, in the runway which contained a lot more slush than the rest of the runway, and that slush was slammed onto the fuselage at a force capable of causing the large bang we all heard. After all that....and it was just another day at the office.

LAS VEGAS, NV (LAS)
OCTOBER 15, 2000

I was flying as captain on the Super 80, (DC-9/ MD80). The trip left Chicago at 1500 hours and went to Las Vegas, to San Jose, and then back to Las Vegas at 2104 hours.

I flew this trip for the month of October. The approach to Las Vegas' McCarran airport was a challenge all month long. There were wind, weather and traffic problems on every trip, but this time was different. The night was calm with clear skies, and I could see the runway from more than 40 miles out. I was looking forward to an easy landing and quick trip to the hotel. It had been a long day, and I was ready for some rest.

I was vectored to final approach to runway 25L for landing. For the first time all month the air was smooth and calm. I could see the runway just about 8 miles in front of me, a piece of cake. A "Cactus" (radio call-sign for America West Airlines) A320 was vectored to final approach in front of me and was descending to intercept the glide slope for landing. I was approaching RELIN (the navigation fix where I would start the decent) at 3,500 feet msl. (1,731 feet above the ground), and the glide slope indicator at one dot high I pushed the autopilot disconnect button to hand-fly the rest of the approach. The control wheel was nearly ripped from my hands as it hit the forward stop. The airplane pitched over to an 11 degree nose-down attitude. I placed both hands on the wheel, braced my feet on the rudder pedals, and pulled with all my strength to move the wheel back and raise the nose above the horizon.

I yelled to Kerry, my co-pilot, "Is the auto pilot off? Is the auto pilot off?" I thought it failed, causing an autopilot induced hard over pushing the wheel full forward.

He yelled back, "Yes! Pull up, pull up."

I yelled back, "I'm trying."

With the nose still down 11 degrees the airplane rolled 5 degrees to the left, I tried to use the wheel to bring the wings back to level, the wheel was moving but the controls were not responding to any of my inputs.

Slowly the controls seemed to start to take effect. The nose went from 11degrees down to 11degrees up and it rolled from 5 degrees left to 22 degrees right. I pushed the rudder pedals full left to counter the right turn. Kerry had disconnected the auto throttles and pushed them to the firewall; full power!

Then with the airplane now pitched up 11 degrees, a right bank of 22 degrees and full power; everything stopped responding. Whatever had us in its grip was still holding on – I had no control. The airplane was just suspended in time and space pointed skyward in a right bank and not caring what I wanted it to do. Seconds passed like hours. I vividly remember thinking to myself as I was fighting with unresponsive controls, "No! Not now". The outcome was in doubt, and I truly thought I might die, along with everyone onboard, in the next few seconds. Later, Kerry, said he saw his whole life pass before his eyes. I felt helpless and expected it to continue the right-hand roll to inverted and crash.

As suddenly as it came, it was gone – whatever "it" was. The airplane was free and responding to my control inputs. In all, 40 seconds had passed. It surprised me how quickly Kerry and I went from fighting for our lives with high pitched staccato communications to just flying a go-around.

I told Kerry to get on the radio and informed the controllers we were on the go-around and wanted to come back for another landing. As we were vectored for another approach, I got on the intercom to tell the passengers as calmly as I could, what had happened and that we were going to make another approach and landing, this time without all the bumps.

The next approach and landing was uneventful. After arriving at the gate, parking the brakes, and finishing the checklist; I got out of my seat and stood in the door, as I always did, to say good bye to the passengers. The passengers were quiet and pale looking as they slowly shuffled out the door. Most said nothing, the ones that did speak only said thank you in a low almost solemn voice. We all knew just how close we came to the end. We were in Vegas and we just won the biggest jackpot of all, we would continue to live our lives!

I talked to the number one flight attendant after the passengers were gone to see what it looked like from his position. He was pale and somewhat shaken. He said it was so quiet you could hear a pin drop. First, they were lifted in their seats, held down only by their seatbelts, then pushed back down into their seats. The overhead bins opened, and some luggage fell out. No one was hurt. There were two flight attendants in the back of the plane. When I went to see them, one was crying hysterically, and the other was laughing hysterically.

"It" turned out to be wind shear caused by the preceding aircraft. You would think that was the end of the story, but it wasn't. I went to operations and contacted dispatch to tell them what had happened and to file my initial report to the company. When I called the tower to find out what airplane was in front of me, he said it was an Airbus 320. He also said the controllers in the tower looking out their windows thought they were watching a crash happen. So did I.

When I got back to the airplane the station manager was there to tell me we were re-assigned to fly to Orange County, John Wayne airport in Santa Anna. I told him we couldn't. The airplane needed a turbulence inspection and the engines needed an inspection because we fire-walled them and may have had an over-temp or over-speed.

He said, "I'll get you another aircraft."

I said the flight attendants were in no condition to fly.

He said he would get me some new flight attendants. He said there were a plane load of passengers that were waiting. He was twisting my arm, and I was wavering. Kerry was still sitting in his seat, I glanced over at him and he was shaking his head no. He was right. None of us were in any condition to fly that trip.

I told the manager, "No we were heading for the hotel."
He said he would be calling the Chief Pilot to tell him I refused the trip. I told him to do what he had to do, but we were going to the hotel.

This was pre-9/11 so the crew van was waiting for us at the bottom of the jet-bridge to take us to the hotel. During the ride my cell rang. It was the Chief Pilot. He had been at a movie with his wife when he got the call from the manager in Las Vegas. He asked me why I refused the trip and I gave him the short version. He said, "Good call." We continued to the hotel, but the adrenalin was starting to let down and the full gravity of what just happened was settling in. I told the crew I was going to change and go to the bar and I was buying if anyone was interested. Kerry was the only one to take me up on my offer. We talked about what each of us remembered and who did what. I took a call from Crew Schedule and they told me the flight attendants

172

were released from the rest of their trip and sent home. They would release us, too, if we wanted. I told Kerry and we thought about it for a while and decided to continue with our trip. Instead of flying to Dallas the next day as we were scheduled to do, we deadheaded on the jump-seats of a 757. I think that was a good thing. It was nice to be in the cockpit and see a normal flight before we would continue on the rest of our three-day trip. We were both a little apprehensive, but by the time we made it to DFW we both felt fine.

I wrote a commendation letter for Kerry for the way he kept giving me critical information while I was fighting to regain control of the aircraft and his subsequent professionalism during the go-around and landing. I received a letter of appreciation from the Chief Pilot in Chicago that he placed in my file at American Airlines. We both did a good job that night. We earned our pay for the rest of our careers, but I always remember, a thousand 'at-a-boys' don't make up for one 'oh-shit', with management and you are only as good as your next landing.

Addendum

Flight Recorder readout

Condition before event onset:
Airspeed 190K, Pitch -1.1 degrees, engine stable at 1.0 EPR

Onset of event: Pitch down -11.2 deg., roll 5 deg left, 0 G pushover

Next- Pitch up 11.3 deg., Bank 22 deg R, 1.3 G pull, engines 2.04 EPR speed 155K
Wind shear warning on for 19 seconds (We did not hear it because of task saturation. Probably why I recall all of our cockpit communications as yelling back and forth to one another.)

Total time of event 40 seconds.
Max control inputs: aileron, 14 deg L, 7 deg. R
Rudder 14 deg L, 22 deg. R
G forces: 0 G, +1.3 G

My Retirement Flight

It was May 18, 2005 and I was leaving on my last sequence I would fly for American Airlines. It was a two-day trip starting with a 1642 departure to LAX. On the 19th I would depart LAX for ORD at 0925 then fly a Tulsa (TUL) turn arriving back at ORD at 2047 for the traditional cake in operations before I would turn in my keys and ID and be gone. At least that was the plan.

The flight to LAX left on time and was one of the most beautiful of my life. The sky had some wispy clouds that made the sunset over the Rockies one of the most gorgeous I had seen. The mountains were bathed in pink, orange and grey light. The snow-capped peaks caught the last rays of bright white sunlight just before going dark. The flight was going so smoothly, and it was so beautiful, that I wondered if I was really ready to give it up.

I didn't have to retire. In fact, I was retiring five years before the mandatory retirement age of 60. There were several factors that entered into my decision. It looked like the company might go bankrupt in the near future and I wanted to protect my pension and not lose it, which happened to so many airline pilots in recent years. The stock market was up, and the value of my pension was enough to live on. If I waited that could all change. One of the biggest reasons was that I'd just had enough. I had enough of being just a number with the company. In the post 9-11 airline industry, I was tired of being treated like a terrorist every time I went through security when I went to work. I was ready to move on and do some things I had always wanted to do but didn't have the time for. Maybe I would go to Alaska and fly a Beaver on floats or sail the Great Lakes. Who knows?

The second day of my last sequence started with an hour and a half gate hold in LAX because of weather in Chicago. After about an hour the number one flight attendant called and said she had a couple of passengers that wanted off. They had missed their meeting and the trip would be pointless. After much persuading via radio I was able to get the gate agent to bring the jet bridge back and open the door to let off those who wanted off. After the door was closed again, we were pushed back from the gate because another flight was inbound and needed it. It was another half hour before we got clearance for engine start and taxi.

We joined the long slow moving line of aircraft taxiing for takeoff. We were only about number five for takeoff when the interphone rang. It was the number one flight attendant. She said the PA wasn't working. I asked if she made sure it was properly connected and she said yes. Great. I started to slow taxi while the copilot looked it up in the MEL (Minimum Equipment List) to see if we could go with the public address (PA) inoperative and what restrictions would be attached to it. The ground controller saw the gap opening up in the line caused by my slowdown and said to speed it up. I didn't. I didn't want to get to the takeoff position and not be able to go until we figured out the PA problem. The ground controller saw what I was doing and directed me off the taxiway to a holding area so other aircraft could get by. The number one flight attendant called back and said the PA had started to operate. I called the ground controller, but it was ten minutes more before he got us back in line for takeoff.

The weather was great, and the flight was smooth until we got to the Mississippi River. I was picking up a broad area of thunderstorms on my radar all around northern Illinois and southern Wisconsin. We were given several turns and speed adjustments to get in line with all the other arrivals. I could see on radar a narrow corridor through the thunderstorms into which the controllers were trying to fit all of the inbound O'Hare[5] traffic. We were able to thread the needle and land on runway 14-R with nothing more than light rain and light turbulence on the approach. Our gate was open, so we taxied in. As I approached the gate, I could see my wife Nancy standing there with a big smile waiving at me. I smiled and waived back as I set the parking brake, shut down the engines and did the after-parking checklist.

We had to change airplanes at O'Hare, and we were already late. American had given Nancy a positive space first class ticket to accompany me on my last flight. We got to the new airplane and I got the paperwork while my copilot did the walk around (before every flight one of the pilots will walk around the outside of the aircraft and check for leaks and damage) and started the cockpit checks.

When I got to the cockpit we loaded our route in the navigation computer, input our performance data into the PDCS (Performance Data Computer System) and set our

---

[5] Chicago's O'Hare International Airport (ORD) named for World War II naval aviator ace, ___ "Butch" O'Hare.

airspeed bugs before doing the Before Starting Engines Checklist. I called for clearance to push, released the brakes and started to move. The ramp controller congratulated me on my retirement, and I thanked him. As the ground crew disconnected us from the tug and saluted indicating we were good to taxi, I saw fire trucks lined up on either side of the airplane with their water cannons at the ready. This was my second to last leg but the last departure from O'Hare, so I was going to get the traditional last flight salute where I would taxi under the curtain of water sprayed up by the cannons. Before we started to roll, the copilot asked if he could make an announcement to the passenger to explain what was happening with the fire trucks. I said yes. I must admit I was feeling a little emotional. As we taxied forward the fire trucks let go with their water cannons and we taxied under the falling water as they saluted. I could hear applause erupt from the passengers. We cleared the ramp and were given taxi instructions to taxiway Mike (M on the airport taxi diagram) to hold, the airport had a ground stop because of the thunderstorms. The ground controller advised to expect an update in thirty minutes. I asked if it was okay to shut down the engines to save fuel. He said yes, no one would be going anywhere for a while. Thirty minutes passed. We were being pelted by heavy rain and wind and I knew we weren't going anywhere yet. We all were advised by the ground controller there would be another update in thirty minutes. I got on the PA and told the passengers everything I knew and urged patience.

After an hour and a half, the skies were getting lighter and the word came that the airport was now open and departures would be starting shortly. We started up one engine for taxi and slowly moved to the front of the line for takeoff. We were airborne after a delay of about two hours. We had to pick our way through a little weather en route to Tulsa, but it wasn't bad. At cruise altitude the number one flight attendant called and said she and the other two flight attendants would be illegal (worked too many hours between rest breaks) to fly back to Chicago. I was not happy. I didn't want to spend my last flight laying over in Tulsa and riding back to O'Hare as a passenger in the morning. I radioed dispatch and urged them to find flight attendants for the trip back to Chicago. They said they would try.

I pulled up to the gate in Tulsa and saw flight attendants waiting, finally something went right. I pulled up the paperwork in Operations and the copilot started the preflight. The gate agents boarded the passengers and we were ready for the flight back to O'Hare. When we called for our IFR clearance back to ORD, Clearance Delivery advised we had a ground hold because of weather at O'Hare. I had seen on the weather section of the release paperwork that the ceilings and visibility were going down. We waited another hour before we were released for departure. The gate agents had called the fire department to give us another water cannon salute since this was my actual last flight. All the agents and ground personnel lined up in front of the airplane and waived as we were pushed back. That was a nice gesture by them, and I appreciated it. Once again, the water cannons let loose as we taxied by. I saluted the firemen as I taxied past them.

We were at the end of the runway waiting for one aircraft to land before we could be cleared for takeoff. After he landed, I heard him say on the radio he had hit a big bird on the runway. The tower controller advised me that there would be a short delay while the runway was inspected for bird debris. About fifteen minutes later we were given clearance to takeoff.

En route to Chicago I checked the weather again. It had deteriorated further but we had done a check of the auto-land system before we left Tulsa, so we could land with an RVR (Runway Visual Range) of 600 feet and the weather was reporting a half mile visibility now (2,640 feet). About half way to O'Hare, a warning flag on my radio altimeter came on. The radio altimeter had failed which would restrict the type of approach we would be able to make at O'Hare. We wouldn't be able to use auto-land now and our minimum visibility would be increased. I checked Chicago's ATIS (Automated Terminal Information Service) that gives the current weather conditions for the airport. O'Hare weather was still good enough for an ILS (Instrument Landing System) approach.

We started our descent and were turned over to O'Hare approach control who then vectored us for an ILS approach to runway 14-R. The approach controller lined us up on the approach just outside of BIFLE, a navigation fix used for 14-R. He cleared us for the approach and advised us to contact tower at CHSTR, the outer marker. I got the latest weather report and set up the approach. This was going to be a difficult one right down to minimums.

We were on autopilot and following the glide slope down to 2,400 feet altitude at CHSTR. I was flying and the copilot monitored the approach and did the radio work. At CHSTR we were cleared to land. I called for landing gear down and flaps 40 degrees for landing. This would lower the nose slightly more than normal flaps 28 and make it easier to spot the runway. We both checked that the autopilot was tracking both the localizer and glide slope within limits. We were still in solid clouds at CHSTR. I turned the nose mounted landing lights off. They would just be reflecting off the clouds and make it more difficult to see the approach lights and runway when we broke out of the clouds.

We continued to descend on the glide slope toward our DA (decision altitude) of 868 feet, which was 200 feet above the runway. At that altitude we would have to see at least the approach lighting system, a series of flashing strobe lights often called the "rabbit," or something identifiable with the approach end of the runway to continue the descent. If we didn't, we would have to make a go-around and fly to our alternate airport. We were getting close to our DA, and I was starting to squirm a little in my seat. I directed my attention out the window to look for the runway, but I could see nothing. The copilot had his hands on the throttles and watched the instruments. His job was to initiate the go-around by pushing the TOGA (Take Off Go Around) buttons on the throttles at the DA, if I didn't push his hands from the throttles and take control for landing.

A heart beat before calling go-around, I saw the approach lights, pushed the copilot's hands from the throttles, and called "Continuing." I could go down to100 feet above the runway now. If I could see something identifiable with the approach end of the runway I could continue and land. If not, it would require a go-around from a very low altitude. Just an instant before having to call for a go-around I made out the runway end identifier lights along with the centerline lights and the runway edge lights. An instant later I could make out the whole touchdown area of the runway. Visibility was poor, but I continued for a smooth touchdown. The auto-spoilers deployed and a few seconds later I could feel the auto-brakes start to grab. I pulled the thrust reverser levers up to unlock and deploy them, and then pulled the reverser levers back, adding reverse thrust to aid in slowing down. At 60 knots, I pushed the reverser levers all the way forward to stow them. At taxi speed, I depressed the brake pedals slightly to disengage the auto-brakes as the copilot stowed the spoilers and retracted the flaps. As we taxied to the gate, we joked that all we needed after today was an engine failure and we would have accomplished everything we would do in recurrent training.

I parked at the gate and finished the checklists while all of the passengers deplaned. By the time I finished with the log book entries and signed it for the last time, everyone was gone. Nancy was waiting for me on the jet bridge. I got out of my seat and stood in the cockpit entry for a moment looking back at my office where I spent over 10,000 hours of flying time. It was dark except for a few indicator lights and the whir of a fan. I looked down the aisle of the cabin. It too was dark and empty. I paused for a moment then turned and walked out the door. I took Nancy's hand and we walked off the jet bridge together. The terminal was completely empty except for a maintenance guy with a floor polisher.

It was past midnight, there would be no cake and coffee in Operations with friends and co-workers to say goodbye and wish me luck. When we arrived home, it was after 2:00 am. Our daughter, Stacie, and some friends had decorated the house and had a special cake and champagne waiting for us, but it was late, and they were all gone. We appreciated the thought and effort. This was the end of one phase of my life and the start of the next.

PART FIVE

ALASKA

Getting a Job in Alaska

I had always said when I retired, I wanted to get a job flying in Alaska. I have been fascinated with Alaska since I was a kid. My wife, Nancy, and I took several vacations to "The Last Frontier" state. In 1998, we delivered a new motor home from a factory in Chico, California driving up the Al-Can Hwy, through Whitehorse, Yukon, to Tok, AK. We decided to turn right and head up to Fairbanks before driving down to Anchorage to deliver the motor home. That was a beautiful 9 day 3,500 + mile trip.

In 2006, the year after I retired, Nancy and I flew our Cessna 185 on amphibious floats to Anchorage and Fairbanks. Our goal had been to keep flying north and dip our toes in the Arctic Ocean but the weather along the route from Fairbanks to Deadhorse wouldn't cooperate. After 5 days of waiting for the weather to clear we gave up and headed back to Chicago. All of that was great, but I never felt a part of it, a part of Alaska, and that is what I wanted.

A year later Nancy was getting tired of still hearing me talk about wanting to fly in Alaska, so she told me to either get a job there or shut up about it. She was right, it was time to do something about it.

I wasn't exactly sure how to go about getting a job in Alaska. I didn't know anyone there. I checked out the web and found "FlyAlaska.com." That website gave me a lot of good information, names and addresses of companies employing pilots. I picked a number of companies I thought I would like to work for and sent out resumes. I received no responses at all.

I was at a ski-plane fly-in in southern Wisconsin when I met a guy who had flown for a lodge in Alaska. I told him I had sent out resumes and how I've not heard a word from would-be employers. He said if you want a job in Alaska you have to show up in person. The operators up there get a lot of letters from want-a-be's. To show you are serious you have to go there in person, usually in January or February. That's when they do their hiring for the next season.

I started to develop a plan. I had gotten a DVD for Christmas entitled, "Alaska Floatplane Flying," that was filmed in Ketchikan Alaska. After watching it about 4 times, I put it in the DVD player one more time and wrote down all the company names I saw on the airplanes in the video. Between that and the information I gleaned from "FlyAlaska.com", I set up an itinerary. I would fly to Seattle then take an Alaska Airlines flight to Ketchikan to stop at each of the companies I saw in the video. Then, I would fly to Juneau and see a couple more, and then on to Anchorage. I would like to describe what my get-a-job with the bush plane companies outfit looked like compared to my get-a-job with the airlines suit. First NO TIE! I wore blue jeans, boots, a winter hooded jacket, and baseball hat. It's cold up there!

It was beginning to get real. I hadn't looked for a job in over 20 years and this job would be 3,000 miles away from my family and from everyone I knew. Still it was my dream of flying in Alaska. I departed with a sense of both apprehension and excitement. What if I couldn't find a job, what if I did?

The flight to Ketchikan went without a hitch. I grabbed my roll-aboard suitcase and headed for the ferry. Yes, that's right, the Ketchikan airport is on Gravina Island, a short ferry ride to Revillagigedo Island where the city of Ketchikan is located. There was a light mist falling as I exited the terminal building, following the path and crowd to the ferry. Then, I paused for a moment. I heard *it* before I saw *it*. There was no mistaking the sound of the Pratt and Whitney radial engine as I picked out the unmistakable site of a Beaver on floats, flying down the channel. This was early March and they were flying floatplanes here in Alaska! I smiled and knew I was in the right place.

I struck up a conversation with the man sitting next to me on the ferry. It turned out he was an aviation insurance salesman here to call on some of his clients. I told him I was looking for a flying job. He asked me a few questions about my background, and then told me I would have a job before I left town.

I left the ferry and started to walk along the waterfront looking for the first place on my list of operators, Promec Air. I didn't have an appointment, but I asked for the chief pilot and was shown to a small office where I was introduced to Tony. He was a gruff man, a little shorter than me with a stocky build and of native descent. We talked for a while, and he said he would like to take me for an evaluation ride later that day. Encouraged, I continued on to my next stop.

The light mist had changed to a brief heavy burst of snow pellets turning the ground white. I stopped at Pacific Airways. The chief pilot was out, so I left a resume and continued my walk handing out a couple more resumes. Next on my list was Taquan Air.

I was met with a friendly "Hi" by the receptionist and, after telling her what I wanted, she brought me to the chief pilot, Tim Boetcher. Tim was a furloughed Northwest Airlines pilot from Minnesota. I gave him my resume and we talked flying for quite a while. He said Taquan was looking for a pilot and he would like to give me an evaluation flight, but they only had one Beaver with dual controls, and it was out flying. I told him I would be happy to come back later. I asked if I could go out on the dock and see the operation. He said sure and went with me. It was very interesting, they had a floating hanger and the docks were floating too. The dock had 5 teeter-totter ramp assemblies built in to them that the airplanes would power themselves up onto which keeps them out of the water. As we were walking out there, Tim saw that the Training Beaver had just gotten back and was already on the ramp and the pilot was tying it up. The pilot was the director of operations, Kevin Roof. We walked up to Kevin and Tim told him that I was looking for a job, and that he would like Kevin to give me an evaluation ride right then. I could see his eyes roll back and reluctantly agree. It was obvious what he really wanted to do was to go home.

Tim gave a quick introduction as we all pushed the Beaver off the ramp and back into the water. Kevin was standing on the float, Tim was holding the airplane to the dock.

Kevin looked at me and said, "Come-on, get in".

Kevin climbed in first through the left door flipping switches and moving levers as he moved over to the right seat. He had the engine started almost before I got in the left seat. Kevin looked over to me and asked how much time I had in Beavers.

I looked at him and said, "About 15 seconds now."

I could see that didn't please him and he wasn't expecting much out of the ride. He said he would do all the radio work and I should just fly to where he told me. He gave me a quick cockpit briefing and showed me how the flaps worked. He set the Beaver up for take-off. He told me where the water rudders were and had me pull them up. Kevin got the clearance to take-off. He told me to start pushing the throttle up, and he would set final take-off power to 36 inches manifold pressure. I held the wheel full back while the Beaver accelerated quickly from full displacement taxi over the hump to planing attitude[6]. Kevin

---

[6]   full displacement taxi is when the full weight of the airplane is supported by the floats. Planing or step taxi is when the airplane is at high speed and the weight of the airplane is increasingly supported by the wings and eventually lifts off the water.

showed me the elevator trim and I set it. I held just a little back pressure and the Beaver lifted easily off the water. I climbed out keeping to the right side of the channel as he had instructed.

It was a good weather day in Ketchikan, so we kept climbing to 1,500 feet. When we cleared Class E airspace[7] around Ketchikan, Kevin told me to make a left turn and head up an inlet. Kevin wasn't very chit-chatty to this point; he just wanted to get this over with.

He said, "Do a steep 360 degree turn to the left."

I turned tight maintaining altitude perfectly, and as I was leveling out on heading, we hit our own wake, signifying that we ended up back in the exact same spot where the aircraft began the maneuver – a perfect turn.

He said, "Okay, now do one to the right."

I did, and again, as I was leveling out, we hit our wake.

"Now do a stall straight ahead."

I reduced the power to idle and maintained altitude by slowly pulling the wheel back until I could feel the buffet of the air stalling as it passed over the wing. As the wing stalled, I pitched the nose down to un-stall the wing, regained flying speed and recovered to level flight with very little loss of altitude.

---

[7]   Except for Ketchikan Class E airspace extends from 700 or 1,200 feet above ground level (AGL) up to but not including 18,000 feet (5,500 m) mean sea level (MSL). Ketchikan's Class E Airspace extends from the surface and a clearance by radio is required to operate within their Class E airspace.

After the stall maneuver, Kevin started to talk a little more about the company, and I could see he was beginning to think this might not be a waste of his time after all. He had me turn left. We crossed a long skinny island, and then turned left again heading back in the direction of Ketchikan. Kevin told me to land here, so I brought the power back to idle and started a decent. As we got closer to the water I started to slow and extend the flaps. The water was clear of debris, smooth, and calm. A few feet above the water I flared and gently set the Beaver down on the channel. As the Beaver slowed it settled easily off the step into the water and all you could hear was the throaty slow idle of the engine (like a Harley Davidson at idle).

Kevin said, "Well it's obvious you know how to fly an airplane."

He then told me to take-off straight ahead. I set the flaps for take-off and added power. Once again, the Beaver quickly got on the step and airborne.

At 500 feet, Kevin pulled the power back to idle and said, "You just had an engine failure, what are you going to do?"

I said, "I'm going to land straight ahead."

I put the nose down and increased airspeed a little to have enough energy to flair during touchdown. Again, as I approached the water, I set landing flaps and flared. The floats gently kissed the water, fell off the step and slowed to taxi speed.

Now Kevin was enthusiastically telling me about Taquan and the job as we flew the short distance back to Ketchikan. Once again, he took care of the radio work. As we were flying downwind past the Taquan base, he said try to land close, so we wouldn't have to taxi very far to the dock. I planned the approach and landing to come off the step about 50 yards off the ramp. I could have landed closer, but I didn't want him to think I was a hot dog. Once we were off the step, abeam of the dock, Kevin took over and taxied to the ramp. He nudged the Beaver up to the end of the teeter-totter ramp, and then applied nearly full power to get it to climb up the sloping ramp. Just beyond the pivot point of the ramp, the Beaver began to pitch down, and Kevin quickly pulled the power to idle to keep the aircraft from running forward off the ramp and across the dock. I could feel my feet on the brake pedals pushing hard to stop, even though I knew there were no brakes on a floatplane. Kevin stopped the Beaver perfectly in position on the ramp.

Tim met us on the ramp. Kevin exited out of the right side door, and the two of them were talking in front of the Beaver. I just sat in the cockpit for a minute, absorbing the flight and thinking how great it would be to fly this every day.

When I got out, Kevin said, "I would like to offer you a job and you'll only have to pay me $2.00 a day."

I laughed and said, "That was great, but you'll have to do better on the pay."

He said, "Okay, $1.00 a day." (It was always hard to know when he was kidding.)

I thanked Kevin and Tim and told them I had a couple of interviews scheduled. I asked when they would like an answer. Kevin said to let him know within a week.

I never made it back to Promech for my evaluation ride. Tony had said he would start me in the Cessna 185 since I already had a lot of time in that type airplane, I decided not to pursue that job. I knew I wanted to fly a Beaver, and that is all Taquan had. If I flew in Ketchikan, it would have to be with Taquan.

I took the ferry back to Ketchikan International Airport and hopped on an Alaskan Airlines flight to Juneau for my next try at an interview. When I arrived in Juneau, it was dark and in the middle of a snow storm. I trudged through the slush and snow in a biting cold wind to my hotel and settled in for the night. I was tired. It had been one long day. The next morning was so cold, windy and unpleasant. I just got back on a plane and headed for Anchorage. That flight was the Alaska Airlines "milk run". We went from Juneau to Yakutat, to Cordova and then Anchorage. Located a short distance from the terminal is Rust Aviation, the biggest operator on Lake Hood in Anchorage. Roughly 25% of the world's seaplanes operate out of Lake Hood. Rust was one of the largest companies and operated a string of Otters, Beavers and Cessna 206s.

I asked the receptionist for the chief pilot.

One of the guys standing in the reception room spoke up, "I'm the chief pilot. What can I do for you?"

I told him why I was there, and we talked for a while. He asked how much Beaver time I had, so I told him about 30 minutes. He wanted to know how much Alaska time I had, so I told him about 30 hours gained on my flight from Chicago the previous year. He told me he pretty much had his pick of Beaver pilots and didn't think he would be able to use me. I asked about his K-2 operation in Talkeetna flying Cessna 185s on skis to Mt. McKinley. I mentioned I had a lot of 185 time and ski time, and that I would be interested if he had an opening there. He thought for a moment and said he thought he was good on pilots at K-2, but he would keep my resume just in case something became available.

I originally planned to spend the night, but I finished everything I came to do, so I just went to the terminal and waited for the all-nighter flight on Northwest Airlines to Minneapolis where I would catch a connecting flight home. Wow what a whirlwind couple of days!

At home Nancy and I discussed the reality of me working in Alaska. She had a job she didn't want to leave, so she would stay in Chicago. For me, the lure of Alaska and fulfilling my nearly life long dream of living and flying there was too hard to pass up. I called Tim at Taquan and told him I would be glad to fly for him. Tim and I talked for a while and discussed what my real pay would be. He laid out when he wanted me there, housing options (Taquan doesn't provide housing) and all the other things needed for such a big move. Thirty minutes after I hung up from talking to Tim, I received a call from Rust Aviation offering me a job at K-2. I thanked him but said I had just taken a job at Taquan in Ketchikan.

He said, "Quit!" I thanked him again and said I couldn't do that.

Flying a Beaver on floats in Alaska was my dream job and I had just gotten it.

Alaska Bound

On my way to Ketchikan

Here is the log of Nancy's and my drive from Chicago to Ketchikan Alaska for my "summer camp." I needed transportation once I got to Ketchikan and I also needed to bring a few things with me, so we decided to drive my Dodge Dakota truck. We both thought it would be a great way to get there and it was.

Here is the log of Nancy's and my drive from Chicago to Ketchikan Alaska for my "summer camp." I needed transportation once I got to Ketchikan and I also needed to bring a few things with me, so we decided to drive my Dodge Dakota truck. We both thought it would be a great way to get there and it was.

As my friends all know, I don't like to drive so Nancy did most of the driving on our 5 day trip to Prince Rupert, British Columbia, Canada.

- Day 1: Wed, 18 April 2007

Well, it is 8pm, so we must be in Jackson, Minnesota. We are about 73 miles east of the South Dakota border. The drive has been easy – gotta love those 70 mph speed limits in Minnesota!

We left Illinois about 1:30pm, stopped for food and fuel (that took 15 minutes) and decided South Dakota was an hour too far, so here we are. The plan is to get up early and see how close to Butte, MT we can get tomorrow.

To be continued………………..

- Day 2: Thurs, 19 April 2007

We left Jackson, Minnesota at 7am. If we thought the 70 mph speed limit was great, South Dakota, Wyoming and Montana has 75 mph (that means that we (Nancy) can go 82 mph). We hit rain at the western edge of South Dakota, rain-snow mix in Gillette, Wyoming, cold at Custer Battle Field (yeah, we stopped) It was very windy the whole trip. We stopped for the night in Laurel, Montana. We decided to deviate from the plan and get off I90 tomorrow. We took US Hwy 191, then Hwy 87 to Great Falls, Montana. We cut off a lot of miles and stayed out of the mountains where they are predicting some snow; then on to Edmonton, Alberta Canada for the night. By the way, we stopped at Wall, South Dakota and Wall Drug Store where I found a nice pair of red cowboy boots.

More later…………….

Custer Monument

- Day 3: Fri, 20 April 2007

This morning we started out from Laurel, MT at 7am. It was COLD but sunny and not a cloud in the sky. The drive was beautiful. About an hour past Laurel we turned north on US Hwy 191. It was beautiful high prairie country. We even saw old bones on the side of the road – of course we had to

play tourist and take a picture! We then junctioned with US Hwy 87 and headed into Grand Prairie, Montana where we picked up I15 to Shelby, Montana. We stopped at the same Pizza Hut for lunch where we ate lunch 10 months ago today when Nancy and I flew up to Alaska in the C185. The waitress remembered us. We then crossed into Canada and cleared customs.

It started clouding up and still very windy and chilly. On the way toward Calgary, Alberta Canada, it started to rain. And there was a lot more snow on the ground. Just before Calgary, the rain turned into snow, then snow-rain mix. And then we hit rush hour traffic in Calgary. North of Calgary we got gas and a quick dinner. We made it to Red Deer, Alberta Canada – about an hour and a half south of Edmonton – at about 9pm Chicago time.

In between the snow showers we saw beautiful vistas; lots of snow on the plateaus. In fact, there is about 3 to 4 inches of snow on the ground here in Red Deer. Glad I brought my winter coat….but where are my boots?

To be continued………….

- Day 4: Sat, 21 April 2007

Today when we started out from Red Deer, there was snow on the truck, and it was dark, rainy/snowy and cold. We got on the road at 7am mountain time, turned left at Edmonton onto Provincial Hwy 16 (also known as Yellowhead Highway). There is lots of snow on the ground and still coming down. But after a couple of hours, the clouds started to break up and the sun even peeked out. The elevation kept going up and soon we were in the mountains on our way to Jasper, Alberta. Such beauty! The mountains were snow capped and there was also snow on the ground.

The wildlife we have seen so far has been; red fox, grey fox, antelope, deer, elk, big horn sheep and even a big black bear.

The road is great. It was mostly divided highway until we got into the mountains, but then it was wide with turn-out passing lanes. After Jasper we entered into British Columbia and the Pacific Time zone. We had a 45 minute stop in the middle of the road. The road had been washed out, and the road crew had been trying to repair it for over a week, 24 hours a day. We got through it and made it to Prince George, British Columbia by 4pm Pacific time. We checked into a hotel, had a stiff rum & coke and now we are on our way to the local steak house for a thick juicy steak and a baked potato (seeing all those Angus on the hoof has made me hungry since Calgary).

Tomorrow we plan on driving 445 miles to Prince Rupert. It should be a short drive compared to the 700 – 800 mile days we've been doing.

More later……………………

- Day 5: Sun, 22 April 2007

As today's leg would be the shortest of the whole trip (720 kilometers, or something like 425 miles), We decided to sleep in an extra hour. We left Prince George, BC at 8am. The day started out beautifully, sunshine and no rain. The trip was uneventful, thankfully, but the scenery was less spectacular. We stopped in Smithers, BC for a nice lunch then headed out on the road again. We've had the aircraft GPS with us on the dash board the whole trip and it has been fun watching the elevation changes. Today the elevation would be constantly going down as we got nearer the coast. Oh, and it started raining – again. This trip has been defined by rain, rain and snow, snow and more rain. Through the mountains today we also saw beautiful water falls coming off the rocks.

Added to our list of wildlife; coyote (We nearly hit him crossing the road), bald eagles and the only moose we've seen was a steel cut-out sculpture.

Tonight, we're staying in a lovely hotel and our room over looks the harbor – it is breathtaking. Tomorrow we get on the Alaska Marine Ferry for the 6 hour sail to Ketchikan. Our road trip is almost over.

To be continued………………..

- Day 6: Mon, 23 April 2007

Well, we made it to Ketchikan! We got to the Alaska Marine Ferry in Prince Rupert this morning (was it really just this morning?) and lined up at 9am. We picked up our pre-paid tickets, cleared customs and drove onto the ship. The sail took 6 hours and it rained the entire way so the view wasn't as great as I'd hoped for. But we met some nice people on board. In fact, we met a gentleman who had worked for Taquan for several years until he retired. However, I believe that he will be conducting the ground school I will attend next week. It was truly helpful to talk with him. He pointed

out some landmarks as we neared Ketchikan and shared some helpful hints. He said that Taquan Air was a great company and very safety conscious. They won't fly when the weather is bad. That laid my concerns to rest. Anyway, the trip on the ferry was fun and relaxing despite the ship pitched and rolled a bit, but not enough for anyone to turn green.

When we got to Ketchikan, the wind was blowing pretty strong and it was raining buckets. We drove off the ship and over to the realtor's office to pick up the key to my apartment. It took us two minutes to look around the efficiency (man, it IS clean – luckily), 20 minutes to unload the truck and one hour to unpack and put everything away. Then it was off to dinner – great Alaskan Snapper (Salmon's not in season yet) and we checked out Taquan Air.

Nancy will be here until Thursday morning. She will have dropped me off at Summer Camp and she will be home by Thursday night. What a difference a jet plane makes. I will send out dispatches periodically this summer to you all. I've taken a lot of great pictures and will have them developed for viewing when I get home. Thanks for coming along with us on our trip.

- Last day in Alaska: 25 April 2007

Hi everyone. Well, today is Nancy's last day in Ketchikan with me. It rained and rained and rained – so what else is new? What else is new you ask? Well, let me tell you. Nancy got to ride along in the Beaver this afternoon! She took me to Taquan this early morning so I could do a ride-along on the morning freight run. This afternoon Nancy was invited to go along on the mail and freight run. Even though it was raining a little, we taxied out and took off, north bound. We flew to a little island that has only one couple living there (with their own zip code, by the way) to pick up and drop off mail. It was so cool. We landed and taxied up to the beach and just, well, beached it. We exchanged bags of mail with the residents then we took off and flew to a fish hatchery to drop off more mail and packages. We pulled up to the dock and the two fellows helped catch/tie down the plane. We all got out because there was a whole bunch of stuff in the back of the plane to unload. The younger guy was so excited to see us because he ordered a bunch of stuff off the internet. We took more pictures and jumped back into the plane to head back to Ketchikan and Taquan's base. Once back, the sun came out and there was even some blue sky. Nancy said "Oh yeah, you're going to have a lot of fun this summer."

The sad news is that Nancy has to leave tomorrow morning for her all day/evening flights back to Chicago. I can't wait until she can come back again.

PART SIX

My going to Alaska to work for the summer was christened, summer camp, by a friend and it stuck. The following I call Letters From Camp Ketchikan. They are a collection of e-mails to friends and family sharing my adventures and observations from "summer camp". I feel it will be a good way to follow my evolution from a flatlander pilot into an Alaska Bush Pilot and get a real feel for flying in Southeast Alaska.

Letters From Camp Ketchikan

April 27, 2007

To All,

Well I guess it's real. Nancy left yesterday, and I am still here. I will miss her but my days will be filled with work.

I have been doing ride-a-longs in the Beaver for the last several days to learn my way around our operating area. Ground school starts on Monday. I have seen a lot of amazing places already. Nancy has and will share the photos. The one constant here is the weather. Not that the weather is constant but that it is constantly changing. The adage "if you don't like the weather wait 15 minutes" was born in Ketchikan. Today started out nice. About a 1,000 foot overcast and visibility of 5 miles and temperature in the low 40's. I got to the Taquan base at 7:00 am and helped load a Beaver for a run to Hyder. We just finished loading it up when it started to hail. That lasted for 5 minutes then stopped. It got good again, 1,000 over cast and 3 miles visibility. Yes that passes for good weather here.

Yesterday I went along on a mail flight to Craig and Thorne Bay on Prince of Wales Island. The wind was blowing about 20 knots from the south. The Tongass Straits was full of whitecaps for takeoff. The ceiling was 1500 feet. The Beaver handled the rough water well. We headed west, passed the Ketchikan airport on Gravina Island and set out across Clarence Strait. The Capstone GPS equipment said the wind was 35 knots and the white caps and wind streaks confirmed it.

We flew over Grindall Island by Kasaan Bay and saw the sea lions "sunning" themselves. As we flew down Kasaan Bay and turned left into Twelve-mile Arm there was a rain shower and the ceiling dropped to about 600 feet and the visibility was about 2 miles, not too bad for here. At Hollis we picked up the road and followed it toward Craig. There were mountains on the left and mountains on the right. The wind had calmed down to 20 knots and we were picking up turbulence, so we hugged the downwind side of the valley to minimize the down drafts and turbulence.

As low as we were and with the turbulence, we could not head directly for Craig but went up Klawok Lake to the town of Klawok. The visibility started to improve to about 5 miles and the wind dropped to about 15 knots as we approached

Craig. We landed in a light chop and came off the step about 50 yards from the dock. There was another Taquan plane there and the pilot helped us dock. We off loaded our freight and mail and were off for Thorne Bay but not until another rain shower passed.

The flight to Thorne Bay was good with 1,500-foot ceiling and better than five miles visibility. The wind had gone down to about 10 and we made a nice landing just off the dock. We off loaded our mail and freight and picked up a passenger. The flight back to Ketchikan (KTN) was good with the exception of some light turbulence over the end of Tolstoi Point.

Once back at KTN we had another load of mail and freight for Hyder. Hyder is on the U.S. Canadian border about 160 miles from KTN the long way or if the weather is good about 95 miles the short way. The problem is the short way is through the mountains. The winds were blowing 30 knots and the ceilings were about 800-1,000 feet. We would be going the long way. Along our route the weather was mostly good. We had 1,500 broken to begin with but lowered to 800 feet in the fjord. The trip went well for the first hour. We had good visibility and ceilings but half an hour out of Hyder we hit a rain squall. We were at 500 feet with visibility decreasing to about a fuzzy two miles. I was getting a little nervous, but we could still make out the mountains on the left side. In about 3 minutes we started to get out of it and visibility was improving. The tide was out at Hyder so we had to land over the mud flats and on to the water at the end of the fjord. After unloading it was back to KTN.

That is a sample of flying up here so far. My definition of good weather has changed. Rain is normal. Wind is normal. Cold is normal. Waives are normal. Good weather here is

205

being high enough to miss the boats and have enough visibility to see the boats before you hit them.

Letters from Camp Ketchikan

May 2, 2007

Since arriving in Ketchikan I have had to temper my enthusiasm with reality. There has been a lot to organize and prepare to live and work here. Luckily Nancy was here and did most of the organizing. By the end of our first day she had the apartment organized. All my clothes were put away, boxes stored and some items we didn't bring with us were purchased. Thank you Nancy.

I have been here 10 days now. I miss my family and friends but many of you have called and I have appreciated that. I haven't had a lot of time to myself. Ground school started Monday. Everyone knows how much fun that is. I can't wait to start flying! That will be soon.

I have had to outfit myself for the rainy climate. The folks at Tongass Trading Post know me by name and my credit card number by heart. I had to get my knee high XtraTuf® rain boots, also called Alaska tennis shoes. They are wonderful I don't even think of the water and mud puddles anymore. Then I had to get my H&H rain coat and pants and let's not forget my rubber gloves and wool socks. Have I told you, it rains here every day? I don't even think of it as rain anymore unless it is coming down horizontally.

Letters from Camp Ketchikan

May 5, 2007

I had my first hour of training in the Beaver yesterday. Everything went well. I did numerous take-offs and landings along with the usual air work. The highlight of the training was when we landed on Patching Lake, a narrow lake with mountains on all sides. We stopped there, at the U.S. Forest Service cabin. The Forest Service dots the Alaskan wilderness with these cabins. They are for rent from the Forest Service for a nominal fee. Usually $15-$25 per day. They provide a boat, oars and firewood, along with a dry place to sleep. The best part is that there is an outhouse near the cabin. I would really like to stay in one sometime soon. They are very secluded. Usually only one on a lake as in this case or at least separated by a good distance.

Today I got another hour in the Beaver. The Beaver and I are starting to make friends. All I have to do is figure out how much rudder to give it. It is an easy flying airplane, but it seems to wander around the sky quite a bit, probably because of the big floats. I had the presence of mind to bring my camera today so I will send pictures soon.

The weather is supposed to deteriorate this afternoon with 30K winds gusting to 40K. So we are finished for today. During my flight this morning I was actually flying through some snow squalls. Okay, not squalls, but there was some light snow.

Letters From Camp Ketchikan

May 9, 2007

Yesterday was a milestone. I took and passed my check ride! I am now an official Alaska bush pilot. I will explain a little of the check ride because I think both my seaplane flying friends and those who don't fly seaplane will enjoy it.

As always, the ride was preceded with an oral examination. It was the usual questions.

What is the gross weight of the Beaver?
Five thousand ninety pounds normal or 5370 lbs with tip tanks full or 5,600 lbs for the two with Whip Air gross weight increase kits.

What is the stall speed?
Flaps down 45 mph. Flaps up 60 mph.

Vx? (best angle of climb)
80.

Vy? (best rate of climb)
95.

What is the fuel capacity?
35 gallons in the front tank, 35 in the center and 25 in the rear. 21.5 in each tip tank if installed.

What are our VFR minimums?
500 feet, two miles visibility normal or, with our exemption, 400 and two miles, or 200 feet and three miles over landable water.
For less than 500 what else must you have?

Wind less than 12 mph and in site of shore. Waves less than 12 inches and landable water.

Okay, let's go fly.

I had run the engine while the airplane was tied up at the dock. It takes about 15 minutes to warm the oil and cylinder temps enough for takeoff. When we climbed in, I wobbled the throttle back and forth twice so the carburetor accelerator pump would put extra fuel in the engine for start. I turned on the master switch and motioned the dock hand to turn us out. As soon as we were pointed for open water, I hit the starter and the engine caught right away. No need to put the mixture to rich because we turn the engine off with the mag switch not with the mixture. It makes for easier re-starts.

On taxi out Tim asked me what time it was. I said ten after. That means it will be five minutes before the airport ferry boat leaves. Enough time for us to finish our checks and depart. The ferry boat route to the airport goes right in front of Taquan's dock. Tim's checklist is easy. Flaps, caps and straps. That means flaps set for takeoff. We don't use the indicator because it is not reliable. We move the control wheel full right and look at the left flap as we pump the hydraulic hand pump lever to lower the flaps to match the droop of the ailerons. Oil cap secure, that's right the oil filler cap is in the cockpit on the floor next to the copilot seat. It is easy to hit it with your feet and have the copilot get a leg full of hot oil! Straps is seatbelts on and we are ready for takeoff. Area clear, water rudder up (or it will cost you a case of beer for the person who sees them down on take-off). Wheel full back and power up to 36.5 inches of manifold pressure. With this light load we are over the hump and on step quickly. Accelerate to about 60 mph and the Beaver lifts off on its own. Climb out and accelerate to

80 mph. Shift the flap control to flaps up and pump them up to climb position. At obstacle clearance altitude accelerate to 95 mph and climb to cruise altitude. It is the first bright sunny day since I have been here so we climb to 2000 feet then Tim tells me to put on the Foggles (hood, to limit my vision to only the instruments inside the cockpit) to do some instrument flying. It figures, the best day I have seen and now I can't see it!

The Beavers have the latest technology; no really! They are equipped with Capstone GPS equipment that shows terrain. Tim gives me some steep turns and stalls under the hood then he has me put in a flight plan to Craig. As I turn towards Craig the terrain color on the Capstone turns yellow and red. I tell Tim we can't go that way because of terrain that is above our altitude as I turn away from the cumulo-granite (mountains). He knew it would have us heading towards mountains that were higher than us. He wanted to see if I was able to see that on the Capstone and make the proper choice to avoid it.

Once the IFR stuff was done we got to do the fun stuff. Tim had me do some landings and takeoffs in confined spaces. Step turns and figure eights on the water. We did approaches over trees to make spot landings. He even threw in a couple of emergencies. We then flew through some passes and into Heckman Lake. This was a real confined area approach. We flew above the lake to check for obstructions and locate a U.S. Forest Service cabin. I was to land on the lake and beach the airplane so that my "simulated" rich New York passengers could get off the float without getting their feet wet. I landed and taxied toward shore sliding to a stop about five feet from the bank. With my new Alaska tennis shoes (knee-high rubber boots) on I jumped down from the float and tied the Beaver to the shore.

The cabin was Spartan, but the setting was beautiful. Mountains ringed the lake. They still have snow on them. The lake drains into a river about 100 yards from the cabin. Tim said there is great fly-fishing for trout in the river and lake. I hope to get the chance to prove Tim right sometime this summer.

After we left Heckman Lake it was back to Ketchikan. I had passed my check ride. Tomorrow I will start my IOE (Initial Operating Experience)

Letters From Camp Ketchikan

May 16, 2007

I had off today and got a chance to sleep in. I didn't get up until 6:30. I know that's not big for most of you but for me it is.

My apartment is right down town and I woke to the faint smell of diesel smoke and knew another cruise ship was in port. At about 7:00 it was confirmed when I heard the clop clop of the horse drawn carriage taking tourists past my apartment to Creek Street, an historic part of town. A short time later I heard the buzz of chain saws and the roar of the crowd at the lumberjack show as the audience cheered for their favorite lumber Jack or Jill. That's right there are even female lumberjacks.

I flew my first solo mail run yesterday. I went to Thorne Bay and Craig on Prince of Wales Island. The weather here has been fantastic by Ketchikan standards. We have had 3 days of sunshine and yesterday was warm enough for me to take my jacket off for the first time since I've been here. That made the mail run easy. In the afternoon I went to Whale Pass and Coffman Cove all on Prince Of Wales Island (POW).

Wait until the weather gets back to normal. I made that same run a few days before on my IOE and had to turn back. The pass to Craig was socked in and we couldn't make it through. We dropped the Craig mail and freight at Hollis and the agent made the 45 minute drive from Craig to pick it up. We were able to scud-run to Thorne Bay for our drop off there. We saw two deer swimming to an island along the way. They had big brown eyes and one of them winked as we flashed by just over their heads. The run back to base was good. As soon as we got over the Clarence Straight the weather picked up.

Letters From Camp Ketchikan

May 21, 2007

First let me say that tomorrow is Nancy's and my anniversary. I love you Nance, thanks for all you do!

It is 17:15 here and I just finished my Marie Callender's frozen dinner. Country pork chop with mashed potatoes and gravy, yummy. Today was a normal, long one. I started at 0545 and got off a little early at 1630.

I am fully checked out now. I have done the mail and freight runs and yesterday and today I was doing tours.

One to the Misty Fjords and two to George Inlet Lodge for all you can eat crab lunch. It wasn't that much flying. I had a lot of sit around time, but I can't think of a place with a better view to sit around. A pod of Orca (Killer Whales) came swimming up the Tongass Narrows today right in front of our docks. What a view! On the first George Inlet tour I saw humpback whales breaking water and blowing waterspouts.

There were three cruise ships in town today but the last of them just left. It is amazing to see the change in town when the ships come and go. When the ships are in it is all hustle and bustle. As soon as the ships leave most of the jewelry shops and all of the tour stands close and Ketchikan gets back to its normal slower pace.

Everything is going good here I hope all is well with all of you.

Letters From Camp Ketchikan

May 26, 2007

I have been very busy since my last letter. I have started to do the tours of the Misty Fjords National Monument in addition to the freight and mail runs. I have been trying to think of how to explain a Misty tour to you and do it justice. I have been searching for the right adjectives to give you a sense of the beauty and grandeur of the place. Pictures would help but I thought it tacky for the pilot to have his camera out taking pictures along with his passengers. I will try a ride-a-long so I can get some pictures. I think I will just try to bring you along verbally with me on a tour of the Misty's.

I meet the passengers on the dock as they are being escorted by our tour people. I am handed a manifest with their names and weights. After some small talk to get a sense of how they are feeling I pick the heaviest person and ask if they would like to be my co-pilot. I haven't had anyone turn me down yet. Hopefully he is traveling with a much smaller person. If so, I put that person in the single aft seat. I then adjust the rest of the passengers to keep the C.G. in limits. After everyone is loaded, I give them a safety briefing and close the door. I take a look at the back of the floats to see how much of the float is above water. This is a good way to double check my C.G. before takeoff.

I climb up the ladder to the cockpit pausing to give the engine one shot of prime. The primer is located on the floor next to the door. Almost impossible to unlock and use from the pilot seat but handy on the way in through the door. Once seated, I motion to the dockhands to untie me and point the Beaver out toward the channel. Master on, ignition on both, wobble the throttle three times and hit the starter. The engine coughs and blue smoke fills the air as the engine comes to life and into the channel we go. Radio master on and listen to ATIS while I get my seat belt on. I put the CD on to give the folks an audio tour of Ketchikan and its history as I get us going toward the monument.

Ketchikan is class E airspace to the surface and is the only airport in the country where all traffic has to get a clearance from Flight Service to enter, takeoff, or land.

"Ketchikan radio, Beaver 667 at Taquan with Delta takeoff east bound."

"Roger Beaver 667, traffic is a Beaver and an Otter taking off from the harbor, also east bound, a Beaver over Danger Island inbound to the harbor and a 737 on final for 11."

"Roger traffic, Beaver 667 on the slide."

Water rudders up, flaps set, trim full forward, throttle to 36.5 inches, wheel full back. After the nose rises to its max, I push the wheel full forward. The nose comes down as the Beaver starts to get on the step. I roll in some back trim to ease the pressure and keep it on the step. The channel is full of floating logs, so I am on alert to turn as necessary to avoid them. At about 50 mph I put in just a slight amount of back pressure and the Beaver breaks free of the water and accelerates quickly to 80 mph. I reach between the seats and very slowly start to pump the flaps up to the climb position. (They are hydraulically operated with a hand pump and a shuttle valve to select up or down.) At about 200 feet I reduce power to 30 inches and pull the prop back to 2000 rpm for the cruise climb. Depending on the weight and temperature the climb rate is 200 to 400 feet per minute.

As we pass Mountain Point, I call flight service.

"Ketchikan radio 667 passing Mountain Point, clear to the east."

"Beaver 667, roger clear to the east at Mountain Point."

I continue my climb as we pass George Inlet and Carol Inlet. When the narration stops, and the music starts to play on the CD I interrupt and have the passengers look to the right at a section of clear cut forest and explain that in ten to fifteen years that area will be so thick with trees that they will have to be thinned out so they won't stunt each others growth.

As the CD resumes its dialog, I continue with my position reports.

"667 Dog Leg for Fish Creek, 1,500 feet"

"667 Fish Creek for the Muskeg 2,000 feet."

I break into the narration again. "If you look straight ahead you will see snow toped mountains. Those are in the Misty Fjords. The water you see is the Behm Cannel. The Behm was formed during the last ice age and is what separated Ketchikan from the rest of the continent. Ketchikan only has about 32 miles of roads. When you come to Ketchikan you must ether come by boat or plane. "

"Dispatch 667 Muskeg for the Mistys"

"Roger 667 Muskeg for the Mistys"

"If you look to the left, you will see New Eddy Stone Rock. Eddy Stone is the core of an ancient volcano. The outer cone was scraped away by the last glacier leaving the much harder core. Eddy Stone protrudes

The New Eddy Stone Rock

over 200ft. from the Behm Canal. This is salt water so be alert for whales and other sea life."

"667 is Eddy Stone for Point Louise at 2,300 switching."

I change frequencies from 122.75 to 122.85 for position reports in the Mistys. I also switch fuel tanks.

"667 Eddy Stone for Point Louise."

"Now if you look right over the nose you will see a 'v' shape cut into the Mountains. That is where Rudyerd Bay cuts into the mountains. That is where we will enter the Mistys Fjords National Monument. If you look just past that first ridge you can see some gray rocks sticking up. That is called The Wall. It is a granite rock wall over 3,000 feet high from summit to the ocean. I'll fly toward the ridge straight ahead so those of you on the right can get a good look at the wall then I will turn right so those of you on the left can see it. Get your cameras ready."

"667 Point Louise for The Wall 2,300."

"There it is. Okay now I'll turn right. Here we go. The rock wall is impressive as we pass 200 yards away. The gray rock is still snow capped with many waterfalls streaming down its face. Look there! There is an avalanche!" A large chunk of snow lets loose from the summit and plunges to the ocean. Each trip is different.

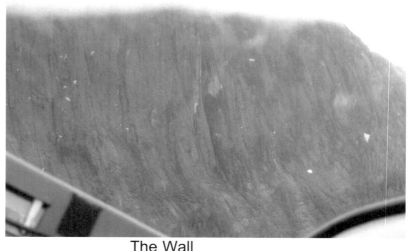
The Wall

"667 The Wall for Punch Bowl Lake 2,300."

"The waterfall you see is coming from Punch Bowl Lake. It is fresh water and stocked with Arctic Grayling. As you can see, part of the lake is still frozen. There is a Forest Service shelter on the lake along with a canoe. It is for day use and is free. The only catch is you either have to boat to the base of the fall and hike up or fly in."

"667 Punch Bowl Lake for the Cut."

As we fly over Punch Bowl Lake everyone is snapping away with their cameras. It is truly a magnificent sight. The lake has some islands on it and the water is reflecting the blue sky. In fact, I can see the mountain's reflection in it. As we approach the Cut, I get very close to the rocks on the right to get a view of any traffic in the Cut and make sure there are no clouds blocking the other side of it.

"667 the Cut for Big Goat Falls at 2,300"

"Now if you look to the right just passed that next ridge line Big Goat Falls will come into view. Big Goat Falls is over 2,000 feet in height and flows from Big Goat Lake to the ocean below. There it is now on the right. I'll fly toward the rocks ahead so those of you on the right can

get a good look at the falls then I will turn right so those of you on the left can get a good look at it." I can see that my "co-pilot" is getting concerned as we come very close to the rocks. I don't blame him. The first time I rode through this I was nervous myself. I think it's a control thing.

"667 Big Goat Falls for the 'Y' at 2,300 descending to 2,000."

As I bank away from the falls, I descend a little and head over the south end of Rudyerd Bay. The passengers are enjoying the views on both sides of the airplane. The exposed rock, the tree-covered mountain sides and the bright blue of the bay below are spellbinding. I glance back to see how they are doing. Everything looks okay.

"667 the 'Y' for Nooya Lake."

Nooya Lake is one of my favorite places in the monument. As you pass the 'Y' you can see a small slit in the rocks. That is the way in. I fly until I am even with the slit to make sure no one is coming out then I bank to the left keeping the rocks off my left side. Once through the entrance it opens into a small 'Y' shaped valley. The snow capped mountains are above us on all sides except the entrance. On the left I can see a small cut out that still has some ice hanging on to it. The ice is a brilliant turquoise color. Looking out my left side window all I see is rock flashing close by (200feet) at 110 miles an hour. To the right is the face of the valley with bare rock in some areas and others covered with snow or trees. I am approaching the end of the valley and put in a little flap to help me make a shape turn to the right. There is no horizon, all I can see is rock walls. I have to check the instruments briefly to make sure I don't loose any altitude. I end the turn with my right wing against the rocks on the other side of the valley. I can't believe I am doing this and getting paid for it, uh yes, I can. I don't think I would be doing this for free. Not four times a day in bad weather. At least the weather has been good today.

"667 leaving Nooya Lake for the 'Y' at 2,000 descending for Bailey Falls"

I start to descend for landing at Bailey Falls. It is a wide and impressive falls of over a thousand feet. If there are no other planes I will land there. Flaps down, engine to near idle, flare, touchdown. The Beaver slows and falls off the step. I cut the engine and turn to the passengers and ask, "How are you doing so far?" The response is all smiles and thumbs up. When we come to a stop I get out and help my passengers out onto the floats to take pictures and absorb the experience.

"How cold is the water?"

"About 40 degrees."

"How deep is it here?"

"Over your head"

"Have you ever had anyone fall in?"

"No, and don't you be the first."

Invariably someone will turn to me in all seriousness and say, "Man you have the best job in the world. Do they pay you for this?"

"Yes, and some days it's not enough."

I have to agree. On a good day like this it is the best job in the world. It is the bad weather days they pay me for.

After five or ten minutes on the floats I get everyone back in get airborne and head for Ketchikan. Each trip is different. Different weather. Different passengers, all with their own point of view. Different landing sites, each trip is beautiful and uniquely different. Each day I go to work with a smile on my face knowing how lucky I am to be here and flying a Beaver.

Letters From Kamp Ketchikan

June 10, 2007

My oldest daughter, Jana, came to Ketchikan to visit for Father's Day. I decided to let her write this issue of Letters From Camp Ketchikan.

JUN 08 - FRI

We took the ocean kayak tour out to Orca cove. The weather could not have been more gorgeous. I guess I brought some sunshine up with me from Phoenix. We saw a pod of killer whales, a Dhal porpoise, bald eagles, and a seal. There were neat sea stars that look like rubbery star fish. They were a bright orange red and purple. The kayaks glided over kelp that grows from the bottom to the surface.

Yes, it is slimy. We surfed the kayaks down the waves of the Nichols Passage and around a reef to a black sand beach that was very peaceful.

From there it was a 30 minute paddle back to the mother ship where we enjoyed a snack of salmon and cream cheese on crackers. After the salmon and crackers it was a rough motor boat ride back to Ketchikan. We were ready for dinner. Salmon of course. I ran into a fellow Sun Devil who was excited to see my maroon and gold T-Shirt (Arizona State University). Then I got caught up on the episodes of Dog Fights (woo hoo!), as the TV resources are limited to the DVDs Dad has on hand.

JUN 09 - SAT

We went out to Taquan base to see the operation, and what was going on. We met a couple of guys sitting around tying ropes. I brushed up on my own rope skills, and learned some new ones. The cruise ships hadn't come in to port yet, so things were low key. We decided to take a drive out to the end of the highway (west) and do some sight seeing. Totem Bight Park was neat to see the totem carvings and pained characters. We walked along the shore which had a type of decomposed granite for sand. When you see all of the Sitka spruce, cedar, alder, and hemlock trees you don't realize that there is virtually no soil, just solid granite, so it would make sense that would be the sand too. Well, it started to rain, and looked like it would pretty much be that way all day. But, no matter, it was so gentle and not cold at all. You just shrug your shoulders and keep going. We took off for the other end of the highway (east) to a salmon hatchery. This is not salmon farming. This is salmon ranching which is a far better process since it produces what eventually become wild salmon. We saw 2" long Coho fries which will be flown to a different stream and released for imprinting. They will spend 18 months at sea and return to spawn. We saw a mother black bear enjoying herself in the estuary. She was probably still pretty hungry from winter hibernation, and the salmon haven't come upstream yet, but she seemed to be fairly uninterested in us. It was great to catch some photos of her.

Across the creek was a zip line canopy tour. Awesome! You go about 140 ft off the ground and get up to 35mph as you are zipping above and between the rain forest hemlock with great views of the sea and snow covered mountains. Ah, what a day

Jana

Letters From Camp Ketchikan

June 25, 2007

Things here have settled down to a routine for the most part. Not boring just routine. I fly 3 or 4 Misty trips maybe a couple of George Inlet Lodge trips for the all you can eat crab feast each day. Today however was note worthy for several reasons.

Today I flew an early morning Misty, 7:15 departure. The weather was good. 2,000 overcast and good visibility. When I got to the Mistys there was a little low scud about half way up the mountains. The view of the mountains, ocean and valleys with the low wispy clouds in the early morning light was indescribably wonderful. Each trip it

226

looks different in some way. One of the passengers was a U.S. Air retired pilot. I put him in the co-pilot seat and told him not to touch anything! (just kidding) After the trip he told me how much he enjoyed the trip and then did something I thought I would never see. He gave me a $20 tip! An airline pilot gave a $20 tip! A U.S. Air airline pilot gave a $20 tip!

After the Misty trip I pulled out the seats and loaded freight for a run to Craig. Craig is only about a half hour away across the Clarence Straight on Prince of Whales Island. It was calm winds, smooth air and good weather. That was the first time I had all of those things at one time going to Craig. Wonderful. Since the weather was so good I took a slightly different route. It is always good to explore and increase your mental map. On the way back from Craig I flew at 500 feet. I saw a deer swimming between two islands.

Once back at Ketchikan I put the seats back in for another Misty trip. The weather had changed some but was still good with some scattered rain showers. Normal. I landed at the head of Rudyerd Bay and spotted three grizzly bears feeding on grasses near a creek. Another $20 tip. This day just gets better and better.

The next Misty trip was routine until I was on final approach back at base. Bobby, a full time dock hand and part time pilot, called traffic in the channel. There was a humpback whale swimming up the channel right where I was going to land. I added a little power and as I passed him he spouted and showed his fluke as he dove down. How many times do you have to dodge whale traffic on landing? Another $20 tip!

Dinner is done, Marie Callender's Chicken pot pie, yummy.

So as I said everything is just plodding along at a Ketchikan pace. I hope all of you are well

Letters From Kamp Ketchikan

July 28, 2007

I can't believe it has almost been a month since my last letter. I guess time really does fly. Part of the reason for the long time span has been that nothing much has changed. Fly, fly, fly and weather, weather, weather. We have had a long span of marginal weather with a few days of CAVU (clear and visibility unlimited). The CAVU makes up for the other. I still find the scenery beautiful.

I have been primarily flying the Misty Fjords tours with some mail and freight runs thrown in. I haven't been able to get out and do any fishing yet. Part of the problem is the lack of an airplane to get to one of the Forest Service cabins outside of Ketchikan and part is just not wanting to fish in a locally accessible stream. I have always thought Alaska fishing is something you do in a remote lake or stream by yourself or with your friends. I may try to get a drop off from one of our mail runs. One of our pilots did that and said it was great. I would have to book a forest service cabin close to a route we would fly on a freight run and the company will let you fly along and have the pilot drop you off as long as it isn't a long detour. I guess I just have to "do it" as they say.

Nancy was able to visit for a few days over the 4th of July weekend. It was nice to have her here but as always it rained for her entire stay. I keep telling her how beautiful it is when you can see it all. She just keeps saying Mmm Hmm. I am beginning to think she doesn't believe me.

I was able to get a few days off strung together and came home for EAA AirVenture in Oshkosh. Nancy had rented a motor home for the event. She has been volunteering at the seaplane base for the last few years. That motor home was a lot nicer than the tent we usually stayed in. We even had air conditioning.

Oshkosh was fun and on Wednesday I was driving home from Oshkosh to pick up the 185 and fly it back with my daughter Stacie. On the way I got a call from a friend. He relayed some really bad news. There had been a crash in Alaska. It was a Taquan Air Beaver with the pilot and four passengers on board. He didn't have any more information at that time but called back a short time later and said he found more information. The airplane had hit a mountain side and all aboard were killed. The pilot was Joe Campbell. Joe started at Taquan the same time as I did. We became fast friends. He will be missed.

I got back to Ketchikan yesterday. There was a memorial service last night for Joe. Joe was a good man and a good pilot. We all have to remember that we enjoy a sport and profession that is unforgiving. The plane that was five minutes in front of Joe made it through. The plane five minutes behind Joe turned around. Joe was caught in deteriorating weather and in an attempt to turn around, hit the mountain. Be careful out there and check your 6.

That's all for now. I'll try to make the next letter quicker than a month from now. Be safe and I will see you all in the fall.

Letters from Camp Ketchikan

Aug. 4, 2007

So far, I have been talking about me and my experiences in Ketchikan. In this letter I am going to tell you a little about the pilots I work with and the call signs I have given them.

First there is Dale, call sign "Radar". Dale has more time flying Beavers than I have flying time, and that is saying something. Dale is a soft-spoken man who shows up every day and does his job. When the weather is down, or unknown, Dale is the one they send out to see if we can fly or not. Dale knows the area better than the back of his hand. So, weather that may be flyable for him is not necessarily flyable for the rest of us. I have had to learn Dale's language. When he says its a little low that means it is impassable for the rest of us. It sometimes seems Dale can see through clouds, hence the name Radar.

Jerry, call sign "Smokey Bear ". Jerry does most of the contract flying for the forest service. Like Dale, Jerry has been flying here since the Wright Brothers invented the airplane. Both Dale and Jerry are very knowledgeable, and I have learned a lot from watching them and asking them questions.

Carl, call sign, well I had a couple of call signs for Carl. The first I came up with was Bull. Not just because Carl is a big strong guy but because of his personality. He is a big BS'er and I didn't want to use a cuss word for a call sign and I didn't think a half a call sign was good either so I came up with a different call sign, "Wild Man." I think Carl will like that one. That pretty much describes Carl. He is a second generation bush pilot with the gift of gab.

Nick, call sign, "Chaw". Nick is a young enthusiastic guy from Minnesota. He always has some chew in his cheek. He is a good pilot and is looking into flying here full time. He looks the part of the bush pilot. He is also the grill master. When we have a cookout, he does the cooking. We came up with the ideas for a TV show staring him as the "Bush Pilot Gourmet". Nick would fly out to a remote location and catch some fish and make it into a gourmet meal. If I ever get stranded in the bush, I want it to be with Nick. I know I won't starve.

Kevin, call sign "Boss". Kevin is the Director of Operations. He has a cutting sense of humor and you never quite know if he is serious or not. He always has a cigarette and Frappuccino in his hand. He is a good D.O. and I enjoy working for him.

Tim, call sign "Cool hand". Tim is a furloughed Northwest pilot. He is from Minnesota. He is a great guy, never gets excited and is able to do his job with grace and style. Unfortunately, he is leaving us to go back to Minnesota next week. Good luck Tim we will miss you!

Now the "NEW" guys.

Andy, call sign "surfer". Andy is from Oregon. He showed up riding a bicycle in the rain wearing a pair of white plastic rimed sunglasses and carrying a copy of "Surfer" magazine. I wouldn't have to point him out, you would know who he was.

Mike, call sign "Spock". Mike is from California and drives a Highbred Ford. He is into Sci-Fi and writes some himself.

Mike is an ex jet charter pilot who was looking for more than a beeper strapped to his side for the rest of his life. Working here is like vacationing somewhere else he says.

Brian, call sign - I haven't found a call sign for him yet. Brian worked for Seaborne Air in St. Croix, flying Twin Otters on floats before coming here. "Otter" maybe that will work? Quite a change! He and his wife Lauren have a new baby girl Amelia. If I had to make a call sign for Lauren it would be easy, "Pillsbury". Not because she looks like the Pillsbury Dough Boy, quite the contrary. She is a lovely petite woman and she loves to bake. She often brings us or has Brian bring us fresh baked goods from her kitchen. We all thank you Lauren!

Bobby, Call sign "Jester". Bobby grew up, well was raised, in Hyder Alaska population 15. He has a work ethic that makes the rest of us look lazy. He worked for the Forest Service maintaining the cabins they rent in the National Forest and is very knowledgeable in wood craft, hunting and fishing. He is always ready to lend a hand. Bobby is also something of a comedian. He is often found making jokes or playing the trickster.

Eric, call sign "Shadow". Eric works the dock part time and flies part time. He is a native of Ketchikan. Eric is one of those guys who shows up and does his job without any fuss. He is always there to catch your airplane as you come in to the dock or fuel it or whatever else it needs. He knows what needs to be done and he does it.

Adam, call sign "Hollywood". Adam is 23 years old and is from Wisconsin. He was a flight instructor at Jack Brown's Seaplane base in Florida before coming to Ketchikan. He showed up later than the rest of us because of his commitment to Brown's. His favorite subjects are computers, paint ball and movies.

Letters From Camp Ketchikan

August 14, 2007

Ah, the end to another long and beautiful day. I am sitting here with my beer and V-8 to write this letter. I know some of you just got sick and the rest just said, "what?" Yes, beer and V-8 but not just V-8. I use a mix of 50/50 spicy V-8 and regular. Nancy made me promise to eat my vegetables and the beer just helps to get them down. But I digress.

I was talking to my friend Jim last week and he couldn't believe I hadn't been fishing yet. I am not much of a fisherman, but not because I don't like to fish. I just don't do it often.

Well I thought Jim was right I should at least go fishing once. After all, the odds of me catching anything without someone's help is next to nil. I asked Mike if he wanted to go with me. He thought it was a great idea. He is also a non fisherman.

We went to Knudsen Cove Marina and rented a 14' skiff with a 15 horse motor. That's right we were in the Pacific Ocean fishing in a 14' OPEN skiff! God looks after his own, I guess. The weather was great. Calm with clear blue skies and about 65 degrees.

We rented everything we needed and had the lady at the counter show us how to set it up. (I wonder what she told her husband about us that night?) We even bought ice for the cooler. No, it wasn't to keep the fish we didn't expect to catch cold. It was to keep my lunch cold. We went to where all the other boats were (Most of them much bigger than ours). We did what they were doing. I figure we must have been doing something right because we were doing pretty good. We caught just as many fish as all of the guys around us. Nothing! We must have looked okay doing it because we didn't see anyone pointing at us or laughing as they went by.

After a couple of hours, we decided to move to a new spot. We motored to the opposite end of Benton Island from where we were. There were no other boats there to scare the fish away, besides the gas was included in the rental. After equally good luck we pulled up to shore. I wanted to check out a tidal pool I had seen from the air. It was hard to walk across the broken rock to get to the pool. It was low tide and the pool was isolated from the ocean. I didn't see any fish and I didn't bring my pole anyway. I wonder if there are any bears on Benton Island?

I got back to the boat and we trolled around some more. Just north of Knudsen Cove I got a strike. I couldn't believe it. I reeled in a Pink Salmon. Mike wasn't feeling well, he got the flu, so we headed in.

Back at Taquan I asked Bobby how to filet my fish. He told me how, so I put on my rubber gloves. I did what Bobby said and it worked out okay. Now I have a half a filet in my freezer just waiting for Nancy. I don't like salmon. I gave Mike the other half. He does like salmon. I figure that salmon cost about $45.00 a pound and damn well worth it.

I think I'll have Marie Callender's pot pie tonight.

Letters From Camp Ketchikan

September 19, 2007

Camp is almost over. Nancy will be flying to Ketchikan on Saturday to help me pack and drive me home. As my stay here nears an end, I have been reflecting on my time here in Ketchikan. I am glad I came, and I will be glad to be back home to see all of my friends. I will also miss it here. As those of you who have come to visit can attest, it is a different place. The pace is slower here in some ways just as the pace is slower in any small town, but it is also richer. How many times have all of you, at one time or another, said, "What am I doing here?" "Why do I live here?" I have not thought that once here. Many times, I will wake up and look out the window and tell God, thank you for this beautiful day. For every day has its own beauty and its own promises.

I look out my apartment window at the cruise ships in port and hear the people walking and exploring. I can hear the creek next to me as it rushes to the ocean. I look up to the mountains with their snow caps and remember what they looked like yesterday as I flew over them. As I drive to work, I see eagles flying pass me. As I fly my plane from place to place, I see whales, seals, eagles and bears. I see God's majesty all about me as I take tourists on an unforgettable trip through the Misty Fjords.

I have changed. Ketchikan has changed me. I have wanted to do this for a long time, and I am glad I have had the chance.

We will be leaving Tuesday for the drive home. It will not be as hectic as the one up here. We plan to see Banff in British Columbia. We will stop and see some friends in Idaho and visit Yellowstone Park. I would like to see Devil's Tower and Mt. Rushmore from the ground if it doesn't take us too far out of the way.

Take care and Nancy and I will see all of you soon.

Dan

Back to Alaska 2011

After 2007 I took 3 years off from flying in Ketchikan, but it was never far from my mind, I wanted to go back. I called Kevin, the Director of Operations, and he said he could use another pilot but it would only be 4 days a week. Perfect! I'll be able to get out more on my own and enjoy more of what Ketchikan has to offer. Nancy will be staying this time. She will be looking for a job once we get there. We set out for Ketchikan on May 8th we arrived on Saturday the 14th of May and I checked in with Taquan. They wanted me to start recurrent training right away so Sunday morning I started a solo review of company procedure and started doing all the written tests that are required.

ANCHORAGE TO KETCHIKAN IN A PA-12

May 24, 2012

I have a couple of days off so I thought I would take a breath and make a posting to catch you all up on what we have been doing. I'll let Nancy fill you in on her stuff.

After a smooth and beautiful cruise up from Prince Rupert, we arrived in Ketchikan on a bright and sunny day. We hoped it was an omen for a good season to come. We hit the ground running. We moved into our apartment and settled in for our first night back in K-town. We awoke to heavy rain and 25-30 mph winds and 42 degree temperatures. That continued for 12 of the next 14 days! The other two were light rain and only 10-15 mph winds.
Taquan was in the process of training five new pilots and I had to go through recurrent training also so things were a little hectic. I wasn't able to fly for a week after I got here. Then my currency check ride lasted only an hour and I was good to go and I have been "going" ever since. After 3 days on the line I asked for 3 days off to help Jared fly his PA-12 from Anchorage to Ketchikan a little over 800 miles. We had a weather window that looked good and we didn't want to lose it.

I took the Alaska Airlines milk run to Anchorage on Wednesday. It stopped in Sitka and Juneau before landing in Anchorage at 9:30 pm, some 5½ hours later. I called Jared but he didn't answer. I got a ride over to the Millennium hotel right on Lake Hood for a burger and a beer. The Millennium is one of my favorite places. You can sit and relax while watching the seaplanes come and go from Lake Hood. They say ¼ of all the seaplanes in the world are based there. That's my kind of place.

While I was having my beer and waiting for the burger I got a text from Jared saying he was in the air and would be at Lake Hood soon. Just as I was finishing my burger I saw the red PA-12 come taxiing in. I called Jared and he met me at the Millennium. He had spent most of the day changing the PA-12 over from wheels to floats and the test flight was from Big Lake, near Wasilla to Lake Hood.

We rented a car and drove to Girdwood where Jared's father lives. He was gone but we stayed at his house. Girdwood is the Aspen of Alaska. There are lots of beautiful houses overlooking the mountain and Alyeska ski area. The view is so beautiful that most of the houses don't have curtains. I slept in the loft with a great view. Alaska in the summer with no curtains. Do you know how long the sun stays up in Anchorage during the summer? Do you? I put a clean sock over my face and got to sleep about midnight. The sun had gone down but it wasn't dark. Needless to say I was up early, which was a good thing. We had a lot to do before we could depart. It looked like the weather report was right on; clear and sunny.

We left Lake Hood at noon and climbed out toward the Turnigan Arm under clear blue skies and no wind. That rarely happens, but it did today. We passed Girdwood and climbed over the Chugach Mountains to Whittier and then crossed the Prince William Sound. We passed Valdez and landed in Cordova, an hour and a half after leaving Anchorage. Part of the lake was still frozen. We taxied to the dock and were met by the operator. Three men in casual business dress approached and asked where we came in from. I told them Anchorage. Then they asked who the pilot was. Not wanting to lie I quickly pointed to Jared and said he was. The man in charge turned to Jared and introduced himself and his companions as being from the FAA and wanted to know how they could help us. That's right we got ramp checked. 47 years of flying and the second time I was ever ramp checked was in Cordova, Alaska flying a seaplane only days after the lake was open for landing and the gravel strip had only half a dozen planes on it. The guys were friendly and didn't give us any problems. They actually were able to help Jared with a few things. We fueled up and were on our way to Juneau, 5½ hours away.

Did I mention we were in Alaska? Yeah that place of ice and cold. Did I also mention that the heater didn't work? I am just glad I brought my winter jacket, fleece vest, extra-tuffs, wool socks and a roll of duct tape. There were so many air leaks in the back seat of that airplane it could qualify as an open cockpit! I taped up the window, stuffed our lunch bag and some old maps against the air leak in the door on the right. Did I say air leak? It was more like a hurricane. I unfolded a sectional on my lap not to navigate but to use as a blanket to keep me warm. Did I say warm? Jared was in the front seat with the sun on him just wearing a wool shirt complaining about how hot he was.

We left Cordova after filling our aux and main tanks with 66 gallons of fuel, and we burned just under 10g/h. That comes out to just over 6.6 hours, and we figured it would take about five and a half hours to get to Juneau.
The visibility stayed better than 10 miles, sometimes way better, but the ceiling came down to about 1,500. The flight from Cordova took us through a slit in the mountains toward the Cordova airport and the Copper River Delta. We saw five moose there. From Cordova we stayed along the coast all the way to Juneau. We passed Yakataga, Yakutat, the Alsek River, Cape Spencer and Juneau. We had the Pacific Ocean off our right the whole way and a beach over 200 miles   long   \

below us and some of the most spectacular scenery in the world out our window. We saw over a dozen black bears, five moose, one grizzly bear, countless eagles and several whales.

We landed on the float plane pond at the Juneau airport. We were able to park in the transient parking on the west end of the pond. We got a ride to the FBO and walked to a motel for the night. The next morning we checked weather, it was still good, and fueled for the leg to Ketchikan.

We departed to the East right over downtown Juneau and out the Gastineau Channel and Stephen's Passage toward Petersburg. We made a few small detours for Jared to check out some possible kayaking areas and also flew by the Le Conte glacier. What a remarkable sight, icebergs floating in front of the glacier, the sharp white walls rising several thousand feet and the pools of bright blue glacial water. Mother Nature at her finest.

We dodged a few rain showers and areas of low visibility but made an uneventful arrival in Ketchikan a little over 3 hours after leaving Juneau. That was a trip I would like to make again someday.

Letters From Camp Ketchikan

May 31, 2011

I went in for my pre-employment drug and alcohol test. I had forgotten just what that involved. I had "gone" just before leaving for the testing facility. Well I realized just how dumb that was when the tech at the testing facility gave me a bottle to fill. Oh s***! The pressure was on and try as I might I failed to perform. That didn't mean just wait and try again. Nope. I had to fill out paper work documenting the incomplete sample. And then wait in the lobby until I felt "ready" to try it again. No pressure right, just drink a lot of water and try again. Not quite. You are limited in the amount of water you can have in any given time period. They don't want you to try and dilute the sample. Hum hum hum, "may I have some more water please?" "No it hasn't been long enough yet." Humm da humm humm, "can I have that water now?" "Just a few more minutes."

As I was waiting for a retest, a young woman came in for the same test. I wished her good luck as the tech called her in. She looked at me quizzically as she went in. A few minutes later she came out and sat in the lobby a few chairs from me. I looked at her and said, "not enough huh." She looked back and said, "yeah."

Another woman walked in and we both watched as she filled out her paper work and then took a seat in the lobby. A few minutes later the tech walked out and called her in to give her sample. The young woman and I both looked at her and wished her good luck.

I wish I was a coffee drinker. I'm sure that would have made all of this unnecessary. The older woman came out and took a seat in the lobby. I looked at her and said, "not enough huh." She looked at me with a flush of embarrassment and said, "yeah." We all chuckled and entered into bathroom banter.

I would sure like to get out of here. I feel like I could go but I don't want to under perform again. Besides being hard on the ego it could have legal ramifications for the drug test.

Could I have some more water now?

I asked the tech if it was common to have someone not fill the cup. He said it was quite unusual. In fact it had happened only once in the last few months.

Great, even more pressure! Humm da humm humm.

I feel like I could do it now but I want to make sure. Could I have another glass of water?

I can do it now, I'm sure, I think! I went up to the window and told the tech I was ready. We went through the whole process again. "Everything out of your pockets, sign this form stating I showed you the rules, wash your hands, now DON'T FLUSH AFTER YOU'RE DONE." He handed me the cup, it looked bigger than I remembered, and I started slowly at first, a drop or two at a time, then more, and more. I made it to the mark. I kept going past the mark. Where was this when I needed it? The cup was nearly full and I had just started. Do you remember the movie "A League Of Their Own?" If you do, then you remember the scene I'm thinking about, uh-huh that much. When I finished I reached for the handle to flush (reflex). Luckily, it was taped as a reminder.

As I left, I wished the girls good luck. Whew that ordeal was over. It would take about three days before the results would be back and I couldn't fly until the company got the all clear on the drug test. I finished all the ground school tests and went along on a couple of trips to get reacquainted with the area.

Two and a half days later the drug test results were back and Kevin, our Director of Operations, put me in the Beaver for recurrent training and a check ride. We did the required hour of training and the check ride and I was on the line. The next day I flew four Misty trips for a total of 5 hours. So far, I have flown over 30 hours this season.

The weather is always the issue here in Ketchikan. A few days ago, we had normal Ketchikan weather, ragged 500 foot ceiling and 3-4 miles visibility and light rain. It was too low to fly the usual route over land to get to the Misty's so we had to stay over water all the way and go around Point Alva to the Behm Canal, then up to Rudyard Bay. This added about 10 minutes to the flight. Even with the low ceilings it was a beautiful trip. We were limited to where we could go in the Misty's but the tour was great. Sometimes when the weather is low it is even more spectacular with the clouds hanging on the sides of the mountains than it is on a clear day.

More later.............

TRIP TO METLAKATLA AND THE MISTYS

June 2, 2011

It has been a good feeling to be back in Ketchikan. I have thought about it often while I had been away. It hasn't changed much. That is, except, for the weather. It has been much better than I remember. They say it will be 70 today and we have had many days in the mid to upper 60s, which is great compared with the last time I was here. I have been told the year I had worked here the weather was unusually bad and it appears this year will be much better. But we still do get the weather I remember from 2007.

A case in point is June 2, 2011. I start my day with a round trip from Ketchikan to Metlakatla (15 minutes away). The ceiling was a ragged 500 to 600 feet with Visibility of 3 to 5 miles and a light rain. It is beautiful with the low clouds and mist with the mountains as a background and the ocean beneath me waves breaking on the rocks. As I was landing my passengers spot a humpback whale spouting just 100 yards away. I landed and taxi to the dock. One of my passengers is a psychologist who uses the airplane for her daily commute to work. After tying up and unloading my passengers, our dock man, Roy, helps me unload the inbound freight and reload the out going freight. I also have two passengers to take back to the airport dock.

After the short taxi from the airport dock to Taquan I stow the cargo net and put all the seats back in. I am ready to start flying Misty Fjord tours. When the weather is good enough, about 800 feet, we fly the short way to the Fjords over land to the Behm Canal and on to Rudyerd Bay. Today we can't go the short way.

The flight to the Misty Fjords takes about 30 minutes with about another 10 minutes flying around the mountains and waterfalls. On low weather days like this I head east from our base right past downtown Ketchikan, at just a few hundred feet, as I climb to my cruising altitude. I continue flying past Mountain Point. I can see 3½ miles through the rain and mist to Bold Island. As I get to Bold Island, I can see Cone Island about 4 miles away. The visibility is not too bad. The ceiling is a ragged, 500 to 600 feet. From Cone Island I continue to follow the coast to Point Alva. We just call it Alva. At Alva I keep following the coast as it slowly makes a 90 degree turn to the Northeast. From Alva I continue to Narrow Pass between Rudyerd Island and Revillagigedo (Revilla). It is about 30 miles from Alva to Rudyerd Bay where the Fjord tour starts. As I pass Rudyerd Island I can start to make out Smeaton Island and continue to the north end of Smeaton and go through Short Pass. From Short Pass I can see across the Behm Canal to Winstanley Island. From the tip of Winstanley Island it is five miles to Rudyerd Bay.

With the low ceiling I will not be able to do the normal tour. When I get to the mouth of Rudyerd Bay I look into the bay and check the weather. I will be able to fly to the "wall" which is a 3,000 foot high, shear faced granite mountain. It, along with New Eddy Stone Rock, are the most recognized part of the monument. I will be able to fly into Punchbowl Cove, just in front of the wall, make a tight turn around back to Rudyerd Bay and continue to the Amphitheater, a rock formation made by glaciers that creates a beautiful natural amphitheater. From the amphitheater I continue past Bailey Falls to the "Y", where I turn around and land in front of Bailey Falls. At Bailey Falls I shut down the engine and let the people out on the floats. It is amazing. Everyone is standing on the floats looking at the falls and soaking up the experience. Two things are inevitable. One, someone will ask, "Has anyone ever fallen in?" and two, "How deep is it here?" The answers are, "No, that is a whole different tour," and, "It's over your head...........about 500 feet."

After about ten minutes, and a lot of picture taking, I get everyone loaded back into the airplane and head back to Ketchikan. I'll make that trip four more times today.

CATCHING CRABS

One nice thing about living in Ketchikan is all the free seafood. Well not quite free, you have to catch it. My favorite is Dungeness Crabs. And I have a unique way of collecting my catch.

Starting in July we start doing bear tours where we fly a load of passengers to a bear viewing area where one of our guides escorts them to a prepared viewing site. The nice thing about that is we fly our first group of passengers out, drop them off and usually fly back empty for the next load. But before I leave I taxi over to my crab traps that I leave nearby. In the morning I bate the traps. I leave early and empty for the last pickup of the day. This allows enough time to land near my traps get out on the floats and pull up the traps to retrieve my catch. I usually get 3 to 5 keepers per trap and I have 3 traps. I put the crabs in the float storage compartment then taxi over to the dock to pick up my passengers.

Back at Taquan once the passengers are gone, I drive my plane up on to the ramp and tie it down. I get the crabs from the floats put them on their backs and give them a good spin like a top. This knocks them out and makes them easy to handle without getting pinched. I then take them to the side of the dock, grab them by the legs and crack their shells open on the dock. This makes it easy to separate the leg clusters from the shell and they are ready to cook.

I worked for Taquan Air for the next two years. I still go back occasionally for visits with the friends I made there. I will always miss that time and place and it will hold a special place in my heart.

PART 7

ODDS AND ENDS

1st SOLO SCHWEIZER 1-19

October 2, 1965 was a warm sunny autumn day in Wisconsin. A few cumulus clouds dotted the pale blue sky and the west wind was fresh and clean. Autumn is my favorite time if the year with cool, clean delicious smelling air and colors no artist ever will be able to capture. A sense if euphoria engulfed my whole being.

I had joined a glider club the week before and had made three flights in the club's TG-3 two place glider. It had been much different from the J-3 Cub that I had been flying with my father. The elevator and rudder were very sensitive but the aileron control required two hands on the stick. A turn was an exercise in contrasts; it took maximum effort on the ailerons and a feather-light touch on the elevator and rudder.

I had my student glider certificate and this weekend, with luck, I would become a glider pilot.

Flying had always been a part of my life. My father owned a crop dusting business so there was always airplanes around for me to look at, work on and dream about. When I was big enough to see out of the cockpit of dad's Stearman and work the rudders at the same time, my father let me taxi it around. I flew as often as I could. Whenever my father went to the airport, I went with him.

When I arrived at the airport with my father on that memorable October day, we went over to the other pilots and talked for a while. On the outside I was reserved and quiet, but on the inside I could hardly control myself. Let's get down to business and fly!

When everyone finally decided to untie the gliders and begin the day's operations, I grew more excited. I knew the time was coming closer. I was the first one to reach the row of gliders. There was a Schweizer 1-19 and then a 1-26 and then the big TG-3 parked on the end. The 1-19 was to be my ship.

I untied the glider quickly and gave it a good preflight. The short rope was hooked to the 1-19 with the other end fastened to a Volkswagen "Bug" we used to pull it over to the runway. My instructor Fred and I discussed the plan of action that would lead to my becoming a pilot that day if I did as I was supposed to. Fred and I pointed the nose of that pretty yellow ship into the wind. I climbed into the cockpit and put on my seatbelt and shoulder harness.

I had been instructed to sit in the 1-19 with the nose into the wind and balance it on its small center wheel. This was to give me a feel for the controls. I sat there for what felt like hours but that was all right. I was in the cockpit by myself, flying all over the world, even if I never left the ground.

Fred was back in a half hour. The question I had been waiting for streamed from his lips, "Are you ready for a tow?" My heart pounded with excitement. I had waited all my life for this moment and I was ready!

My first solo flight will not go into any record book, except possibly for being the shortest flight in history. The tow was to be behind the VW "Bug." I was to get only about 10 feet in the air and halfway down the grass strip, then I was to release and land straight ahead. The towline was attached. The release had been tested. The VW started to move slowly, taking up the slack. I was exited but serious. The slack was taken up and I moved the rudder from side to side in the signal to go. My father was holding the wing. The VW moved a little faster. The excitement swelled as I began to move. My father ran beside continuing to balance the wing until there was enough airflow for controls. The 1-19 accelerated and my father released the wing. I was on my own.

The left wing dipped. I reacted instantly with right stick to raise it. At that slow speed, it took full deflection. The wing came back to level. Airspeed was up to 40 mph and I pulled the stick back gently and the glider lifted off.

I raised the 1-19 only 10 feet over the runway, but I was flying. Halfway down the runway, I pulled the release. It made a loud bang as the release finger struck its metal mount. I decelerated very quickly. I pointed the nose down to keep airspeed. I didn't have far to go before landing, but I didn't want to make any mistakes. I felt the grass on the wheel and then I was down. I pushed the stick forward. The 1-19 went up on its nose skid (a wood plate about 4 feet long and mounted from the wheel forward to be used as a brake) and came to a stop. I sat there balancing the wings. I didn't want it to be over already. The entire flight was entered in my logbook as "two minutes solo."

We pulled the glider back down the runway edge in preparation for another flight. Briefing completed. Rope hooked up, rudder signal given and I started my second solo flight. This time I was to go to 50 feet over the runway, release at the midpoint and glide in for a landing. It was beautiful flying solo, you made your own decisions. My second fight was 50% longer than the first. It lasted three minutes, block-to-block, and I now had five minutes solo time in my logbook.

My third solo flight was to be even longer. The 300 foot rope we had been using was replaced with an 1100 foot rope. I would be able to get up to 600 or 800 feet. After takeoff, I was to pull back on the stick. The farther back I pulled the stick, the faster I would go in a slingshot effect.

I wagged the rudder full left and then full right as I felt the excitement build. This time I would really fly. My 1-19 and I began to accelerate and I felt the controls start to take effect. A little back pressure on the stick and up we went. Back on the stick more and the airspeed increased to 75 mph. The altimeter was winding up quickly – through 300 feet, 400 feet...I looked down for a moment to find the tow car, but I couldn't see it...600 feet, 700 feet...the rope is almost vertical...800 feet; BANG! The release snapped as I pulled the red ball on the lever. The acceleration stopped and the airspeed settled at 50 mph.

I was struck by the silence. A slight whisper of air passed my open cockpit. The wind welcomed me and I could see for miles. Lake Michigan was 12 miles to the east. I looked around at all the things that I had seen many times before, but they looked different now – better. A shout of joy and awe filled my soul.

I banked into a tight 360 degree turn to the left and then back to the right. My little 1-19 responded instantly. At 400 feet it was time to begin my landing approach. The nose was pointed down, the airspeed was 60 mph and I was in a right down-wind for runway 27 with spoilers on full to help slow me down. There was only a slight burble caused by the spoilers. At 250 feet I turned a tight base and then a quick, short final. At about five feet, I broke the descent and settled gently to the grass. The stick went forward and I used the nose skid to slow and stop. The right wing settled slowly to the ground. I just sat there, savoring every moment of that all-too-short flight. I was on the ground, but my spirit was still in the air.

My father was the first to meet me with a smile, a handshake and a pat on the back. He too had waited a long time for this day.

A lot has happened since that day. I have flown a lot of airplanes in many places. My flight path has taken me from that 1-19 through years of crop dusting, flying freight and commuter airlines, right up to the cockpit of a Boeing 767. I have flown the Alaskan bush in Beavers on floats and competed in aerobatics, but October 2, 1965 is as vivid now as it was when I first went aloft alone.

THE CUB WINS THE CUP AT BROKEN PROP

Wisconsin is a fantastic place to fly in summer, but as anyone who has spent much time that far north can tell you, summer doesn't last.

What happens in the winter when the temperature hovers at the zero mark for weeks and the ground is hidden beneath a carpet of white? Are the airplanes all put away and forgotten until spring when the lakes thaw and the ground once more shows its face to the sun?

Well, Wisconsinites are a hardy bunches who love airplanes and flying. They do not hide from the winter cold but change wheels for skis. The flying continues and so do the fly-ins; ski plane fly-ins.

One such fly-in is held at a small, privately owned airstrip named, Broken Prop, (I can only guess how they came up with that one), near Berlin, Wisconsin. The fly-in has been held for some years now and keeps getting bigger. There are Cubs, Champs, Citabrias, Super cubs, Cruisers and more, all on skis. The pilots gather in the hangar, have

255

some good homemade chili, stoke the fire and, like pilots everywhere, trade stories.

One pilot tells of his first time on skis (one take off, no landings), circling a small lake when one of his ice fishing friends motions him in for a landing.

"Why not, there is plenty of room. Carb heat on, power off, plenty of room over the trees. Now hold the nose up, use power to control the descent, just like a glassy water landing in a seaplane. Closer, closer, finally the skis touch and what! Slush starts spraying from the heels of the skis! Full power! Take off! The airplane does not respond. It slows; two frozen rooster tails are flying from the skis. Still at full power the Cub slows nearly to a stop. It does not sink! The reason becomes clear. Two inches of slush lie beneath the snow on the lake and the ice. The Cub slows to a stop, power off. The slush is frozen to the bottom of the skis.

"How to get out of here? I cleaned the ice from the ski bottoms as well as possible and I attempt the takeoff. Full power and nothing happens. The man on the lake rocks the wings to break the skis loose. Nothing happens. While the wings are still rocking I bounce the tail up and down with the elevators to try to help break it loose. Finally it starts to move. It responds slowlly; a fast walk, a slow trot. More speed. Bounce the tail more.

"The slush covered lake feels more like a field of mud, holding the Cub back. The lake is a mile long, plenty of room to clear the trees if only the Cub would accelerate. The end of the lake comes closer. Better not stop. Full power skidding turn; keep what little airspeed I have. Twenty miles an hour; the slush starts to spray from under the skis. Twenty-five miles an hour; nearing the middle of the lake. Come on airspeed! The Cub feels lighter. Come on! Thirty miles an hour; the skis seem to be breaking the suction of the slush. It is accelerating faster now. Thirty-five miles an hour; boy those trees look big. The skis break free of the slush and start to accelerate on the snow. Forty miles an hour; ease the stick back, get the skis up. Too late to stop now; make it or end up in the trees. The Cub starts to rise very slowly. Come on! More! We are flying. Those trees are looking bigger. More altitude. The dark barren fingers of the trees pass inches below the skis. Let's go home."

The stories continue for some time, each adventurer taking his turn, each is more excited than the last.

The days are short in February and there is more to do. The spot landing contest is being organized. But this is no ordinary contest. Two dark lines of ash are trailed across the snow covered runway. The contestants must land past the first line and stop before the second without swerving or turning the engine off.

Ten planes enter the competition. In the first round only five are able to keep the dark lines of ash from sliding under their skis; a Champ, Super Cruiser, Vagabond, PA-11 and a Cub.

The distance is shortened and the five take off to try again. The lines look so close. It must be only 300 feet. With no brakes and little wind it looks impossible. The Champ is first. He is a little high and fast. The pilot starts to slip, but too late and he lands long. The end line slides beneath his skis. He's out. The Super Cruiser is next. The approach looks good. Two feet in the air over the end line. Touch down. The snow puffs from under the skis, beautiful but too fast. He can't stop before he too passes over the end line. Next up is the Vagabond, but this airplane is too fast and its stall speed is too high to make it. His approach is excellent but he is too slow, he can't fly that slowly. More power or it'll stall. Incredibly the skis touch just past the start of the landing zone. This Vagabond has a skilled pilot; he is still in the contest.

The PA-11 is on approach. Its original blue and yellow paint is beautiful. Retractable skis. A nice looking ship, framed against the crisp pale blue sky and soft white snow. The approach is good. Speed just above a stall. Stick back, power off and the PA-11 comes to a stop 30 feet from the end line. He's in.

Last is a yellow Cub with a black lightning stripe on the side. The Cub is 200 feet from the threshold line and only two feet over the snow. He is going to be short. The airplane slows, 100 feet from the threshold line. The engine gets louder as the pilot adds power. The Cub touches down just past the threshold. He slides to a stop between the lines. He too is still in the contest.

The distance is again shortened. Now the lines are 200 feet apart. This is the final round and the shortest landing wins. The Vagabond makes the first try. The approach is flawless. Incredible how slowly he can fly with such short wings. The touchdown is perfect, but the lines are just too close. The Vagabond slides over the end line. The PA-11 is up. Again he makes a good approach. His touchdown is good but the end line is approaching quickly. He is still going. Stick back, dig that tail ski in. Power off, slow down. The PA-11 stops 10 feet short of the end line.

The Cub is already on the approach. If he misses, the PA-11 wins. The yellow Cub is no show piece. The fabric is old, the color faded, yet the plane exudes quiet confidence. It seems to say "I know I'm not the prettiest or the most expensive, but I know myself, and what I can do, and that is all that matters." The Cub is making another low approach. The nose is coming up. It is just above stall speed and still 100 feet away from the line. The engine speed increases, the added airflow keeps it from stalling, but for how long? The nose comes up further, more power is added. Just a few more feet. The airplane is barely eight inches over the snow, touch and its over, he'll lose. It is an endeavor of pride. The Cub stretches its glide. The heels of the skis touch just as it passes the line. He is over to the right a little. The snow is deeper there, more drag, shorter slide. The stick is all the way back. The tail wheel presses deep into the snow. The Cub slows quickly. The engine is turning so slowly that you can see the propeller blades. The airplane stops with 50 feet to spare. The spectators are amazed and the judges declare that the Cub has won!

Stories traded, chili eaten, feet warmed and trophies awarded, old friends and new ones say good-bye and good luck as all head for home. See you around. Be back next year for sure!

JUST ANOTHER BOAT AT THE BAR

June 29, 2010

It is difficult for me to just get into an airplane and fly. I have to have a goal of some kind even if it is just to do takeoffs and landings. I need a plan. That is why my flight of June 29, 2010 was so out of character for me. The extent of my plan was to load my camping gear in my J-3 float plane and head for the Wisconsin River, then follow it to the Mississippi River and hopefully find a sandbar to camp on. I didn't know anything about the area, and I had never gone airplane camping before. It was going to be a great adventure.

The morning was warm and blue, with light winds. I had four hours of fuel in my tanks. My camping gear and food were stowed in the float compartments. My backpack was strapped into the front seat and my snacks were in a plastic coffee can within reach (I didn't know when or where I would find lunch and I get testy when I don't eat).

I backed the Cub onto the ramp, completed the pre-flight and hit the starter. Yes I wimped out and installed a starter when I rebuilt the Cub. It makes it so much easier when you are on floats, especially when you are doing instruction. I didn't install a generator, so I don't need a transponder and encoder to operate in O'Hare's class B Vail.

I pointed the nose into the wind on Pistakee Lake and pored on the coal. The 90hp Continental with the Aqua 1500 floats made takeoff a quick and easy event. I climbed north over the lake to gain some altitude before heading northwest towards the Wisconsin River. The air was warm and smooth as I passed over Geneva Lake and headed toward

Lake Delavan. I passed over the airport there (C59) as I continued to lake Koshkonong. Jana (58C), (also my daughter's name), and Verona (W19) passed by without a ripple in the sky. I could see Madison and searched for the 1299 foot high towers southwest of the city. I was slightly above them but they still made me nervous. I like to know where they are.

This was becoming unfamiliar territory for me. Most of my light plane flying has been east of here. Once I passed west of Madison and junction with the Wisconsin River near Sauk Prairie it was virgin country for me. The landscape had changed. The relative flatland had given way to rolling hills and valleys with much of the land being forests. The farm fields wiggled left and right with the contours of the hills. Corn, grain and hay fields began to stir with the first hints of the morning breeze. The temperature was climbing. The sun was warm so I opened the door to cool off and get a panoramic view of the world beneath me. A smile came to my face as I thought how lucky I was to be able to see God's pallet before me like this.

The Wisconsin River surprised me a little. It was over 100 yards wide but was much shallower than I had expected. There were many sandbars and a lack of a clear main channel in many areas.

I continued toward Prairie du Chien winding past Lone Rock (KLNR) and Boscobel (KOVS). The topography changes in that area. The rolling hills are pushed back from the river by a flood plane. I flew over some large flat fields of rich black earth.

Nearing Prairie du Chien, the view from my window changed yet again. The river broadens and becomes a tangled maze of braided channels and swamps thickly populated with trees and brush. I could see the cliffs on the western shore of the Mississippi ahead but I couldn't see the river yet. My map showed I was approaching the Prairie du Chien Airport (KPDC). As I flew by the airport, I was looking for a place to land for fuel. Some place where I wouldn't have to walk too far. It didn't look promising. I still had over two hours of fuel, but since I didn't have a plan I figured I needed to have options.

I broke out over the Mississippi. It was wide and fast and beautiful. There had been a lot of rain in this area lately. The water was brown with silt and a lot of debris, whole trees were racing down stream. I could see the current tugging at the channel markers and large waves coming off them. The strong current could be a problem. My altitude over the river was less than the height of the ground on the west bank. I never realized it was so much higher. I turned right and headed up river. The main channel was wide and fast but there were lots of back channel areas with slow moving water that were good enough to land in, but it was deserted and no visible beaches. I flew a few miles more and came to a dam that was over a mile wide. There was a beach with a few boats on it but the water was fast and dark and not inviting for a floatplane. I turned down river to see if that looked any better.

I passed Prairie du Chien and continued down river. I looked up to my right and saw a river observation deck with people looking down at me. I waived and continued on my way. I wondered what they thought of me.

It was looking promising. The river widened out and slowed down. There were more pleasure boats. I saw a nice looking sandbar on my right. There were several boats tied up and people out playing on it. I circled a couple of times checking for a landing site. There was a little back channel that was long enough to land in and it looked like there were no obstructions. Boy, a little local knowledge would be nice. I lined up and set the Cub down without incident. As I taxied to the sand bar, the other boaters watched and as I shut off the engine to drift the last few feet into the beach. I jumped into the water, grabbed my bow line and tied up to a log. I was immediately offered a beer by one of the boaters. It was hot out now and that beer sure looked cold but I regretfully declined and asked if he had any water instead. His bikini clad wife grabbed an ice cold bottle from the cooler and offered it to me. Ahhhh! That was good!

It was lunch time and I was getting hungry. I asked my new friend if there were any restaurants on the river I could get to with my plane. He said the marina just north of Prairie du Chien had a good restaurant and the channel was marked with white buoys. I remembered seeing it as I was south bound from the dam. I asked if they had gas too. He said they did. I had a plan. After a brief rest I pushed back from the bar into the current and started the engine. I taxied back into the slack water channel I landed in and took off north bound again. When I got to the north side of Prairie du Chien, I saw

the white buoys marking the channel to the marina. I circled, checking out the channel and the marina to see if I would be able to land and taxi in. The entrance to the marina was a little tight but doable. I landed in a little crosswind up river in the channel. The current was light and it was no problem. As I approached the entrance to the marina it was clear and a little bigger than I had thought from the air. The fuel dock was straight ahead and open enough to make a fairly easy approach with the light wind I had. There were several tall posts that the floating dock rode up and down on with the river fluctuations but I could avoid them. I turned into the marina. Shortly after I entered the channel to the marina, a cabin cruiser appeared from one of the slips to my right, turned into the channel and proceeded right towards me. I stayed as far to the right as I could but he came right down the middle of the channel. It didn't appear as though he saw me. He kept coming right for me. I couldn't stop, I couldn't turn and he kept coming. He was on the fly bridge with his wife and I could see them both now looking at me and pointing. It took a while for him to realize he wasn't going to clear my wing. He finally turned right to give me some room. As he passed, he gave me a big smile and friendly waive. I waived back. As I approached the gas dock, I adjusted course to head straight into the dock, cut the engine and climbed out on the float to stop the airplane and tie up. I love it when a plan comes together!

I climbed the steps to the second floor bar and restaurant and grabbed a table overlooking my plane. When the waitress came to take my order I asked about getting some gas. "Sure, no problem just let me know when you're ready." I sat back, enjoying my iced tea while waiting for my pulled pork sandwich, thinking how great this trip was already.

After my meal, a few pictures and answering some friendly questions, I was ready to gas up and head out down river.

With full fuel tanks and a satisfied stomach I pushed back from the dock. I floated backwards a few yards before starting up. The taxi out was uneventful. The wind was light so as I made it to the channel. I did a quick run-up and took off down river. The door was down and the warm air filled the cockpit. I passed the river overlook again and waived to the people as I continued to the sandbar I used earlier. I was kind of getting used to this exploration stuff.

When I got back to my sandbar there were still a number of boats there including a houseboat. It would be a bit of a squeeze but there was still room to put the Cub on the bar. I circled and landed in the same back channel as before, with a little more confidence that there were no obstructions hiding just below the surface waiting to ruin my day.

As before everyone was watching as I approached. After tying up at the same log a young family of four came over and asked some questions about the airplane and where I was from, you know the questions. They were nice people and asked if they could take a picture of their boys next to the airplane. I said I had a better idea, why don't I take a picture of all of you by the airplane. I had the boys stand on the floats and put the parents alongside. When I was finished with the pictures I asked the boys if they wanted to sit in the Cub. Their eyes got big as they enthusiastically said yes! Dad might not know it yet but that might have just cost him a lot of money in flying lessons. Do you remember when you first sat in an airplane and decided you had to fly?

I spent the late afternoon relaxing and talking with the folks on the bar. As the boats began to thin out I unloaded my camping gear and set up my tent on a patch of sand I smoothed out with a slope towards the river. I was trying to secure the Cub for the night and having difficulty finding something strong enough to tie to when one of the boaters offered me a long screw-in anchor. I thanked him and asked if he would be back tomorrow so I could give it back to him. He said he would be back in the afternoon but not to worry about it just keep it. I thanked him for his generosity but I didn't really have room for it. I told him I would leave it behind a tree since I was planning on leaving before noon.

As evening approached I gathered some sticks and dried drift wood and built a small fire. The houseboat and I were the only ones left and we were both spending the night. I cooked my canned chili and sat staring into the fire reflecting on this perfect day. I retired early.

The ground was a little lumpy. I didn't bring an air mattress, no room. I drifted off to sleep with a smile as I recalled the day's adventure.

Hooooooonk, Hooooonk, Hooooooooooooook. I awoke with a start. It was a freight train passing by. I had noticed the tracks on both sides of the river but I was not prepared for the noise. The cliffs on both sides held the noise in and it reverberated from side to side. The horn and clickety clack of the cars on the rails seemed to last for ever. I settled back in and fell asleep.

Hooooooonk, Hooooonk, Hoooooooooooooook. I awoke with a start again! It had only been about an hour since the last train. In all there were at least four trains that night. By the third one I just rolled over and tried to fall back to sleep.

It was 2:30 AM when all of a sudden the whole tent lit up with the brightest light I had ever seen! I knew it was 2:30 because I looked at my watch. I didn't even have to use it's built in light. I unzipped the screen and pushed back the flap to see a string of barges and tow boat with a gazillion candlepower search light aimed right at me. He must have seen the plane and wanted a better look. I waived, I have know idea if he saw me, I was nearly blinded. The next time I was awakened it was by the sun.

I laid there for a while until I just couldn't ignore my growling stomach any more. I got up and made some instant oatmeal for breakfast. I cleaned myself and my dishes in the river and talked to the guy from the house boat for a while. I decided to break camp and head down river to see what was there.

It was another perfect day. I loaded all my gear in the Cub pushed off the bar and decided to take off into the slight breeze and also into the current of the main channel. In seaplane training you are told if the wind speed is less than twice the current take off with the current. I learned why that morning. The current was strong enough that with the engine at a fast idle and pointed into the current I was standing still in relation to the shore. I did my run-up and pushed the throttle up for takeoff. The Cub got up on step quickly and kept accelerating, at least in relation to the water. The drag from the water was so great that I was barely able to get enough airspeed to lift off.

I made a circle of the sand bar and headed down river. I came to an island with a wide grass runway on it. Checking my map I confirmed it as Guttenberg (GAA). It was ringed by houses and looked like a charming and inviting place. I saw a Cub on wheels sitting on the grass getting ready for a flight.
Next up was Cassville (C74). I was at about 500 feet and the smoke stacks near the airport were 355 feet. They looked taller.

My view of Cassville was like a Norman Rockwell version of Middle America. I can only wonder at what it would be like to walk the streets and talk to the people.
There were a few sandbars and islands as I continued south, but for one reason or another they didn't suit me. I landed at one such island to check it out but the current was strong and it was open to the main channel.

I talked to some of the people tied up there and they said when the barges come through there they can throw quite a large wake. I got back in the Cub to keep on looking.

As I passed Dubuque, IA I saw how different it was from the rest of the river I had flown over. There were some back channels but they were clogged with traffic and covered with high tension wires criss-crossing everywhere, including the river. I pressed on toward Galena, IL. My wife has a friend there and I briefly considered stopping and asking for a room for the night, but what kind of adventure would that be? I told myself I would go another 10 minutes and if I didn't find a place I liked, I would head back toward Prairie du Chien and camp at that first sandbar I stopped at yesterday.

I made it to Bellevue IA (80 miles) before my time was up. With no good spot in sight I turned around and started back up river.

I now had some familiarity with the river. I had some idea what to expect around each bend. I spotted a small island with a sand beach. I circled several times to check it's suitability for camping. It was small but big enough but there was already a boat there with two tents set up. I thought it might be a little small if I decided to drop in and stay. I kept going up river.

As I flew over the sandbar I used yesterday I noticed some of the same boats were there today. I circled and landed out front in the main channel. I do like to make an entrance. I taxied to the now familiar beach and tied up. I was greeted as an old friend by those I met yesterday. Several people were interested in rides and I accommodated them. It has always been a pleasure to introduce people to aviation, especially in a float plane.

Once again as the boats thinned out I set up camp. Again there was a houseboat I would be sharing the bar with this night. I relaxed just watching the river go by and thought of Mark Twain. I slept okay. I'm still not used to this camping stuff but I know I will learn to like it or at least the adventure that comes with it.

I woke early and just enjoyed the peace and quiet of my little sandbar. I gave rides to the people from the houseboat before packing up and heading to the marina for gas and lunch.

After lunch I plotted a course directly home. How lucky could a guy get, three beautiful days in a row during Wisconsin's summer?

.

Selfie on my way home in the Cub

7,000 MILES IN A BushCat LSA

10C TO ANC

I was in the office at Galt Airport (10C) and over heard Jeremy and Dani discussing getting the BushCat to Valdez, Alaska for the Valdez STOL contest. They were having reservations about the pilot that the company had lined up to make the trip. I had flown from Galt to Anchorage twice and thought it would be nice to do the trip again. I piped up saying I would fly it to Alaska for them. They both looked at me and said really? I said, in a heartbeat.

A day or two later Jeremy asked me if I was serious. I said yes I was. I wanted to attend the Alaska Airmen's Association Trade Show on April 30 and 31st. We worked out the details on when he needed the airplane in Valdez and picked a departure date based on our expected time enroute of 6 days plus 3 more days for weather delays. I knew that April was not a good month weather wise to fly to Alaska, but the events dictated the timing.

I didn't want to fly the trip alone so I asked my friend, Parker, if he wanted to go along. I asked Parker because he has had a lot of experience hunting and fishing in Alaska and if we were delayed enroute at a remote spot or, worse, were forced down, he would be a great asset in our survival. Parker was also an experienced light airplane pilot and most importantly he was retired and had the time to make the trip.

With the date set and the crew arranged, Jeremy set out installing a heater and a few other things we needed in the airplane for the Alaska trip. Parker and I discussed what camping and survival gear we would need. (I will put this list in the appendix)

Parker has a radio show about flying that he records at the Huntley, IL radio station, so he also brought his recording stuff hoping to be able to do some interviews.

DAY 1

Our departure time was set for 0800 on April 22, 2016. Parker had arranged for some press and his radio station to have a representative on hand to watch our departure. We departed into overcast skies and light headwinds. We were off on a 6-day, 40 flying hour trip at 0815. As we proceeded west toward Beloit, WI the ceiling and the visibility lowered as we were flying into light rain and mist. We turned south to try to get around the weather. It only continued to get worse. We always had an escape route to better weather but it always went back toward Galt. Now just 30 minutes into a 40 hour trip we were contemplating our first landing at Poplar Grove (C77) just 21 miles from our starting point, not a good omen for what was to come. Keeping Poplar Grove in sight we continued on toward Rockford. I thought I saw a slight thinning of the clouds there. As we got close to Rockford the ceilings and visibility did start to increase. Little by little we were able to inch westward while keeping a line of retreat open. We proceeded cautiously minute by minute preparing to turn around if necessary. Parker kept track of our position and where the best diversion airports were and the antennas. Slowly the ceilings and visibility increased and with them our sprits and hopes that we would be able to continue.

By the time we got to Platteville, WI we had over a 1,500 foot ceiling and visibility over 6 miles, we would be able to keep going. The weather reports showed good VFR to our west and by the time we made our first fuel stop at Mason City, IA the sky was clear and the visibility was unlimited. We fueled both the airplane and ourselves with a quick lunch at the airport diner and were off for Mitchell, SD

Every town, Iowa. A railroad track, grain elevator, church and ball park.

At every stop people commented on our zebra stripe paint job. We would tell them that the airplane was made in South Africa and the BushCat name referred to the African bush where the airplane was flown extensively. We would tell them of our planned flight from 10C to Anchorage and tell them they could follow our progress on the **BushCatUSA.com** web site.

Our plan was to refuel at Mitchell, SD and fly on to Wall, SD where we planned on spending the night. This is where our ground support team (my wife Nancy) proved invaluable during the whole flight. Once we knew we would reach Wall we texted her and she found a motel with airport pick-up for us. It made the trip so much easier not having to put the airplane away then try to find a place to stay. We were tired

278

and hungry and having the hassle of finding a place to stay would have been difficult.

When we landed at Wall we were met by the ex-mayor and he helped us tie down and filled us in on what to do and where to eat. In the meantime I called the number Nancy texted me for the motel. Our driver was the owner of the motel. It was a clean and low cost motel that was very comfortable.

The plan for the morning was to fly to Rapid City, SD fuel up then fly over Mount Rushmore and then on to Devils Tower. Parker and I met in the motel office at 0630 for a continental breakfast of orange juice and granola bars. Not exactly the breakfast of champions to propel us on a long day of flying.

DAY 2

It was cool and calm for our 35 minute trip to Rapid City. Most of the places we stopped for fuel were self-service. I like them because we could get in and out quickly with a minimum waist of time.

Departing Rapid City we asked for, and were given, a vector to Mount Rushmore. The work of carving the presidents into Mt. Rushmore began in 1927 and was completed in 1941. During the 14 years of construction the 400 workers earned $8.00 a day while carving the monument out of the granite.

We had to climb to 7,700 feet to fly over the monument and at full gross weight it took a while. We were sure glad Jeremy installed the heater in the airplane. It was near freezing as we climbed to 7,700. The sky was clear and we got some great shots of the Presidents on Mt Rushmore.

From there we cut right across the middle of the Black Hills enroute to Devils Tower in northeast Wyoming. As we crossed the Black Hills there were very few roads or fields to make an emergency landing. The day was warming fast and we started to get buffeted by thermals and mechanical turbulence. The black of the trees contrasted with the still present white snow in the high country, the greening grass of the valleys and blue sky made the Black Hills beautiful. We flew over a few ranches and camp sites but most of the terrain is untouched. We were still at 7,500 feet but we were at times just a couple of thousand feet above the ground.

As we flew north the Black Hills gave way to much lower rolling grasslands with rock escarpments sticking up through the grass. We saw I-90 snaking past Sturgis and

Spearfish South Dakota as we continued toward Devils Tower. We needed to see if there really was a base for alien space craft on top!

Devils Tower slowly took form as we approached the single 1,267 foot rock column. We circled and took a lot of video and pictures. We were both impressed with its grandeur. It was a short flight from Devils Tower is Hulett Wyoming. Hulett is at 4264 feet elevation (high) and the temperature had risen into the 80's. There was no wind and no traffic so we landed toward the end of the runway where the fuel pumps were located. There was an operations office that was unattended and locked but, as we found very often on this trip, the combination was a code that a pilot could easily figure out. We

refueled and were on our way in about 30 minutes. There was still no wind so we elected to takeoff from the close end of the runway to minimize our taxiing. We knew the density altitude was about 4,900 feet. That means the airplane would perform like it was at 4,900 feet. As the density altitude increases the performance of any aircraft decreases. We would have a slower acceleration to our takeoff speed. We would use more runway and we would climb slower. Checking the surrounding terrain we chose the takeoff path that involved the least amount of climb needed. Even though our takeoff run was longer than normal it wasn't bad at all for our weight and density altitude. We pointed our nose northwest and began our trek to the Custer Battle Field and Laurel, Montana.

It was a little over 2 hours flying over some of the most desolate terrain in the lower 48 states. It was rolling hills with brown grass and dirt roads. Occasionally there would be a ranch house. The question that kept going through my mind was why? Why would anyone live here? It is dry, dusty, desolate, cut off and alone. A trip to the grocery store would take all day.

We could see I-90 and make out the Custer Battle field in the distance. We flew over the trails and markers and I could almost see the battle of June 25, 1876. The land was rolling and grass covered, easy for men on horseback to maneuver and approach unseen. Nancy and I visited the Battle Field on a previous trip. It is a very interesting place and worth a stop, unfortunately there is not an airport close enough for us to land at and go to the battlefield.

Laurel Montana was another quick gas stop. We couldn't get a ride into town for lunch so we just ate several of the protein bars I brought along. This became the norm. I sure am glad I brought a lot of them.

The takeoff from Laurel was another at high density altitude, as most of the rest would be. Again we had a long roll and slow climb. I had checked weather and knew we would be flying into rain showers and an approaching cold front. Jeremy was working with XM radio to activate our XM weather on the GPS and with impeccable timing the XM came on just after leaving Laurel, just in the nick of time. We could see on the GPS the rain around Great Falls and Cut Bank, Montana all the way into Canada.

The Judith Gap is a gap in the mountains between Laurel and Great Falls Montana. This gap is orientated roughly east and west and with either north or south winds they pile up at the gap and accelerate. As we were approaching the gap so was the cold front. The wind steadily increased and the ride got more and more turbulent. Parker and I were searching for a way through the gap and associated strong wind and rain. Our ground speed went from 85mph to 32mph. We turned right to go parallel to the front looking for a break in the rain. We had a clear escape route to the south back to Laurel but we gave ourselves 10 minutes to find a path through or we would make a dash for Laurel. It was getting so rough that we slowed to 80mph for turbulence penetration. We hit several down drafts that were so strong that even with full power we were still descending at 600 to 800 feet per minute and we were only about 2,000 feet above the ground. We were over mostly open fields that would have made a successful emergency landing possible if it came to that. Parker and I made a 180 degree turn and our ground speed zoomed up to 128mph. This front was only about five miles wide and I spotted what looked like a way through. Parker and I quickly conferred and

decided to commit to it. Our ground speed was again down to 32mph and the turbulence stayed with us. Slowly we penetrated the front with the rate of climb jumping around from 800 feet down to 600 feet up with the turbulence ever present. As we proceeded mile by mile the ground speed slowly increased. First it was 40mph then 43mph, a few minutes later it was 48mph then 50mph. Finally we were through it. Our ground speed stopped at 63mph. It was a far cry from 85 of only a few minutes ago but that was it. I recalculated our fuel burn and came to the conclusion that we would not be able to make it to our intended overnight stop of Cut Bank Montana. We headed for Ft. Benton, Montana.

We texted Nancy and asked her to find a place for us to stay in Ft. Benton. The XM weather showed a few showers on our path but it wouldn't be a major problem. When we landed I checked my phone and found Nancy had gotten us a motel room. She said there wasn't much there and she hoped it would be okay. I called the number she provided and the owner came right out to meet us. They were very nice people and we appreciated the ride into town. However, when we pulled into the driveway I saw what Nancy meant. My first thought was the Bates Motel. It was straight out of 1958. I inspected the room. It was clean and turned out to be comfortable. The only place to eat was the VFW club. It was about a half mile walk and we appreciated the chance to stretch our legs. Even though the BushCat is comfortable, we'd been sitting in that cockpit for two long days.

We had some good fried chicken then took a leisurely walk back along the Missouri River. There was a cool statue of Lewis and Clark along with Sacagawea and a replica river boat.

DAY 3

We woke up early and wanted to put a lot of miles behind us, but that is not what Mother Nature had in mind. I checked the weather and found scattered rain showers and low ceilings around Ft. Benton and they got more numerous to the north going right up deep into Canada. We got a ride to the airport from the motel manager. We did our pre-flight on the airplane even though we knew we wouldn't be leaving right away. I checked the radar on my phone then on the GPS-XM. Our planned jump off point for our boarder crossing of Cut Bank Montana was not going to work, but Shelby looked okay. We decided to call Nancy and have her make the necessary changes to our e-APIS notification before we left Ft. Benton. After several hours we departed for Shelby Mt.

The visibility was good after takeoff but the ceiling was only about 900 feet. With a combination of rising terrain and lowering clouds we ended up flying under 600agl at times. Parker was navigating and checking the map for towers and I was flying the terrain and dodging the few towers on our route. When we landed at Shelby Montana it was raining and cold. There were a couple of local pilots in the office and Parker talked with them while I tried to dry out our maps. I had the office looking like a laundry room with maps spread out everywhere. There was a courtesy car at the airport so Parker and I took it to town for some breakfast. If there is one thing I have learned in aviation it is that, whenever you have an opportunity to eat or pee, take it because you never know when the next one will come around.

We ate at the local truck stop. The food was pretty good. We were in no hurry; it was raining harder than ever. I called Nancy to change our e-APIS border crossing time again. I called Canadian Customs to do the same.

In all we hung around the Shelby airport for almost 6 hours and changed our proposed boarder crossing time at least four times. Nancy became an expert at it.

Finally the weather broke enough for us to give it a shot. I called Great Falls radio from the ground to activate our cross border flight plan but there was no answer. That was not unusual so we departed to try and activate our flight plan once we were airborne but we still couldn't make contact. We couldn't go without activating our flight plan and we weren't sure if our radio was working. We returned to Shelby. As soon as we landed Parker pulled his headset jack out from the plug to see if it was loose and reseating it would make it work. As he did that we discovered the problem, a stream of water came poring out of the jack. With all of the rain some had made its way into the radio headset connection box and shorted out the headsets. I hoped the radio was okay and by drying out the box it would work. Exasperated, I called Nancy to change our border crossing time once again. I called Canadian Customs from the plane and changed our arrival time in Lethbridge, Alberta to 1700 local time. We dried out the box and tested the radio. It worked! We wrapped the box in plastic to prevent a recurrence of the problem. Instead of changing our time again we waited for our last proposed departure time to come and we were off. I was able to contact Great Falls radio and activate our flight plan and get a transponder code.

There were scattered rain showers enroute that we had to dodge and the terrain was increasing giving us less and less ground clearance. As we got lower Parker said he was glad I had been a crop-duster. We were almost close enough to the cattle to read their ear tags. Lethbridge weather was still reporting good VFR and about 30 miles out our flight conditions started to improve.

We landed at Lethbridge right on the time I had given them. We closed our flight plan and asked for directions to the customs ramp. There was no customs agent to meet us. That is often the case. I got out of the plane and walked to the customs door but it was locked and there was no one around. I called Canpass and reported our arrival. The customs agent asked a few questions and gave me a number to put in the window of the plane to show we had cleared customs. I asked if we were free to move the airplane. He said, "Yes, you are good to go."

Parker and I taxied over to the FBO and tied the airplane down and fueled it. Nancy had gotten us a motel room but we had to call for a cab. Forty-five minutes later we were on our way to the Holiday Inn Express. We were tired and hungry so we wasted no time checking in and heading to the restaurant. While we were eating I got a call from a number I didn't recognize so I didn't answer. I didn't have a Canadian calling package and the roaming charges were $1.00 a minute. There was a voice message so I decided to listen. It was the district supervisor for Canadian Customs and he didn't sound happy. A dollar a minute or not, I called right back. He started by asking why we were not at the airplane when his officers arrived and why we were two hours late on our planned arrival time. I told him I had changed the arrival time by phone and had landed right on time. I further stated that I called Canpass and the officer told me we were cleared in and could leave. He asked the name of the officer. I said I hadn't gotten his name but I did get a clearance number. He said with surprise, you did, what is the number? I explained that I was at dinner and didn't have it with me but I could get it. I also explained that I had put the number in the windshield of the airplane as required. His attitude changed and he asked me to call back with the clearance number. I said I would.

I hurried the rest of my dinner while Parker taunted me saying I was going to be arrested. Back in our room I called the customs supervisor back and gave him the clearance number. He thanked me and said, "Sorry for the confusion and welcome to Canada". I wasn't going to jail!

DAY 4

I woke at 0600 and looked out the window; rain, low ceilings and fog. I didn't bother waking Parker. I crawled back into bed and went to sleep.

0800 I got up again and looked out the window, the same weather greeted me. I got my phone and checked the aviation weather forecast. It told the story, low IFR everywhere. We had a leisurely breakfast and just waited for the weather to clear.

DAY 5

Day five started like day 4 but the forecast was for improvement in the afternoon.

We stayed at the Holliday Inn until checkout time then took a cab to the airport. Not wanting another radio problem and having days of rain I had moved the airplane into the hanger the previous night. I kept checking weather and updating our flight plan to Red Deer, Alberta.

Early afternoon the weather looked good enough to take off. Parker and I were doing the preflight when I came to the right wheel. I looked at the clean concrete floor to see a little puddle of red fluid. I bent down to examine it further and sure enough it was brake fluid and it was coming from our right brake line. I exhaled in frustration and let out a few expletives. Can't we catch a break? Without brakes the airplane cannot be taxied because there is no steering system except for differential braking. I talked to the mechanic and he said he didn't have the parts to fix it. We needed a compression fitting, a length of brake line and a union to join it to the old brake line. One of the off duty line boys was there and offered to take me to town to try and find what we needed.

My phone wasn't working well since we flew over Devils Tower. Parker says it was because of the aliens. I think it was just poor AT&T coverage. It turned out later that I was wrong, the phone had gotten damaged and only worked sporadically but maybe Parker was right and it was the aliens.

After an extensive search of every auto parts store and truck repair place in Lethbridge, I returned to the airport to find that twenty minutes after I left to find the parts a private mechanic who worked on a corporate Lear Jet arrived and offered Parker the parts we needed to fix the brake. Because of my faulty phone he wasn't able to get the message to me.

As it turned out we were able to pull enough excess brake line through the float to repair it without splicing. Thirty minutes after I arrived back at the airport, with the help of the mechanics, the brake line was repaired and we were ready to depart.

It was a long taxi to the runway in a strong crosswind which was a good test for the repaired brake. It was working perfectly. Parker made a good crosswind takeoff and pointed us toward Red Deer. It was VFR with scattered light rain showers.

As we neared Calgary the weather improved with more widely scattered rain showers and, by the time we got to Red Deer, we were in good VFR. We had put the rain showers behind us, at least for now. We wanted to put as many miles behind us as possible because the bad weather was supposed to be back tomorrow. If we could get to Whitecourt today we should be north of the weather predicted for tomorrow, so we pressed on. Between Red

Deer and Whitecourt the sky turned blue and it warmed up considerably in the cockpit.

As we approached Whitecourt, we were advised of air tanker activity to our east and there were several Lockheed Electra air tankers that landed just in front of us. We learned of two fires in the area. One was a wooden train trestle and the other was a dumpster fire behind Wal-Mart. Air tankers put both of them out.

Luckily we had texted Nancy to get us a hotel room in Whitecourt before leaving Red Deer. As we learned at the hotel desk, because of the train trestle burning, the rail road had booked every room in town for the next few weeks to house the crew that was on the way to rebuild the trestle.

DAY 6

The day was beautiful, clear skies and unlimited visibility. We got a bit of a late takeoff due to a minor problem that the FBO at Whitecourt helped us with. Our route was direct to Grand Prairie, Alberta and then to Dawson Creek, British Columbia which is Mile Post 0 and the start of the Alaska Highway.

The construction of the Alaska Highway, aka the Alcan Highway, started on March 8 1942 just after the U.S. got into WWII and was finished eight month later on October 28, 1942. For decades it was a dirt and gravel road, but in recent years it has been updated to mostly paved highway.

We fueled the plane and then took a break for lunch. There was a nice deli in the terminal and there was even a comfortable pilot lounge where we could check the weather and file a flight plan for Fort Nelson, British Columbia, our stop for the night. As usual we called Nancy to find us a room in Fort Nelson.

We passed over Fort St John, B.C. and followed the highway north. We could see the front range of the Canadian Rockies, on our left, all day. Knowing we would be flying through them tomorrow filled us with a sense of excitement and a little apprehension. We were flying through the heat of the day and the trip to Fort Nelson was a bit rough because of a lot of thermals and maybe some mechanical turbulence from the mountains and irregular terrain we were flying over.

At Fort Nelson we tied down the airplane and called the number Nancy had texted us for our cab ride to the hotel. The air was hot, the wind was calm and the mosquitoes numerous as we waited forty five minutes for our ride.

The hotel was new and very nice. It had internet service so checking weather and filing our flight plan in the morning would be easy.

DAY 7

The weather was good and the winds moderate so we decided to follow the Alaska Highway through the mountains to Watson Lake, Yukon Territory. We were between 5,000 and 6,000 feet as we worked our way through the mountains. This is easily the most beautiful part of the trip. We passed the Toad River airstrip and then Muncho Lake. Muncho Lake is a brilliant green blue color owing the green to copper oxides. The Alaska Highway offered the only emergency landing area since we were in the heart of the Canadian Rockies, surrounded by mountains that were much higher than we were.

At the North end of Muncho Lake we had to make a couple of jogs to get through the pass that led us out of the mountains for now and over Liard Hot Springs.

There is a large park and campground at the hot springs. On a previous ground trip Nancy and I stopped and walked the board walk to the hot springs. I didn't have a swim suit, I was going to Alaska, and the Canadians frown on skinny dipping so all I could do was dip my toe in. It was quite hot. The setting is in a swamp and pine forest. It is very picturesque. As there is no airstrip close, I checked with Nav. Canada to see if it was permissible to land on the road in front of the park and found that it is not permitted near the park. Landing on roads in other areas is not specifically permitted or specifically denied. In other words it's good unless something happens then it's bad.

The highway snaked through rolling hills and along side the Laird River on its way to Watson Lake, our next fuel stop. We didn't exactly follow the road. We tried to cut some of the corners but we stayed close enough so we would either be able to make the road for a forced landing or at least have a short walk if we couldn't make the road. How lucky we felt determined how far we would stray from the road.

Watson Lake is little more than a wide spot in the road. On a previous trip I was able to borrow a car from the guy that operated the Nav. Canada facility, and at that time operated one of two fuel concessions, to go into town and see the Sign Post Forest. The Sign Post Forest was started during the construction of the Alaska Highway when some home sick soldier put up a sign pointing the direction to home and how far it was. It soon got out of hand and there were hundreds of signs put up. The practice has continued to this day and if you bring a sign with you they will give you a hammer and nail to hang it. There are thousands of signs there and it is pretty cool. A cab ride into town was around $50 so if you can't borrow a ride, have a lot of cash.

Parker and I circled the Sign Post Forest and called it good. We circled Watson Lake at low level and took a look at the remains of a WWII bomber on the south shore. The lake was still frozen so we couldn't make out the tail submerged under a few inches of water. We landed, refueled and ate another protein bar before saddling up for the leg to Whitehorse, Yukon.

It was a two hour and twenty minute flight from Watson Lake to Whitehorse with good weather. When we departed

Watson Lake we angled to intercept the highway. We saw our first moose just south of Watson Lake and circled for a picture. As we approached Teslin Lake I could make out the bridge and clearing where the town of Teslin is located. It looked like a nice little town with an unpaved runway next to the highway and near the north shore of Teslin Lake by Nitsulin Bay. Teslin Lake is over 70 miles long and the town of Teslin is located a little over half way up the lake.

We followed the north shore at low level admiring some of the log homes and fishing lodges we passed over and shaking our heads at some of the neglected rundown shacks that also occupied the shoreline.

At the northwest end of Teslin Lake we made a ninety degree left turn to follow the Alaska Highway as it passed through the mountain pass toward Whitehorse, the capitol of Yukon. At Marsh Lake we were able to pickup Whitehorse ATIS and contact Whitehorse tower for a landing clearance. They had us come in right over town that allowed for some great photographs. We were to land to the southwest. The runway began at the top of a cliff of several hundred feet in height. It was a very deceptive visual approach. We were about three hundred feet over the town but only about one hundred feet over the runway. We were pointed right into a 15 mile per hour wind and I was ready for a down draft just before the runaway because of the steep drop off. We got a little down draft but with the extra speed we were carrying we easily compensated and make a good landing. We got clearance from ground control to taxi to the self service fuel pumps at the end of the ramp and refueled for our departure the next morning. Fueling completed, we taxied to a parking spot just under the tower and secured the BushCat for the night.

My phone still wasn't working well but Parker was able to get Nancy on his phone and as usual she had gotten us a room.

DAY 8

It was cold, just above freezing. At the airport we made our way to the FSS office just to the right of the tower. We checked weather and filed our cross boarder flight plan to Northway, Alaska where we planed to clear customs. Nancy had updated our boarder crossing time with e-APIS, she was becoming a pro at that, and I called Northway customs to coordinate our arrival with them.

As we departed Whitehorse we could see the Yukon River and Lake Laberge, made famous by the Robert Service poem *The Cremation of Sam McGee.* The sight of the Yukon River and Lake Laberge made me think back in history to the 99ers as they ran the turbulent Yukon River right here, in anything that would float, in a quest to "make it rich" in the gold fields. The rapids that gave Whitehorse its name are long gone. A dam was built to supply electricity and calm the waters, but if you look hard, you can still make out a ghostly image of the 99ers on the river.

It was a long leg and we would be tight on fuel so we cut the corners off the highway as we headed for Northway. We had our vests and jackets on and were doubly glad Jeremy had installed the optional heater in the BushCat before we left. We had good visibility but overcast skies and intermittent snow showers. We were hampered by head winds and some light turbulence. We dodged a few snow showers and flew through a couple of others until we got to

Kluane Lake. I could see dust being kicked up on the southeastern edge of the lake at the settlement of Silver. There was a cut in the mountains there and the wind would often accelerate off Kaskawulsh Glacier, down the mountain slope and come roaring out across the Alaska Highway and Teslin Lake. We hugged the northeast (down wind) side of Kluane Lake so the wind would both have time and distance to dissipate and we would be on the up flow side of any wind that remained. Surprisingly the ride wasn't any worse than light turbulence.

We could see dark snow showers ahead that appeared to block our path. We passed the airport at Burwash Landing and could see the showers went from left to right covering the entire valley we needed to cross to make it to Northway. We poked our nose in and the snow was heavy and the visibility was poor. We turned around and started to climb. We were going to try to get over a ridgeline to our south and maybe get around the snow but that didn't work. Not wanting to waste fuel we made a hasty retreat to Burwash Landing airport. In my haste to land I forgot to call the airport common frequency for an airport advisory, a point the local Nav Canada radio operator reminded me of.

There was a nice little terminal building occupied only by the radio operator. Unlike the U.S. almost every airport has a radio operator. They are not controllers but attempt to organize traffic and provide local winds and traffic, much like our Unicom, but with much more reliability. As usual there was no food available so we each had another protein bar. We talked to the radio operator and he said that the snow had been there all morning and wasn't expected to clear until the afternoon. We had a border crossing time so I texted Nancy and asked her to file an update. I called Northway, Alaska customs and told them we were forced to land because of bad weather and would not make our landing time at Northway. The customs agent sighed and said that that was too bad because an agent had just been sent to Northway for us and she couldn't recall him, and it was a two hour round trip. I was surprised. I had cleared customs at Northway before and there had been an officer stationed there. The customs agent said they didn't do that any more and they were now dispatched from a border crossing station on the highway. It was an hour and thirty minutes flying time from Burwash Landing to Northway so I would take that into consideration with my updated arrival times and notifications to customs.

The next thing on our list was fuel. After talking to the radio operator we were informed that there was a local air tour operator who would sell fuel if he had extra. We called him and were in luck. He said he would be out in about an hour and would sell us ten gallons of 100LL. That would give us plenty of fuel to make Northway and then Tok. Northway doesn't have fuel anymore which makes it very inconvenient for us and other pilots transiting the area.

In all we waited for six hours at Burwash Landing for the weather to improve enough to continue our flight. We kept everyone updated and had no problem crossing the border. By the time we landed at Tok, Alaska, we were tired and hungry and decided to spend the night. There is a great restaurant just across the Alaska Highway from the airport at Tok and it also had rooms. This one we did on our own without Nancy's help. We ate a good dinner and had time to do our laundry. This was the second time we did laundry on this trip. We were very limited on our baggage but found it easy to find laundry facilities enroute.

DAY 9

We got an early start with clear skies and crisp air. We took the Glenn Highway cutoff from Tok through the mountains to Gulkana. As we were twisting our way through the mountains, following the highway, we encountered some mechanical turbulence. We were at 5,000 feet but still below the mountain tops. The upper level winds were hitting the mountain tops and rolling around and down on us. The ride was a little uncomfortable but the scenery was spectacular. We were able to get some video and stills despite being bounced around.

After a quick fuel stop at Gulkana we were back in the air for our final leg to Anchorage. Just west of Gulkana we passed the Alaska Pipeline. It runs from the Arctic Ocean to Valdez Alaska on the coast of the Gulf of Alaska, a distance of about 800 miles. It was starting to get windier and the turbulence increased. The Tazlina Lake and Tazlina Glacier soon came into view to our south. We got some great pictures but because of the winds and turbulence we didn't want to try to fly over them, besides we wanted to get to Anchorage.

As we proceeded over the highway toward Anchorage the mountains continued to grow around us until they were well above us and we were flying over the highway hidden in a small valley. We were slowed to 80mph for turbulence and got continuous light turbulence with an occasional moderate bump. As we were coming out of the mountains onto the Anchorage plain I could see a wall of dust blowing up from the Matanuska River as the wind carrying it hit the hundred foot tall bank as the river made a sharp left hand turn. We made our turn toward Palmer and Anchorage short of the wall of dust and turbulence then hugged the mountain face on the upwind side rather than the downwind side. Because the mountain was so much higher than we were flying we thought this technique would give us the best ride and keep us clear of all of the controlled airspace coming up. It worked. We had a fairly smooth ride.

We contacted Anchorage approach and asked for radar flight following to Anchorage Ted Stevens International Airport. This is actually a complex of three airports co-located. The Ted Stevens Airport is the main airport. It is a large international airport serving international flights to Asia. Fed Ex also has a base there for their international services. There are two major runways. Runway 33/15 is 10,960 feet long and 150 feet wide. Runway 07/25 is 12,400 feet long and 200 feet wide. In this complex is also a gravel runway for light planes using large tundra tires and skis in winter. There is also the Lake Hood seaplane base. It is the biggest seaplane base in the world with hundreds of seaplanes based there. We had a good view of the city of Anchorage to our right as we kept close to the mountain and east of the highway to stay clear of all of the controlled airspace in the area.

We were cleared to land on runway 33 with a 30 degree right cross wind of 17 gusting to over 22K. On final approach we slid downwind of the left side of the runway, then we lined up into the wind and across the runway, pointed for the taxiway we planned on using to exit the runway. The runway is 150 feet wide and with the wind we had, we could have landed on it widthwise. It would be no problem landing on an angle and getting to taxi speed before exiting the runway.

We secured the BushCat in transient parking and, just as we finished, Parker's phone rang. It was our friend Mike from Galt airport. He said, "I see from the Spot track that you have landed in Anchorage. Where can I meet you?" We didn't even know he was going to Anchorage. Mike graciously offered to pick us up and we ended up spending the rest of our time in Anchorage with him.

We made it, at least we made it most of the way. Parker was an iron man. Of the 40 hours it took us to get to Anchorage, I flew all but about 2½ of them.

We spent half of Saturday, our arrival day, and all of Sunday at the Alaska Airman's Association trade show. It was full of aircraft and aircraft mods and accessories especially suited to Alaska. It was an interesting experience. Of course I had to buy a $50 raffle ticket for a newly rebuilt Super Cub that I didn't win. We spent six days in Anchorage, four of them waiting for good enough weather to get to Valdez, Alaska for the STOL competition and show. That was the goal of the whole trip.

Jeremy and Dani arrived on Wednesday by commercial flight and went to Valdez on a Raven Airlines flight on Thursday morning. We told them we would keep trying to make it to Valdez for the show.

DAY 14 FRIDAY

We had been in Anchorage waiting on the weather to improve enough to fly to Valdez. The weather in Anchorage hadn't been all that bad with VFR conditions and intermittent light rain. The weather in Valdez wasn't that bad either, mostly VFR with occasional light rain. The problem was getting through the pass at Whittier and across the upper Gulf of Alaska. The winds had been blowing at 30 knots for the past four days making getting to the pass impossible for us. The weather cameras in the pass showed almost nothing but clouds. We had been checking with FSS (Flight Service Station) several times a day for the past four days and they could offer little encouragement for an improvement in the weather.

Today was different. The winds had slackened and the weather in the pass at Whittier was supposed to start to improve. We checked out of the room Nancy reserved for us at the Holliday Inn Select, near the airport, at 1300 and had them bring us to the airplane. We loaded our gear and checked with FSS again. We were hopeful. It looked like the weather might let us get through, but not quite yet. The next hourly report showed everything good except for the pass itself; it still showed a lot of cloud cover. We decided to go take a look. We could always turn around if the pass was closed. Even though we were eager to go, we were not going to push further than was safe. We texted Jeremy that we were going to give it a try and head for Valdez. He texted back, LOL. I thought LOL? Why would he text that?

We departed the gravel strip at Lake Hood and headed east. It was overcast with light winds. We made it to Whittier with no problems. I had flown over the pass once before but never through it. We entered cautiously, always

305

having an escape route. As we got into the pass, a lake appeared beneath us. With our floats it would make a good landing spot if we needed it. As we flew deeper the clouds started getting thicker. We saw that the lake was made by a glacier. Parker got a few quick shots with his phone's camera. When we got to the end of the lake we looked left through the pass. The clouds were everywhere but there was a soda straw opening to the ocean that was clear. We could clearly see the ocean and we knew there was an airport just the other side of the pass. We made a quick left turn and flew through the straw while we descended with the mountains just off both wings. As we came out over Whittier we were at 1,500 feet and our course over the ocean towards Valdez looked good with just a little light rain and five to eight miles visibility.

It was an hour flight from Whittier to Valdez. About thirty minutes out the ceiling started to drop and the visibility was down to about 3 miles and rain. I asked Parker to keep his finger on the map where we were and keep an eye out for cabins or villages if we needed to land on the ocean. We flew over a nice bay with a small fishing village and a couple of cabins.

As we got to about 30 miles from Valdez the ceiling went down to about 200 feet and the visibility was only about three quarters of a mile in rain and mist. Parker had his finger on the map and I was following the coastline. We were flying in a gray sky over a gray ocean next to gray mountains. It was a surreal sight. It was a tense few minutes but we soon flew out of the rain shower and the weather began to rapidly improve. The ocean surface was covered with chunks of ice that had calved from the many glaciers. The ceiling had increased to over 2,000 feet and we could climb higher to take in the beauty all around us. That is why I fly in Alaska, the challenge and rugged pure beauty of it.

As we approached Valdez we got the ATIS (Automated Terminal Information Service) weather and a landing clearance. We had finally made it. We taxied to the parking area, tied the BushCat down and called Jeremy. He said he couldn't believe we were there. He, Dani and Mike were driving to town to get some parts at Radio Shack for a video system when he looked up and saw an airplane. He recognized it in a second as his BushCat. Everyone else said no way but Jeremy was right, it was us. They had been following the weather too and thought we were kidding when I texted that we were going to give it a try. I told Jeremy I never kid about flying.

DAY 15 SATURDAY

We got to the Valdez Airport about 0800. Jeremy signed me up for the STOL competition that day and signed himself up for the flour bombing on Sunday. We were in the class with the experimental and light sport airplanes. Many of them were specially modified for the competition. One airplane had NO2 injection for more power and all of them were striped down to make them as light as possible. One of them even removed his tail wheel to save a few ounces. We knew that with our amphibious floats we would not be able to win the competition so we decided to show what the BushCat could really do. We loaded the BushCat with our survival gear, camping equipment, fishing poles and tackle, and half a tank of gas, then Parker and I both got in. We were just under max gross weight when we pulled up to the start line. The starter looked at us and just shook his head.

The winner was the Just Highlander Super STOL with a combined takeoff and landing distance of 103 feet. Second was a Chinook with a score of 144 feet. Third was the other Chinook with a score of 273 feet. Fourth was the Piper J-4 with a score of 319 feet. We finished fifth with a score of 775 feet, not bad for a fully loaded airplane ready to fly you to your fishing hole for the weekend.

Jeremy overheard a spectator looking at the BushCat and laughing saying it can't win, it is way too heavy. After Jeremy explained what we were doing by showing what performance we could get out of a fully loaded airplane ready to take you on you adventure instead of just jumping off the ground, as light as possible and unable to go anywhere, he thought for a second and said that was a great idea.

The STOL competition is a great event and it is fun to see how short a distance a plane can take off and land, but I hope in the future they will add a competition where you have to do what we did. Takeoff loaded for a fishing and camping trip with enough fuel to get there and back.

DAY 16 SUNDAY

Although Jeremy had signed up for the flour bombing contest with the weather looking like it was going to deteriorate in the Whittier pass later in the day, we all decided that Parker and I should leave as soon as we could so we wouldn't be stuck by the weather. We all had flights to make the next day.

It was a better flight to Anchorage than from Anchorage. The only problem we had was getting through the pass at Whittier again. The winds were okay but the clouds were moving in again. By the time we got there it was in the process of closing down. We heard a Cessna 180 on the radio going through the pass about five minutes ahead of us. We reached him on the radio and he said the pass was still open and the weather on the other side was good. When we arrived at the entrance to the pass the sky was a thin milky color. I knew it wouldn't be long before it would cloud up and be closed. We could see through the pass to the mountains on the other side and I knew there was a lake we could land on if necessary, so we continued. Whittier was still good and the pass was still open, but just barely. We made it through and were flying into improving weather. It was then that Parker told me he had to pee. There was no way we were going to go back through that pass to Whittier. He knew he would have to hold it. It was about thirty minutes to Anchorage and I could see he was in agony but there was nothing I could do. All he could say was, "I wish I didn't have that third cup of coffee!" We touched down on the seaplane pond at Lake Hood and I step taxied to the far end where the ramp was. As soon as I came off the step Parker opened the door and got out. He said he couldn't hold it anymore. I thought he was going to go right there on Lake Hood but he held it until we powered up the ramp and I set the brakes. He jumped down and made it to the port-a-potty with no time to spare! Note to self; make sure you have an empty, BIG, wide mouth bottle on board.

We secured the airplane and got a hotel for the night. I was leaving on an all-nighter for Seattle and Ketchikan, Parker was taking the all-nighter the following night back to Chicago.

What a trip!

BUSHCAT ANC TO 10C

The Flight Home

Three weeks after we departed Alaska, having left the BushCat there, Parker and I went back to Anchorage to bring it home to Galt Airport near Chicago.

The trip to Anchorage took about 6 hours on Alaska Airlines. Our trip home would take about 6 days if the weather held up, more if it didn't.

It was the first week of June and the weather had changed. It was warmer and dryer. It was now the tourist season so one more thing had changed too, the prices. The hotel we had stayed at for $99 a night was now nearly $200 a night. Nancy did her magic and got us a room at the Lake Hood Inn. The Lake Hood Inn is a nice bed and breakfast located right on Lake Hood. It has a nice deck overlooking the lake and headphones so you can listen to the float planes taking off and landing on Lake Hood. They had just changed to summer rates but Nancy sweet talked them into giving us the off season rate. It was a great room right next to the Lakeside Millennium Hotel.

When we arrived at Anchorage we went over to the airplane and gave it a thorough per-flight inspection and loaded our camping gear and a few other items we would not be needing for the night. We were also fortunate that a fuel truck pulled up and asked if we needed fuel. We were planning on getting it in the morning from the self-serve pump by the gravel runway but this was even easier. We said sure, we'll fill her up.

I woke up at dawn and checked the weather (looked out the window) then called flight service for a complete briefing. The weather looked great but turbulence was forecasted for our first leg from Anchorage to Tok.

We took a cab to the airplane and loaded up. Day one and only 3,400 miles to go. The transient parking ramp is not controlled and the taxiways are shared with the cars and trucks of people using the airport. We taxied to the gravel strip and got our clearance to depart. We also asked for flight following. The airspace around Anchorage is very densely packed with the mountains to the east and two controlled airports, an Air Force Base, an army airport and several other private and public airports. Once you get about fifty miles north of Anchorage and make the turn toward Gulkana you go from heavy traffic to flying in the bush. Two different worlds right next to each other. I once heard it said by some Alaskans that the nice thing about Anchorage is that it is so close to Alaska. I can see what they mean. Anchorage is much like any other medium size city. It has a lot of great restaurants and shopping. You can find anything there. Fifty miles away and you are in a different world.

The reported turbulence never happened. We made several pilot reports along our way to Tok and just enjoyed the scenery and our good fortune with the weather. The landing at Tok was more hazardous than we expected. The wind was out of the south and a direct cross wind for our landing. As we approached the runway, the trees on the south edge churned the wind into a swirling mess. The BushCat was rocking and rolling all the way to the runway. The landing wasn't one of my best but at least the airplane was re-usable.

We fueled up and I called Canpass, Canadian Customs, to give them the required two hour notice of our arrival. I also called Nancy so she could update our U.S. departure with e-APIS. Then Parker and I walked across the Alaska Highway for lunch at Fast Eddy's.

While we were having lunch it had gotten hotter and windier and as anyone who has flown an amphibious float plane can tell you, it is very difficult to taxi in a crosswind and we had a strong crosswind. We used a lot of right brake and blasts of power taxing down runway 25 for a runway 7 departure; even then it was hard to keep it going in some semblance of a straight line. We thought the takeoff would be a little easier than the taxi because we would have full power and the help of the ailerons by keeping the stick into the wind to help keep us straight. The crosswind and turbulence caused by the trees on the upwind side of the runway made it more difficult than we expected for takeoff. It was difficult to keep the airplane straight as we accelerated down the runway. Once we rotated and got airborne it was even worse. We were heavy and the hot turbulent air bounced us around and made it difficult to climb. To make things worse we hit a downdraft and were barely able to hold what meager altitude we had, let alone climb. We started to sink and we were beginning to question weather or not we would make it. Abruptly, the downdraft released us and we began a slow but steady climb, still bouncing around while heading to the Canadian border.

We crossed the Alaskan/Canadian border on time and, dodging a few rain showers, landed at Beaver Creek, Yukon to clear customs. Beaver Creek is along the Alaska Highway and the Canadian Customs checkpoint is visible from the airport. The runway is gravel, unattended and there is no fuel available. After shutting down the engine I called Canpass to report our arrival. Instead of an agent coming over to check us in we were given a clearance number and released into Canada. This was the second time on this trip that we were cleared in without anyone coming out to inspect us. I guess the Canadians are just more trusting then we are.

The trip home followed the same route as our trip to Alaska, so I will only add a few instances of note from our trip back to home.

We had filled our fuel tank at Tok, Alaska and none was available at Beaver Creek, Yukon. We knew fuel could be a problem if we were going to make it to Whitehorse on one tank of fuel. We cut the corners on the highway as much as possible but we ran into headwinds that were stronger than expected. Luckily the fuel tank is transparent and visible from the cockpit. I never trust gauges especially when fuel is going to be tight. Having the tank and fuel quantity visible gave me a lot more confidence in my fuel calculations. We turned a corner and ran into even stronger headwinds. It was looking like we would be under what we considered to be a safe reserve at Whitehorse. Haynes Junction is shown in the supplement as not having fuel available but it was the only airport between us and Whitehorse. We figured if we had to we would get into town somehow and get some car gas. I heard an aircraft call Haynes Junction traffic for landing. I called on the radio to that traffic and asked if there was fuel available. He said not normally but he could sell us some if we needed it. I thanked him and said we wouldn't be there for about twenty minutes he said he was still about ten out himself and that wouldn't be a problem.

We made another big turn along the highway that put us on a heading towards Haines Junction and Whitehorse. Our ground speed picked up a little more than ten miles an hour. I made a new fuel calculation and it showed, with the new ground speed, we could make it to Whitehorse with adequate reserves. I made another radio call to our new friend, thanked him, and said we wouldn't be needing that fuel after all.

We made it to Whitehorse with just under four gallons of fuel, enough for forty five minutes of flying time.

It was light turbulence form Whitehorse to Watson Lake with a few moderate bumps thrown in due to the daytime heating. There were also some widely scattered rain showers. We fueled up and checked weather for the leg from Watson Lake to Fort Nelson, BC. It called for possible scattered thunder showers, winds aloft at 10k and winds at Fort Nelson were calm. It looked great so we decided to follow the highway through the mountains just like we did on the way up.

It was about an hour and a half of flying until we got to the Liard Hot Springs and turned south to enter the mountains. We were having the usual light turbulence due to daytime heating but clear skies and 10mph winds. As we worked our way into the mountains over the highway we started to get some moderate bumps. We passed it off to the tight canyon wall as we entered the mountains. The forecasted winds aloft were only 10k and Fort Nelson was calm, this shouldn't last long. We headed down Muncho Lake and the turbulence became continuously moderate with a lot of up and down drafts. The surface of the lake had some whitecaps but didn't look as bad as the ride we were experiencing would indicate. By the time we got to the south end of the lake it got really bad. We were in continuous moderate turbulence and downdrafts that made it impossible to hold altitude. We tried to hold 75 to 80 miles per hour for best rate of climb and turbulence penetration. We were at 4,500 feet but it was impossible to hold that. We would be at full power and sinking at 600 to 800 feet per minute, and then in an instant, we would be climbing at 700 feet per minute with the power near idle to keep our speed at turbulence penetration. It seemed the down drafts lasted longer than the up drafts and at times we thought we would be smashed into the ground. We couldn't keep the wings level or the attitude stable. We just held on and rode this bucking bronco through the mountains. We were afraid to try to turn around thinking we might be flipped upside down or stalled out in the shear. At one point, only half jokingly, I told Parker it was nice knowing him. We both kept calm and did our best to make it through. Parker navigated, telling me what to expect up ahead and I tried to steer a path on the down wind side of our route that would give us more up drafts than down drafts.

Time slows down, at times like this, you live every second, second by second. I don't know how long it took to get through those mountains, an hour, a life time, I don't know.

Parker kept telling me we were just about out of it but it continued. The valley was wider and I could see the end of the mountains but the turbulence would not stop. We cleared the last ridge between us and Fort Nelson but still the turbulence would not stop.

Finally, Fort Nelson was in sight and we were out of the mountains. The ride was better but it stayed rough until we were parked and the BushCat was tied down. We were beat physically and mentally. We were ready for a cocktail and a good night's sleep.

The next morning the leg from Fort Nelson to Dawson Creek presented its own challenges. We got an early start and the cool air gave us a better ride for a while. The wind had shifted and was now out of the west. There were forest fires along our route and a restricted area that we couldn't go around. We would have to climb to 7,000 feet to go over it. At 7,000 we were experiencing light mountain wave and it was very difficult to maintain altitude, in fact we couldn't maintain altitude. The wave would give us 500 feet per minute up followed by 500 feet per minute down. We would have to go from full power in the sink to half power in the lift, all the time trying to stay above 7,000 feet.

When we landed at Dawson Creek it was so windy we couldn't leave the airplane untied. We fueled up and taxied through the rough grass to a tie down spot. Dawson Creek has a nice deli where we had lunch and a pilot lounge where we took a break for a couple of hours hoping the wind and turbulence would subside.

The next four days we had continuous light to moderate turbulence due to winds and daytime heating.

We landed at Clyde Ice Black Hills Airport at Spearfish, SD for fuel and lunch. The density altitude was about 6,200 feet with no wind and higher terrain all around. We had waited several hours for the temperature and turbulance to go down, we were tired of the rough ride. Because of the high density altitude we did not fill our fuel tank, instead we just put in enough to make it to Rapid City, SD with a good reserve. The wind was only about 3 miles per hour favoring runway 31 but we chose to depart on 13. The reason we

317

chose to take off with a slight tailwind along with the high density altitude is because on runway 31 there was an up slope and we would be pointed to higher terrain. By taking off on runway 13 we would be down slope and heading into a valley of slightly lower terrain that was big enough to circle in if we needed to before continuing to Rapid City. This worked well and we did have to circle to climb over the terrain and continue to Rapid City.

By the time we made it home we were beat. It finally smoothed out about an hour and a half from home. We were met by our wives, Jeremy and Dani and a few friends. Nancy had a cold dirty martini in her hand waiting for me when we shut down the engine. We both just sat there for a minute happy that we made it home and trying to get the old bones moving again. Nancy really knows how to take care of me.

CONCLUSION

The BushCat proved itself on this trip, especially on the trip home, dealing with all of the turbulence. It wasn't made for this kind of trip but we showed it was capable of it. We also found the BushCat to be quite comfortable for the long days in the air. In good VFR weather any competent pilot with proper planning can make this trip of a life time. Know your limitations and DON'T PUSH THE WEATHER. That being said I have described flying through some weather that was less than good VFR but I always had an out, a place to go if it deteriorated to un-flyable where I was. Fly the terrain. When you are out of the flat lands the best route between two points is not necessarily a straight line. Make sure you have plenty of time. As I described, you can be grounded for several days. Make the best of it. Bring that book you always wanted to read, rent a car, take a tour or enjoy the pool, don't push the weather!

APPENDIX

Distance: 3,280 statute miles each way to Anchorage
            140 statute miles each way to Valdez

Days traveled: 9 days up and 6 days back, 6 days in Anchorage, 4 of them waiting for weather to proceed to Valdez

Valdez STOL competition: 5th place in the Exp/ LSA division (out of 5 competitors)
We were loaded to near gross weight, with 2 people, all our survival and fishing gear, plus full fuel, the others were striped and some   had NO2 injection.

Time: 39.7 hours 10C- PANC

Fuel used: 406 gallons 10C-PANC-PAVD-PALH-10C

Fuel cost: About $2,275

Route: fuel stop to fuel stop. RON= Remain Over Night

From	To	Time		Distance (SM)
10C	MCW	3.1		256
MCW	MHE	2.7		239
MHE	6V4	2.3		210
6V4	RAP	.6	RON	40
RAP	W43	1.6		99
W43	6S8	2.7		216
6S8	79S	2.6	RON	173
79S	SBX	.9		74
SBX	CYQL	1.0	RON-2	86
CYQL	CYQF	2.1		183
CYQF	CYZU	1.8	RON	156
CYZU	CYDQ	2.2		206
CYDQ	CYYE	2.8	RON	231
CYYE	CYQH	3.0		266
CYQH	CYXY	2.8	RON	232
CYXY	CYDB	2.0		148
CYDB	PFTO	2.4	RON	185
PFTO	PAGK	1.3		115
PAGK	PANC	1.8		165

TOTAL   39.7 HOURS   3280 SM

BAGGAGE

12 ga. shot gun and ammo
Flare gun and 3 flares, 3 railroad flares
One burner gas camp stove, mess kit for two
Freeze dried food for 7 days each
Gallon jar filled with protein bars

Sleeping bags
3 boxes of waterproof matches and 1 pack of fire starter sticks
Tent, tarp and parachute line
Fishing poles filet knife and lures
Inflatable life jackets
Rain jackets, mosquito head nets
Winter coats and vests
Rubber boots, 2pr
Paddle and float pump
Engine oil
Duct tape, you never know when you will need it
Tools kit and spare parts, multi-tool, lighter, saw and pocket knife
Two small duffle bags for clothes each
SPOT ELT and extra batteries
Canadian charts, notebook and pens
i-pad for internet, weather and pictures
Camcorder

THE PILOTS

Parker is a retired construction superintendent with a commercial pilot's license. He was in Special Forces during Vietnam and is an avid sportsman. He has hunted and fished all over the world including several trips to Alaska. He also hosts a radio show called *Aviation Life* on FM 101.5 Huntley Community Radio and on the web at www.huntleyradio.com.

Dan Johnson is a retired American Airlines Captain. He started his aviation career as a crop-duster and freight pilot for 10 years before joining the airline. After retiring from the airline he worked in Southeast Alaska for three years flying a Beaver on floats.

JUDGEMENT

We hear a lot about judgment and risk management in making aviation decisions. Just what is it and where do we buy it?

Judgment, it is something we as pilots all need to have and learn to develop to help us avoid trouble or limit its effect once we get into it. I'll relate a recent event that happened to me.

I needed to get night current for a flight I wanted to take. I waited until an hour after sunset and began to taxi my Cessna 185 on amphibious floats to the end of the runway. The 185 sits up high when it's on amphibious floats and it makes a narrow runway look even narrower. The runway and taxiway were freshly repaved (black) and Notamed that the runway markings were not painted. To top it off, the new taxiway did not have lights on it. I taxied slowly; however, it was still hard to follow the taxiway.

I continued to the run-up pad and finished my "Before Take-off" checklist. I turned my taxi light back on and went into position on the runway. It was dark – very dark. I turned on the landing light and it still didn't illuminate the runway very well. To make matters worse, the sides of the runway had been filled with new black dirt and seeded. The grass hadn't come up yet and that made it hard to identify where the unmarked runway ended, and the "grass" began. I really wanted to get this night currency so I could take my wife to a dinner party at a nearby airport the next evening. I thought about it for a moment and decided the conditions weren't good enough. I really wanted to do this but the decision not to go was a good one. (Judgment)

I started to taxi back to the hangar. It was hard to see, even at taxi speed. As I approached the taxiway, remember that it had no taxiway lights, I started my turn. A moment later I realized that I had missed the turn and was sinking into the mud. I didn't push the throttle to the stop to try to power it out. (Judgment) I closed the throttle and shut down the engine. As I walked back to the hangar with my trusty little flashlight in hand, a car approached down the taxiway. It was my friend, Mike, wondering where I was. I quickly explained what had happened.

I called Flight Service to advise that the runway was blocked and made plans to get the plane out of the mud. Mike got help from our friends, Mike, Shawn and, later, Joe.

We brought a pickup truck down the runway with a couple of ropes to try to pull it out. We attached the ropes to the spreader bars and slowly started to pull. The ropes took up a strain but the plane didn't move. I stopped the truck. I didn't want to break anything! (Judgment)

It was going to take a lot more effort to get it unstuck and back in to the hangar. We tried to jack it up and put plywood under the wheels. The floats have a trailing link landing gear so, as we jacked the floats up, the gear just kept extending. We ran out of jack travel before we could get the wheels out of the mud. That wasn't going to work. We finally had to get the airport Bobcat with forks and a strap to lift the 185, one float at a time, high enough to get the plywood under the wheels. Once the plywood was under the wheels it was easy to pull the 185 back onto the runway and back to the hangar. It took three hours to get it out of the mud and another hour to clean it up the next day. No damage was incurred during the process. I have had to take the expected ribbing and my 185 has a new nickname, "Mud Dauber."

The point of the story is this; use your good judgment to avoid getting into trouble. If you do get into trouble, again, use your good judgment to keep it from becoming bigger trouble. Don't get in a hurry and make things worse. Slow down and think! Remember that you are only as good as your next decision.

Oh, by the way, afterwards the pizza and beer were on me!

DO I REALLY NEED ADVANCED SPIN TRAINING?

January 9, 2004

I met with Bob Hart at the local greasy spoon to finalize my purchase of his Pitts S1-C. Bob had spent nine years building the Pitts and it showed every loving minute Bob took with it. He asked if I minded if he brought Gerry Molidor, who is Bob's friend and also the president of the International Aerobatics Club (IAC) along with him. I had met Gerry a few times at the airport and quickly agreed.

We sat down and ordered our lunch. Bob and I finished the paper work and the three of us began to talk about how I was going to get checked out in the Pitts. We also talked about aerobatics and the Pitts. Bob loaned me his copy of "Spins In The Pitts Special" by Gene Beggs. Gerry loaned me "Fly For Fun" by Bill Thomas and some back issues of "Sport Aerobatics" magazine. Bob and Gerry were both very helpful and offered their assistance in getting me properly checked out in my new Pitts. I enthusiastically accepted their offer.

My insurance company requires 5 hours of instruction in a two place Pitts before insuring me. I thought that was a good idea anyway. Both Bob and Gerry suggested, as part of that 5 hours, I should get some advanced spin training. Although I am a very experienced pilot, I am not a very experienced aerobatics pilot. Even though I don't intend to become a competition aerobatics pilot, I thought the training would be fun and good insurance.

The Pitts is a beautiful airplane; small, powerful and agile, real eye candy in the air as well as on the ground. I began looking at it a little differently though as I taxied it from Bob's hanger over to mine. The Pitts S1-C has a short wing span, just over 17 feet, with a full span aileron on the bottom wing, so the roll rate will be fast. The main landing gear is close together and the ground clearance at the wing tip is only 18 inches so I will have to be careful of obstructions while taxiing and during landings, especially in cross winds, I will have to be careful not to put the up wind wing too low. The distance from the main gear to the tail wheel is also short, 12 feet 4 inches so the tendency to ground loop will be high. The Haigh tail wheel is locking and extends about a foot further aft than the Scott tail wheel, both those features will help to keep her straight on takeoff and lessen the ground looping tendencies. The Lycoming O-360 180 h.p. engine with a fixed pitch propeller will generate a lot of torque and P-factor. Rotating from the three-point position to a tail high attitude for takeoff will also introduce gyroscopic precession into the equation, wanting to turn the Pitts even more to the left during that maneuver. I had better be ready on that right rudder. Yes, my Pitts S1-C is beautiful and seductive but I'm beginning to see the fire-breathing dragon in her.

When I got home, I started looking through all the material Bob and Gerry had given me. I pulled out Gene Beggs's book on spins. After the introduction and table of contents, the only thing written on page one in red lettering is this, "WARNING This Book should not be regarded as a substitute for dual instruction. Dual instruction from a competent professional should be considered mandatory. Experimenting on your own is very dangerous!" On the very next page is this,

"EMERGENCY SPIN RECOVERY IN THE PITTS"

1. POWER- IDLE.

2. REMOVE YOUR HANDS FROM THE STICK.

3. APPLY FULL RUDDER OPPOSITE THE ROTATION UNTIL ROTATION STOPS.

4. NEUTRALIZE RUDDER AND RECOVER TO LEVEL FLIGHT"

Warning, Emergency, yeah, that cinches it, I WILL be getting some advanced spin training before I start flying my Pitts. When respected people in the aerobatics field such as Gerry Molidor and Gene Beggs tell me I need to do something, I had better listen.

Paging through the IAC magazines Gerry had given me I saw an ad "Join the Chandler Air Force, Advanced Spin Training w/emergency Recovery, Chandler Air Service, Chandler Arizona." Perfect!

My vacation is in January and my wife and I were planning to visit our daughter in Tempe Arizona, a part of the Phoenix metroplex just as Chandler is. A few emails later and it was all arranged. By the time I had arrived at Chandler Air Service, I had read Gene Beggs's book three times. I introduced myself to the person behind the counter who was friendly and helpful. She paged Steve Smith, he would be my instructor. Steve is the Assistant Chief Flight instructor at Chandler Air Service instructing in aerobatics and advanced spin training. He has also flown competitive aerobatics for several years. Steve and I went to his office and briefed all of the various spins and spin scenarios we would be doing. This took a little over an hour and we finished about 10:30 am. This was two and a half hours before our scheduled 1:00 p.m. flight. I would have preferred flying right after the brief while everything was fresh, not to mention before eating lunch.

We met back at the office at 1:00 p.m. and walked over to the hanger. The Pitts we were to fly was a nearly new S2-C with less than 100 hours total time. It was an attractive white with blue trim. I would be flying from the rear seat which is where the main instruments and controls are located. We did a thorough cockpit brief, including avionics, since I would be doing all of the radio work. With the cockpit brief and the preflight done it was time to put on our parachutes and strap into the Pitts. If you have never strapped into an aerobatics airplane before it is quite an experience. With parachute on, I stepped up to the left wing, leaned forward so the chute would not hit the canopy, then bent my right leg up and swung it over into the cockpit, and on to the seat. Thankfully Steve was there coaching me all the way. When both feet were on the seat I moved my right foot to the cross tube, careful not to step through the Lexan floor, then started my left leg through the rudder tunnel. Then with arms on the side of the cockpit, I slid my right leg down and settled in. The aerobatics seat belt system is quite different from the normal seat belt. First the lap belt is really two belts in one. The normal looking one is the safety belt and attaches with the release to the right. The second belt and buckle is where you attach the shoulder harness and crotch strap This release lever is to the left side. This belt also has a ratchet device on it, similar to a cargo hold down strap, so you can cinch it down tight. When they say, "you wear the Pitts", they mean it. After I was all situated, Steve climbed into the front cockpit and strapped in with much more grace and speed than I was able to manage. We ran the check list, started the engine, tuned the radios, and were ready to taxi.

Chandler is a controlled field, so I got the ATIS and contacted Ground. We were cleared to runway 22R for take off. There was no forward visibility from the back seat at all. I S-turned (swerved back and forth) so I could see in front of me, all the way to the end of the runway. Steve talked me through the run-up and we were ready for take off.

"Tower, Pitts 44MV ready for takeoff, 22R"

"44MV cleared for take off, 22R. At 2500 cleared left turn south bound departure"

"Roger, cleared for take off, 22R, left turn south bound Pitts 44MV."

I taxied into position, but Steve made the take off with me following through on the controls.

Powering up the 260 ponies was smooth and rapid. Steve fed in some right rudder with the power up then he did the Pitts rudder dance to keep us tracking straight down the runway (note to self: start flying from a wide grass runway). After about 3 seconds, Steve pushed forward on the stick (more right rudder) and the tail came up. Now I could see a little bit in front of us. About another 3 seconds, and Steve added a little back pressure and we were airborne. At 300 feet, Steve told me to take over. Okay, I have the flight controls. I pulled the manifold pressure back to 25 inches, set the prop to 2500 rpm, adjusted our pitch, and trimmed to climb at 120mph. At 2500 feet I initiated a left hand turn to the south. With gentle pressure and a small deflection of the stick, I was in a 45 degree bank. WOW! I expected a quick response, however this was quicker than I had expected. From then on all I did was think about turning and the Pitts read my mind and was obeying my command.

At the practice area, at 4000 feet, agl, Steve took control again for a quick roll to inverted, held it for a second, then back right side up. I needed to tighten my seat belt a little more. Now for what I came for. I brought the throttle to idle, left rudder to counter the pronounced yaw from reducing power. Hold altitude and let the airspeed bleed off. Nose high attitude, there is the buffet, rudder full left for the left spin. The Pitts shuddered a little then fell off on the left wing. The nose went to about 60 degrees below the horizon and the left rotation started. It takes one whole turn for the spin to fully develop then the rate of rotation increases slightly. After three more turns, Steve told me to recover. Full right rudder, stop rotation, rudder to neutral, push stick forward to neutral. The second of many surprises today is that the stick is being held full aft by the air pressure and requires some force on my part to bring it forward to neutral. With the Pitts' wing unstalled and pointing at least 60 degrees nose down, the airspeed began to build. I started to pull the nose level and add full power simultaneously. As the nose reached the horizon, I continued the pull into a normal climb to 4000 feet. We had lost about 700 feet in the first turn, and about 300 feet each turn after that, approximately 1600 feet total. After another normal spin to the right, we climbed to 5000 feet. Next we did a flat spin to the left and recovered using the emergency spin recovery procedure described by Gene Beggs in his book "SPINS IN THE PITTS SPECIAL." I pulled the power to idle holding altitude until the Pitts stalled. As before, I added full left rudder. After one turn Steve told me to move the stick to the full right position. The pitch angle flattened out a little, not as much as I thought it would. The rotation increased to about half again as much as in a normal spin. Next, Steve had me add full power. The spin flattened a little more and the rate of spin increased even more. After about three turns I initiated the recovery. Power to idle, remove my hand from the stick and put it on my knee, then full right rudder. After a little more than a turn the rotation stopped abruptly and the stick jumped to neutral on its own. I grasped it and, adding power, I pulled the stick back, recovering into a normal climb to 5000 feet. The accelerated spin is truly amazing. I never knew an airplane could spin so fast or that I would be able to control it, well, at least recover from it. As in all spins we started by stalling the airplane and this time I added right rudder. Once the spin is developed, after about two turns, Steve told me to

move the stick from full back to full forward. The effect on the Pitts was literally mind boggling. The rotation increased so quickly and to a rate so fast that I could not tell how many turns we did. In fact the ground was only a blur. The nose was pointed straight down. I was thankful the practice area was a wide open space with few features on the ground to focus on. Had this been the Midwest with it's patchwork of colored farm fields and roads instead of the Arizona desert I would have been even more scrambled than I was. Recovery was made by moving the rudder to full left and the stick to neutral. Rotation stopped quickly. Rudder to neutral, back on the stick, power up and recover to level flight. That was as intense, extreme and mind blowing experience I have ever had in an airplane. It is one of those things that defy description and needs to be experienced to be truly understood. It took a couple of minutes for my inner ear to settle down from that one. It was some of the most intense flying I had done and the training could be a life saver. The briefing before my flight was a little over an hour and the flight lasted just under an hour. I'll need to go back for some inverted spin training, as my stomach and time gave out before I could get to that. Did I need advanced spin training? Yes! And everyone flying a high performance aircraft like the Pitts should get it. When I do these spins solo or inadvertently fall into one I won't be surprised and recovery will be a piece of cake. As to my beautiful Pitts S1-C, I'll have to wait until spring to see if she is a lady or a dragon.

CHECKING OUT IN THE PITTS

Spring is here and I can't wait to check out in my Pitts. The insurance company wanted me to get five hours of duel in a two place Pitts before they would insure me in my S-1C. I found a guy who had a Pitts S-2A in Springfield, IL. I arranged to fly the required five hours with him. Flying the S-2A from the front seat is a very similar site picture to flying the single seat S-1. I found it to be sensitive on the rudder and light on all of the controls.

After the five hours of countless takeoffs and landings I felt confident to transition to my S-1C. I was going to take off from 10C and fly to Dacy airport just a short distance to the west to do my first few landings. Dacy has three long grass runways. Grass is much more forgiving than a hard surface runway so if I don't touch down perfectly straight it wouldn't swerve as quickly and try to ground loop. (A ground loop is similar to doing a donut in a car on ice and usually ends in significant damage) Two of my aerobatic friends, Gerry and Doug were going to take their Champ to Dacy and watch from the ground. We would be in radio contact so they would be able to give me advice as needed. I was a little disheartened when I saw them getting into the Champ with a fire extinguisher and a crash ax. I took off first. I lined up on the 35 foot wide runway, locked the tail wheel and paused for a moment. With the checklist completed and the area clear I pushed the engine to full power. The acceleration was rapid and so was the swerve to the left. I over corrected to the right then back to the left. By that time I had enough speed to lift off. I gently eased the stick back and I was in the air. This was not like the S-2. It was shorter, lighter, quicker, and almost the same power as the S-2. It was a dragon. I had a lot of tail wheel experience and I was going to need all of it today.

Gerry and Doug would take longer to get to Dacy than me so I gained some altitude and did some turns, stalls and other air work. I tried to familiarize myself with my Pitts before I was going to attempt to land it.

I could see Gerry and Doug were in position about fifty yards from the west end of runway 09. My wife, Nancy, had also arrived. I went through the procedures in my mind as I positioned myself on the down wind leg of the traffic pattern. In the Pitts you do a 180 degree overhead approach to landing. That means when you are opposite

334

the spot you want to land at you cut your power and start your descent. At about a 45 degree angle from the end of the runway you start a turn and keep turning until you are lined up with the runway. In this way you can keep the runway in sight. Once you are lined up with the runway and are close to the ground you flare to the landing attitude and no more. The airplane will settle to the ground and touch down. That is when the real fun starts. You have no forward visibility. You have to use your side vision and peripheral vision to keep the airplane straight. Your feet are active on the rudder peddles to counter any movement left or right of the nose.

I called my ground crew and told them I was coming in. They verified no traffic. I brought the throttle to idle and the Pitts started to descend with the glide ratio of a brick. I descended at 100mph and slowed to 90mph over the fence. Gerry called on the radio, "looking good. Five feet, hold that attitude." I held the landing attitude and as the airspeed bled off, the Pitts kept settling. Touchdown, the runway was bumpy especially for my 5 inch wheels. I worked the rudders and held the nose straight until I reached taxi speed and turned off the runway. Gerry called out on the radio, "good job." I was now officially a Pitts pilot, one take off and one landing. I was very happy the fire extinguisher and crash ax were not needed. I made several more takeoffs and landings under the watchful eyes of Gerry and Doug before heading back to Galt airport. (10C)

The landing at Galt wasn't as easy or good as it was at Dacy. Galt is a narrow hard surface runway. All I could see was a little of one edge of the runway as I landed and rolled out trying to keep the Pitts straight.

I had been flying the Pitts for a while but my takeoffs and landings were not very good. On takeoff it would swerve left then right gaining enough speed for me to pull back on the stick and get into the air before it got really bad. I made one landing that I can only describe as a crash that hadn't fully developed. I made the usual 180 overhead approach and touched down a little nose high with the tail wheel hitting first pushing the main wheels down. When the main wheels hit the Pitts started a slight bounce and swerve. I used heavy braking and a lot of rudder movement to try to keep it straight. By the time I got it stopped it had one wheel off in the grass. I taxied back to the hanger and analyzed the situation.

First I needed to sit higher. I cut several foam pads to raise my sitting position until my head nearly hit the top of the canopy. Next I analyzed my takeoff technique. The Pitts is short with a big engine and propeller. On initial power-up the P-factor from the prop along with the torque of the engine exert a large turning force to the left so I need to put in about half of the available right rudder **before** I add power. The propeller is large and heavy producing a lot of gyroscopic precession. That means when I push the stick forward according to the laws of physic that force is applied after 90 degrees of rotation. So when I push the stick forward to raise the tail I need to add more right rudder. I have been flying in tennis shoes with thick soles, I can't feel the rudder peddles and I'm not getting any feel back through the peddles. I have a nearly worn out pair of deck shoes. The soles are so thin I can feel ever pebble I walk on. They ought to be prefect. I'll leave them in the seat so I won't forget to put them on.

My next takeoff and landing were great and I haven't had a problem since.

IFR HAMMERHEAD

I was competing in an aerobatic contest with my Pitts S-1 C. The ceiling was a ragged overcast but reported good enough for us to proceed with the contest. I was flying in the Sportsman category and the sequence had a hammerhead maneuver in it. I had done hundreds of hammerheads and I enjoy them. To do a hammerhead you get up as much speed as you can and then pull the airplane into the vertical. As the speed dissipates you have to start to feed in some right stick to counter the roll produced by the engines torque. When the airspeed is nearly zero you push full left rudder to pivot on the left wing tip to the vertical down line. At the same time as you push the rudder you need to push the stick nearly full forward to counter the gyroscopic precession of the propeller. After doing this maneuver many times in practice you develop a muscle memory so you barely need to think about it.

I was proceeding through the sequence of maneuvers required for the Sportsman class. Next up was the hammerhead. I had a lot of speed and full power as I pulled vertical. The speed was dissipating as I held my vertical line straight up. Without notice the world disappeared. I had flown into a cloud while going vertically up and my speed was decreasing. My first thought was, "well this is interesting". I didn't change anything, I couldn't, I had no instruments to level off and descend. I continued with the hammerhead. As the speed bled off I continued to move the stick to the right counteracting the torque even though I had no visual reference to verify I was using the right amount of movement. When the airspeed nearly reached zero I put in full left rudder. I couldn't see anything so instinctively I added forward stick. If I did it wrong I could end up in an inverted spin. I had done inverted spins before; it would not be a big deal to recover from that. When I thought I was pointed straight down I centered the controls and waited. I was flying a Pitts, the worst that could happen is that I would break out of the clouds in an unusual attitude and have to recover. I was confident I could do that. A few seconds later I popped out of the clouds holding my vertical line and on my heading. I continued and finished my sequence. The judges radioed that a cloud must have gotten in the way and asked me to repeat the hammerhead. I smiled to myself and replied "Rodger." This time I started a little lower.

The adventure continues. I hope you enjoyed the ride.

Made in the USA
Columbia, SC
11 July 2024

38497892R00185